Supporting Students with Literacy Difficulties

Supporting Students with Literacy Difficulties:

A Responsive Approach

Ted Glynn, Janice Wearmouth and Mere Berryman

Open University Press

Open University Press
McGraw-Hill Education
McGraw-Hill House
Shoppenhangers Road
Maidenhead
Berkshire
England
SL6 2QL

email: enquiries@openup.co.uk
world wide web: www.openup.co.uk

and Two Penn Plaza, New York, NY 10121-2289, USA

A catalogue record of this book is available from the British Library

ISBN-10: 0 335 21919 5 (pb)   0 335 21920 9 (hb)
ISBN-13: 978 0335 21919 3 (pb)   978 0335 21920 9 (hb)

Library of Congress Cataloging-in-Publication Data
CIP data applied for

Typeset by RefineCatch Limited, Bungay, Suffolk
Printed in Poland EU by OZGraf S.A.
www.polskabook.pl

Contents

Dedication

We acknowledge the contributions of the very many children, family members and teachers who have participated in our research activities over the years, and from whom we have all learned so much.

We also acknowledge the unstinting support we have received in writing this book from our partners, Vin, John and Chris.

1   Understanding responsive social contexts for literacy learning

In this book we examine different ways in which teachers and other adults, at school and at home, have created effective, responsive, social contexts for literacy learning. Within these responsive social contexts, students experiencing learning difficulties have been able to participate more fully in reading, writing and oral language activities. Throughout the book, we strive to assist teachers and schools to engage with children and their families and communities in ways that ensure that literacy tasks and pedagogies employed will affirm the knowledge and experiences within children's homes and cultural backgrounds.

The current chapter presents the framework of sociocultural theory that has guided our understanding of the causes of the difficulties with literacy that many students encounter at school. This chapter also presents the rationale underpinning the various effective teaching programmes and strategies for addressing these difficulties.

Chapter 2 introduces responsive social approaches to classroom teaching generally; Chapters 3 to 6 focus on responsive approaches to oral language, reading, writing and spelling; Chapter 7 focuses on responsive approaches to assessment; while Chapter 8 addresses effective school and community literacy partnerships. Finally, Chapter 9 summarizes the key elements of sociocultural approaches and their particular importance for understanding literacy.

Traditionally, literacy has been understood as a unified individual achievement which paved the way for the development of cognitive and intellectual skills. Prevailing educational practices emphasized the acquisition of basic technical literacy skills as prerequisites to becoming literate. Gregory, Long and Volk (2004) note that literate people were thought to engage in thought independently from the context to which it related, to think logically and in abstract terms, and to see things from variable points of view, and that these outcomes were due to literacy itself.

Sociocultural perspectives, on the other hand, argue that it is not literacy *per se*, but engagement in particular literacy practices through interaction with others in social situations, that leads to cognitive and intellectual skills (Scribner and Cole, 1981). For this reason, in this book we lay a particular emphasis on the kinds of interactions that support literacy development. Sociocultural perspectives also support the notion of 'multiple literacies', which result from children participating in the many different social and cultural contexts and communities of literacy practice, even prior to entering formal schooling (Heath, 1983).

Interpersonal and intellectual learning are interdependent from birth and continue to remain so throughout life. In this book we view both children and adults as active agents who come to know the world in terms of their own operations upon it. We emphasize especially the use of language in contextualized social interactions with other people, namely parents, other family members, peers and friends.

In Western societies children's learning was traditionally the domain of psychologists, whose emphasis was on children's individuality, as well as on the universality of human cognition and development (Gregory et al., 2004). These were seen as largely independent of the different influences of particular social and cultural contexts and environments. However, individual child-centred approaches to literacy learning may have under-valued the view that, when engaging in any literacy activity, children bring to that activity not only their own prior experience and understanding, but also the experience and understanding they have shared with others in their families and communities. Children enter school often already competent and literate within a number of different communities of practice. We offer a number of illustrations of this. Some indigenous children, for example Māori children in New Zealand, might enter mainstream primary schooling already competent and literate performers of tribal stories and chants, action songs, and customary forms of greeting as well as being able to recite genealogy and oral history. Their homes and communities might be very rich in terms of literacy practices that are crucial to the maintenance of their culture. There has been a great deal of research on children as individuals learning from parents or teachers, either at home or at school, but there has been relatively little research on young children as literacy learners within communities or networks that include peers and other people in their schools, neighbourhoods and extended families (Gregory et al., 2004).

Another important feature of sociocultural approaches to learning and development is that children are seen as assuming autonomy over their own learning, and as entering into learning interactions, activities and routines, and developing social relationships with more skilled members within their cultural communities. The role of adults and others with more expert knowledge is fundamental to learning:

Crucial to a socio-cultural approach, therefore, is the role of the mediator (a teacher, adult, more knowledgeable sibling, or peer) in initiating children into new cultural practices or guiding them in the learning of new skills.

(Gregory, Long and Volk, 2004, p. 7)

The extent to which children manage their own learning has been viewed in different ways (Rogoff, 2003). Many studies have supported Vygotsky's conceptualization of the adult as providing supportive scaffolding which is then gradually removed, leaving the child working independently of adult support (Wood, Bruner and Ross, 1976; Bruner, 1996). Other studies have shifted the focus on to children as active initiators of their own learning. Some forms of engagement that are not directly focused on instruction are also important to children's learning. Children themselves may take the initiative in observing and becoming involved in ongoing activities (Rogoff, 1990; Rogoff et al., 2003). Rogoff (1990) has proposed the concept of 'guided participation' to highlight the different ways in which children learn as they take part in, and are guided by, the practices of their own communities:

The concept of guided participation is central to my proposal that learning is a process of changing participation in community activities. It is a process of taking on new roles and responsibilities.

(Rogoff, 2003, p. 284)

In this book we look at a number of ways in which more skilled and interactive learning partners such as children's challenging and exploring peers can serve both as guides and collaborators. Children, together with collaborators who mediate their learning, draw on cultural resources and experiences to co-construct learning and make sense of their world. In this way children:

... appropriate an increasingly advanced understanding of and skill in managing the intellectual problems of their community

(Rogoff, 1990, p. 8, cited in Gregory, Long and Volk, 2004, p. 7)

One important way in which children achieve this level of understanding and skill is through participating in contexts where there is regular and sustained interaction with more-skilled individuals around genuinely shared activities. Lave and Wenger (1991) argue that learning is the process of change in the degree to which individuals can actively participate in 'communities of practice'.

Genuinely shared activities are those that are meaningful and purposeful for both the less-skilled and the more-skilled participants in such communities. Regular interactions around these shared activities can lead to children developing and refining their knowledge and skills within specific domains, such as literacy learning. In this book we discuss some of the contexts in which learning interactions have reciprocal benefits for participants, so that the more-skilled participant can be both guide and collaborator. Regular participation in these activities affirms and extends the interdependent positive social relationships between learning partners. These important interactive and social contexts for learning have been identified as responsive social contexts (Glynn, 1985, 1987). We see how the knowledge and skills that children acquire through social activities are also those that provide generic process knowledge about how to exercise a measure of autonomy in learning. Paradoxically, these contextualized *social* interactions are increasingly seen as fundamental to the acquisition of *individual* intellectual knowledge and skills (Bruner and Ross, 1976; Bronfenbrenner, 1979; Vygotsky, 1981; Wood, 1988; Bruner, 1996; McNaughton, 1996, 2002).

Pedagogical challenges

The view that failure in literacy learning results more from social and institutional arrangements than attributes of individuals (Lave, 1993, p. 10) is a very positive approach. It takes away a feeling of helplessness and gives a sense that students will acquire literacy if appropriate strategies are devised to facilitate their increasing participation in activities that will support learning. In this book we put a particular focus on strategies, including classroom pedagogies and the whole school literacy curriculum, that have been used very successfully in schools. From a sociocultural perspective, differences between skilled and unskilled literacy performances are more likely to be understood in terms of the characteristics of the particular contexts in which performance occurs, rather than in terms of differences in intellectual capacity between individuals (Wood, 1992). Children may fail in their literacy learning if certain literacy practices are privileged over others, for example when children's literacy achievements in family, home and community contexts are neither acknowledged nor affirmed in the literacy practices of the school. When this happens, teachers are challenged to find ways of including students from diverse social and cultural backgrounds into the community of practice in their classrooms.

This is particularly difficult when the language and culture of the teachers and the school differ from those of their students. Differences in the complexity of language used by different 6-year-old children to talk about the activities they are engaging in, either at home or at school, might reflect the different amount and quality of language exchange they have had with their family members or teachers around those activities. These differences might also reflect the differences in caregivers' and teachers' knowledge and experience in interpreting and responding to the language initiations that each child makes within the context of a particular activity. In many schools, teachers may have so little authentic knowledge and experience of the family and community contexts in which their students live that they are unable to participate in those literacy contexts and practices in which their students are already successful.

We illustrate ways in which this dilemma has been addressed successfully. One approach, for example, is for teachers, students and community members to collaborate in constructing new literacy contexts and initiating literacy practices in which all parties can participate. We show how this requires schools to acknowledge and affirm the funds of knowledge (material and intellectual resources) that exist within communities (Moll, 1992, p. 214) rather than regard literacy practices of diverse communities as deficits or as unacceptable deviations from the standard literacy practices of the school. In order to engage students from diverse communities in the literacy practices of the school, some schools have first explored and engaged in the literacy practices of those communities. They have included in their literacy curricula some of those stories, oral histories, songs, chants, word games and other genres from the families and communities of their minority students. This has proved to be a strong first step towards the successful inclusion of minority students and their families within the literacy practices of the school.

Further pedagogical challenges to ensuring the inclusion of children in communities of literacy practice may also arise where some students experience acute difficulties in acquiring the mechanics of written language. As Salmon (1998) points out, the traditional Western psychology of intellect presupposes that there is only one way of being intelligent. Schools equate competence with traditional kinds of educational success that are reliant on literacy and numeracy skills. Schools give priority to formal educational skills that involve the manipulation of symbols, and set literacy above spoken language. We discuss Riddick's (1996, p. 32) view that among clinicians and educationalists there is general agreement about the 'devastating effects' that serious difficulties in literacy development can have on children and their families. In a study of the personal experiences of 22 students identified as 'dyslexic', and their families, the students reflected on their feelings of disaffection and of dread of 'visible public indicators' (Riddick, 1996, p. 124) of their difficulties in literacy, such as reading aloud and always being the last to finish work. These students had very strong views about which teachers were best able to support them in ways that were positive and productive. The key qualities of the 'best' teachers were a propensity to offer praise and encouragement linked with understanding of the difficulties experienced by the student. We might add to this a knowledge and understanding of ways that teachers can address the difficulties often experienced by students, in sound-symbol identification, sequencing, directionality, symbol orientation and general organization, but without being constrained by a solely phonics-based approach and without losing sight of the communicative function of written text. As Vygotsky (1978, p. 118) commented: 'Writing should be incorporated into a task that is necessary and relevant for life.'

We have already noted the importance of the social and communicative relationship between learners and mediators, whether adults or peers, working on genuinely shared literacy tasks.

> According to Vygotsky (1978), a child and partner interact within a communicative relationship because of the partner's language knowledge and sensitivity to the child's capabilities and because of the child's innate desire to become part of the communicative world. Working within this supportive relationship extends the learner's knowledge into the zones of proximal development – 'those particularly promising areas just beyond the child's reach'.
>
> (Gregory et al., 2004, p. 16)

However, the type of supportive learning relationship envisaged in this statement is not restricted to partnerships between young children and adults, but can operate also between children and their peers. Gregory et al. (2004) note that research on reciprocal teaching and learning between siblings describes a synergy taking place in which children play active, complementary and balanced roles in building on what they both know and in fostering their mutual learning, not just the learning of the one who may be a novice. Numerous studies of the effects of peer support or peer tutoring on students' reading and writing testify to the power of this synergy, leading to measured literacy gains for both tutee and tutor children (Wheldall and Mettem, 1985; Glynn, 1992; Houghton and Bain, 1993; Houghton and Glynn, 1993; Westera and Moore, 1995; Glynn et al., 1996; Medcalf, Glynn and Moore, 2004; Pickens, Glynn and Whitehead, 2004).

Not all adult or peer tutoring interactions introduced by schools for students experiencing difficulties have this particular synergy and mutually beneficial outcomes. In this book, we discuss how some interactive tutoring contexts lead to literacy learning that is dependent on the continued control and direction of a more-skilled partner. While this partner may have a guiding role, there may be little or no evidence of a collaborative learning role and the interaction may actually promote a kind of learned helplessness. For example, in a supportive one-to-one oral reading tutoring context, one tutor might respond immediately to every reader error by supplying the correct word and reinforcing the reader for imitating the word supplied. Another tutor might first wait, delaying his or her response and allowing a little time for the reader to think about whether what he or she had just read 'made sense'. Students working with the first tutor might go on to learn the dependent strategies of appealing to the teacher or tutor for every word they do not know or just waiting for the tutor to tell them the correct word. However, students working with the second tutor might go on to learn more independent strategies like reading on from the unknown word, or going back to the beginning of the sentence to seek additional information to help them solve the word. The differential nature of tutor responsiveness is further illustrated when, in the first case, tutor praise is likely to reinforce the student strategy of imitating the correct word supplied, while in the second, tutor praise is likely to reinforce the student strategy of searching the text for further information. In the second case, the tutor might also provide the reader with further information or clues about word meaning, but still without supplying the word itself. Because the second tutor and the reader have discovered that they have common experiences and shared interests in the topic they are reading about, the second tutor might try also to link the additional information supplied to the student's prior knowledge and experience of the topic, or to the wider context of the story. The learning contexts created through these two student – tutor interactions are clearly quite different, the second context being far more responsive, social and interactive than the first.

Characteristics of responsive social contexts

It is important at this point to explore what, in general terms, are some of the characteristics of responsive social contexts which facilitate active engagement with communities of literacy practice in order to support and promote literacy learning. Glynn (1985) has identified four features:

1. Responsive social contexts provide opportunities for learners to initiate

Whether the context is one of infants learning to speak their first language, students learning to speak a second language, or young children learning to read or write, or learning to draw or paint, if these learners are to have agency over their own learning, they must be able to initiate interactions with others, around learning activities, and not simply respond to adult or peer questions and directions. Many classroom learning contexts are such that learners have no opportunity to initiate, but can only respond to questions and directions from someone else. A teacher may ask a child to draw a picture of their pet, but then impose a series of direct, closed questions; 'Is this your cat? Does she have sharp claws? Does she have sharp teeth? Is she sitting on a chair? Does she like catching mice?' These questions may or may not respond to the child's drawing in any way at all. They leave little or no room for a conversation about the drawing, in which the student might have some degree of control over what is said. A more responsive teacher might set out some interesting materials, and then wait until the student has selected a topic and has begun work. Then, rather than asking questions, this teacher might show she is really interested in the picture, by moving close and looking at it carefully and waiting for the student to initiate some statement or comment. The teacher would then respond to that initiation, in a conversational manner.

In a responsive learning relationship, children not only learn how to use language to obtain particular information, or to access materials and activities, but they also learn a powerful general strategy for engaging and maintaining adult attention. This learning can readily be used with new materials, with new adults and in new contexts. One key to promoting child language initiations in interactive contexts is for the teacher to delay intervention to allow the child time and opportunity to initiate. Delaying intervention is an important strategy by which teachers can relinquish total and direct control over interactions. With delayed intervention from the teacher, there is more time for the student to initiate as well as more opportunity for the teacher to respond, rather than direct.

2. Shared activities between less-skilled and more-skilled learners

A responsive social context should provide opportunity for the learners to engage in shared activity with more-skilled performers with whom they have a positive social relationship. The notion of shared activity implies that the learning activities or tasks be functional for both the less-skilled and the more-skilled participants. When parents and family members are 'captured' by their children into telling them a favourite family story, or into helping them to write a letter replying to an invitation, the task is often both enjoyable and functional for both participants. The child learns a little bit more about the writing process, and a lot more about eliciting parental help with an important task. The parent might learn how much the child really wants to go to a friend's birthday party, and learn, for example, more about how to turn an incidental request into an interesting conversation. A relaxed conversation can be an enjoyable shared task, in that control over the topics and direction of the speech are shared between child and parent because both obtain some information about how the other partner thinks, feels and acts. Regular and extended conversations around genuinely shared tasks affirm and strengthen the relationship between a parent and child. In contrast, language interactions in which an adult continually asks 'leading' questions, which minimize the opportunity for the child to contribute, are not genuine shared tasks. Similarly, a teacher 'testing' a student by asking a set of questions when the student is well aware that the teacher already knows the answers, is not a shared task. This strategy does not predispose to engaging conversations.

3. Reciprocity and mutual influence

Responsive social contexts are also characterized by reciprocal mutual influence. Each party in an interaction has an impact on the other, and modifies the learning and behaviour of the other. Successful peer tutoring of reading, for example, can result in social and learning gains for both tutors and tutees (Limbrick, McNaughton and Glynn, 1985; Wheldall and Mettem, 1985; Houghton and Bain, 1993; Houghton and Glynn, 1993; Glynn, Berryman, Bidois, et al., 1996). In a study of peer tutoring of spelling, Dineen, Clark and Risley (1977) found that when children undertook both tutor and tutee roles, their learning gains were just as effective on lists they taught to someone else as they were on lists they learned themselves. Reciprocity and mutual influence have also been reported in the area of peer management of students' classroom behaviour, where unprogrammed positive changes occurred in peer managers' own behaviour as well as in the behaviour of target students whose behaviour they were monitoring (Sanders and Glynn, 1977). Studies showing reciprocal learning gains for tutors and tutees also commonly report, *post hoc*, that these were accompanied by positive social outcomes.

Roger Hall's play *Multiple Choice*, about the friendship that develops between two adolescents who have dropped out of school, beautifully illustrates reciprocity and mutual influence. Roberto teaches Paul to repair cars, and Paul teaches Roberto to read (Hall, 1983).

A second illustration comes from a short story by Apirana Taylor (1992) which tells of a young grandson who pesters his grandfather to teach him to wield the *taiaha*, a weapon used in *mau rakau*, a traditional form of martial arts among Māori (people of the land, indigenous people of New Zealand). At first the grandfather is reluctant, and feels he cannot remember all that he himself had been taught. However, in response to persistent demands from his grandson, he begins teaching, and finds that he gradually recalls not only the correct moves, but also all the *karakia* (prayers) and instructions that must accompany this training. Grandson and grandfather grow very close, working together on what has clearly become a shared task of importance to them both. It is certainly not the case that time and effort spent working on shared or reciprocal learning tasks with others is time out from advancing one's own learning.

4. Amount and type of feedback

A fourth characteristic of responsive social learning contexts is the quality of feedback received for learning by both participants. Underachievement in written tasks in some school settings may be in part a function of feedback that is excessively delayed or infrequent. Some students experience learning contexts in which there is so little feedback of any description that systematic efforts simply to increase the rate of feedback students receive will have positive outcomes. For example, merely increasing the immediacy and frequency of feedback to a class of low-achieving fourth formers on the rate and accuracy of their completion of writing tasks yielded dramatic gains in work completed and minor gains in accuracy, even though accuracy was already quite high (Scriven and Glynn, 1983). As this class completed more and more written work over time, with the increased rate of feedback, their teacher was observed to make fewer and fewer control or management comments. It appeared as though these students were becoming more motivated by completing set tasks, and having this regularly acknowledged, so that there was less need for the teacher to comment on their off-task behaviour.

Glynn (1985) has also identified four specific types of pedagogical strategies that are consistent with following a responsive, interactive role, rather than a directive or managerial role, in a learning context. These responsive teaching strategies are:

1   Providing interesting materials that promote engagement by the learner (for example, a literacy environment rich in interesting reading texts, matched to the interests of the readers).
2   Delaying and reducing direct teacher instructions and directions so as to allow opportunities for learners to initiate (for example, opportunities for a student to attempt an unknown word while reading, before being told what the word is).
3   Maximizing opportunities for shared activities between less-skilled and more-skilled learners so there can be reciprocal learning and enjoyment of the task (for example, devising learning tasks that are authentic for both teacher and learner, such as co-constructing a story, and oral or written text that represents the life experiences of both).
4   Responding to initiations by the leaner so as to encourage reciprocity and mutual influence (for example, placing the learner in the teaching role, and having the learner teach the teacher some knowledge or skill in which the learner has more competence than the teacher).

Utilizing all these strategies would shift teachers a long way from the model of tight instructional control displayed in many educational settings. Teachers displaying these behaviours would be providing 'loose' training (Stokes and Baer, 1977), in that they relinquish direct control over the precise timing and sequence or specific context of all the learning interactions. But in handing over a much greater share of control to the learner, they would be providing for strong generalization of what is learned into new contexts, particularly into contexts in which the learner must perform independently of teacher support (Glynn, 1985).

Conclusion

In this book we adopt a sociocultural approach to literacy learning. This implies a reconceptualization of previously taken-for-granted assumptions about teaching and learning. Literacy learning is seen as situated in a social and cultural context and as dynamic and interactive between learner and context. This means that difficulties in literacy learning are situated here also. The importance of arranging learning environments as the context in which students construct knowledge was long ago highlighted by Dewey (1933). A situated view does not indicate which practice in literacy learning should be adopted. However, 'it does say that the activities of different learning practices are important . . . because participation in these practices is fundamental in what students learn' (Greeno, 1998, p. 14).

Where, as in this book, students' literacy difficulties are seen as situated and the nature of these difficulties is seen as changing in relation to the learning context, there is a need for teachers to be reflective in their practice in order to cope with the uncertainties of real life and the complexity and diversity of the multiple literacies students bring with them into classrooms. For teachers, accustomed to assuming the role of the all-knowing 'other', being prepared to move to the 'unknowing' position may be very uncomfortable:

> The image of wise judgment under conditions of considerable uncertainty stands in marked contrast to the preferred public image of a reliable, quasi-scientific knowledge base.
>
> (Schön, 1983, p. 17)

As Wearmouth (2003) notes, however, it is crucial to maintain a reflective stance towards one's professional practice in the area of literacy learning in schools. Otherwise, it is difficult to see how we are to understand the difficulties experienced in learning by so many students in the world of schools, and it will be difficult for us to open up their opportunities for learning and show genuine concern and respect for the professionals who have to deal with them.

2 Responsive classroom pedagogies

Introduction

This chapter is concerned with responsive approaches to literacy learning in classrooms. It examines some of the key parameters of the responsive learning contexts that teachers, other adults, peers, and students themselves, can create to support literacy learning for students who experience learning difficulties generally, as well as for those who experience specific difficulties with literacy.

Understandings of 'inclusion' vary according to the extent to which students are able to participate in the classroom. A sense of belonging and acceptance is a basic human need. The identity of community members is influenced by the extent to which interactions within the group engage and acknowledge them. To achieve this level of engagement, the social context of the classroom needs a prevailing ethos of care and respect for its members (Cavanagh, 2003). Of central importance here are pedagogies that reflect a view of students as having active agency in their learning and a view of the learning environment as playing a key role in understanding students' literacy learning as acquired through social interactions. We discuss, for example, classrooms that include cooperative group learning activities and a focus on the construction of knowledge about literacy through scaffolding by, and dialogue with, peers (Stevens and Slavin, 1995a, 1995b).

This chapter offers examples of research studies reporting on literacy gains arising from students engaging in authentic learning tasks supported by interactive adults and peers who provide frequent *responsive*, not simply *corrective*, feedback. The chapter demonstrates reciprocal benefits for teachers and learners, for students and tutors, arising from shared tasks in socially responsive contexts.

Building on prior experiences

Literacy is part of the 'cultural toolkit' (Bruner, 1996) that is crucial for full participation in society. Human action is mediated by tools and signs – semiotics. Semiotic means include language, writing, and all sorts of conventional signs (Vygotsky, 1981).

> These semiotic means are both the tools that facilitate the co-construction of knowledge and the means that are internalised to aid future independent problem-solving activity.
>
> (Palincsar, 1998, p. 353)

As already noted in Chapter 1, the approach to student learning taken in this book emphasizes the learner's active role in his or her own learning through meaningful interactions with others. It is probably at classroom level that the most important interactions affecting pupils occur (Florian and Rouse, 2001). Children's learning goals and expectations often stem from the goals and norms of the community. It is essential, therefore, that when young students enter school, classroom literacy practices can build on their own pre-existing experiences.

Unfamiliarity with classroom literacy practices on entering school can result in complete bewilderment, an inability to understand what is on offer, and an inability to connect this with personal experience. Gregory (1996, p. 33) notes, for example, how Tony (not his real name) arrived at his school in England, aged 4 years and 10 months, with an 'eye for detail' and a 'disciplined and structured approach to reading from his Chinese school'. In that school he had been 'given an exercise book where he had to divide the page into columns and practise ideographs over and over again until they were perfect' (Gregory, 1996, p. 32). The carefully and clearly delineated and confined tasks set by the teacher contrasted sharply with the range of personal choice given to Tony and his classmates in the mainstream classroom in Northampton, England. His aimless wandering around the classroom while peers chose activities for themselves indicated that he appeared unable to cope with the non-realization of his expectations about what school should be about.

There is no possibility of making sense of what bears no relation to one's own ways of making sense of things. The way in which a lack of understanding can feel threatening to oneself and can lead to feelings of anxiety or hostility is illustrated by the recollections of school experiences by an inmate of a UK prison. He recalls 'a cocktail of . . . um . . . conflicts there all the time' as he tried to cope with the expectations of a mainstream London school that conflicted with those of home:

> I was weak in certain subjects, like English mainly, because I tend to write the way I speak. I'm born here my parents are from the West Indies. I am in an English school I had to cope with the different . . . criteria because at home it was like a cross between Caribbean where we tend to speak more Patois or broken English. School was like trying to do it faithfully. . . . You get to learn . . . how important language is for you to fit. . . . and then, like . . . I might get homework to do and I'll ask my dad and he will say no, it's done this way, which is, their schooling was from the old grammar, and it's always a conflict and I would always believe what my father had said because he was a father figure. . . . Yes, and then it was completely wrong, and eventually you get frustrated, and I am not going to do this, and you just sort of throw it out.
>
> (Wearmouth, 1997, p. 32)

A number of issues crucial to enabling all children to situate themselves in the social context of classroom reading arise from this discussion:

> The need for teachers to learn of the literacy practices taking place in their pupils' lives outside school;
> The need to find strategies to build on strengths that each of the children in the group bring to school;
> The need to make school interpretations of literacy explicit to children and their families.
>
> (adapted from Gregory, 1996, p. 45)

In a study of early literacy learning in three classrooms of 4- to 5-year olds in the UK, Gregory, Williams, Baker and Street (2004) show how one teacher in 'Tarnside', South London, was able to build on children's pre-existing frames of reference of what constituted learning, which they brought from home and their church Sunday school classes. This teacher was able to develop high standards of literacy achievement in the classroom. This is particularly significant given that these children often lived in short-term hostels with mothers whose economic, social and cultural resources were meagre. Seventy per cent came from minority ethnic backgrounds, the majority being African, African-Caribbean or dual race families, a small percentage from the Asian subcontinent, and the remainder from Anglo backgrounds. Regular church attendance played an important part in their lives. Few families had books or computers. Nevertheless, these children achieved literacy level scores at school that were 'more or less equal to the national average in the National Assessment Tests' (Gregory, Williams, Baker and Street, 2004, p. 94):

> These children, though desperately short on resources, were racing

ahead with a teacher who respected and shared a similar interpretation of 'work' (trying hard) as the children's families.

(Gregory, Williams, Baker and Street, 2004, p. 106)

This teacher's classroom fitted well with the overall structure of the English National Literacy Strategy, and included drilling in phonics and other formal patterns of language structures. On a social level, the teacher seemed aware that most of the children were stepping into a new world in school, and facilitated what counted as 'school learning' by consciously teaching the rules and expectations of her classroom:

> . . . the teacher . . . carefully unravelled and explained aspects of the English language and literacy and children were praised as they mastered them. English politeness customs, procedures and behaviour were also explicitly taught and practised.
>
> (Gregory, Williams, Baker and Street, 2004, p. 94)

There was no sense that the children were seen as deficient as a result of cultural differences. The teacher expected that all the children could, and should, achieve well, and in this her philosophy and approach were in accord with those of the families. Academic learning was central to this very orderly classroom:

> First thing in the morning, the children got a book out of the box and read together or alone. . . . The children spent lengthy periods in discussion with the teacher on the mat. During this time, intensive and explicit teaching took place (when someone interrupted, the teacher said: 'Excuse me, I'm in the middle of teaching'). Although she showed that social behaviour and manners were important, this was a small part of classroom culture . . . Instead, every opportunity was taken to switch into academic discourse. Nothing was taken for granted. . . . children were encouraged to take artefacts from home into the classroom and, during newstime, to show what they could do. For example, one child showed how he could whistle and everyone clapped. Similarly, the teacher shared her own experiences from outside school with the class and encouraged the children to do the same. She also lost no opportunity to model what counted as learning in her classroom.
>
> (Gregory, Williams, Baker, and Street, 2004, p. 95)

In a classroom at 'Mountford', located in an estate of social housing in a seaside resort in southern England, children came largely from very low income families, with few books. The ethnic background was 97 per cent

Anglo with the remaining few primarily from the Asian subcontinent. Here, in contrast with 'Tarnside', pupils' achievement levels on National Tests at age 7 were 'poor'. The cultural setting of the classroom is described as a 'haven', taken from the philosophy of the Plowden Report (DES, 1967) in which:

> children in 'disadvantaged' areas were assumed to enter school from homes which provided 'little stimulus for learning' (DES, 1967). These children were seen to need a 'sanctuary' (sometimes referred to as such) of peace, an escape from the perceived harsh realities of home. . . . the teacher, who was warm and caring, saw herself as socializing the children into the learning habits of school rather than focusing strictly on academic work. She made excellent provision in terms of learning materials for the children and gave them the opportunity to talk freely without having constantly to supply the 'correct' response. Interviews with the teachers, however, revealed a considerable gulf between home and school; there was little knowledge of what literacy and learning practices took place at home. On the other hand, parents felt that school expectations were not made clear and they were consequently unsure of what counted as successful learning in school. Parents were excluded from classrooms for security reasons and on the grounds that their presence might upset children and prevent them settling into school routines. The 'haven' created for the children was, therefore, one which was denied parents and families as their children entered school.
>
> (Gregory et al., 2004, pp. 91–2)

This was a situation in which the school perceived itself, not families, as knowing best what was needed for children. The school did not see itself as needing to work in partnership with its parents and communities. The focus on the social learning of the class often meant something different from behaviour at home. A child, for example, was told that using the word 'dumbo' was unkind and was made to apologize for this with no explanation offered as to why this word was unacceptable:

> . . . 'home' rules were very different from those in school and there was no reason as to why the latter should be preferable or superior. Being a successful learner if this classroom . . . meant showing you knew how to behave appropriately in the classroom and using correct formulae, more than displaying academic knowledge. There was . . . comparatively little direct literacy work, especially with reference to phonics and word recognition.
>
> (Gregory et al., 2004, p. 96)

Deficit notions of the children and their families prevailed over recognition of potential for learning:

> ... as if families needed to be given access to the ways of behaving and corresponding politeness formulae of the dominant class before and, to a certain extent, instead of academic knowledge.
>
> (Gregory et al., 2004, p. 96)

There was little understanding that parents and/or older siblings might have the potential to induct younger family members into literacy learning, as Gregory (2004) notes in the context of studies into literacy learning among Bangladeshi children in East London.

Teachers in the 'Mountford' school were sure that students would never approximate to reaching the national requirements in literacy and numeracy before the end of the reception year. Yet verbal questions from the teacher revealed 'lively, intelligent minds' (Gregory et al., 2004, p. 105). At the end of this year, this group was 'still struggling to understand what counted as learning in the classroom'. It seems that this school did not recognize the potential level of expertise in literacy activities that exists in homes with all cultural groups, and did not see itself as part of the learning and teaching problem to be addressed.

Classroom support for literacy learning

There is no single clear-cut way of ensuring the inclusion in classroom activities of students who experience difficulties with literacy, in classroom activities. Using support staff, such as learning support assistants (LSAs) in the UK and teacher aides in New Zealand, is common practice in many classrooms. A central issue for this chapter is that teachers working with LSAs in mainstream classrooms should ensure their classroom pedagogies are responsive to students' needs and that responsive social contexts are created for all students. LSAs and teacher aides need to understand and be able to work alongside teachers in implementing these pedagogies. However, there seems to be little clarity or consensus among teachers, parent helpers and pupils about what exactly the role of teacher aides and LSAs ought to be. Sometimes there may be little appreciation of the power that support staff selected from children's own communities have to bridge the gap between home and school. In-class support is sometimes imposed on the class teacher from without to accompany the 'integration' of pupils with 'difficulties'. On the one hand, support teachers and LSAs may lack status and authority in the eyes of staff and students (Lovey, 1995). They may also lack specific knowledge of how to support literacy. On the other hand, support staff may find themselves propping up the system by helping students through inappropriate lessons, thus, unwittingly, contributing to students' problems in the long run (Allan, 1995). In this context, even the best qualified, most experienced support person can be humiliated by lack of definition of role, being treated like one of the students, and not being able to act in the familiar capacity of authoritative adult (Best, 1991; Thomas, 1992; Wearmouth, 2000).

In practice, the work of LSAs and teacher aides in class varies enormously from one school to another. A University of Manchester, England, research report on LSAs (Farrell, 1999) confirms that many play a key role in acting as the main source of support for students with exceptional needs in mainstream schools. Although teachers are often responsible for planning schemes of work to be implemented by LSAs, in many cases, 'they [support staff] took the lead in adapting programmes of work and in planning new programmes' (Farrell, 1999, p. 17, reported in Mittler, 2000, pp. 126–7), especially when LSAs were working in non-resourced schools or employed by LEAs.

Farrell's (1999) report reflects a strong consensus among teachers and support assistants on how effective in-class support should be organized. The report summary indicates that:

- LSAs and teacher aides must be fully informed about the aims and objectives of a lesson and about the learning needs of students who experience literacy difficulties.
- LSAs and teacher aides need to be familiar with any additional or alternative materials and equipment that have been designed to support students with difficulties in literacy.
- Teachers and LSAs or teacher aides must be able to trust each others' judgement and have enough time to plan activities involving literacy.
- Support should be offered to students very sensitively. Some students and teachers preferred support assistants to 'float around a class' but be immediately available when needed.

The report concludes with an agenda for evaluating practice under three major headings: role, management and training. However, working one-to-one with individual students within a mainstream class is not the only way LSAs and teacher aides can support the teacher to establish a responsive classroom. In some countries, for example in New Zealand, teacher aides frequently contribute to the management and teaching of the whole class or groups of students within the class so that the more qualified teacher can spend time with individual students who have difficulty with literacy.

The authors of this book have worked with three schools in one community where teacher aides from within the students' home community (mothers, aunts, uncles, grandparents) who had previously been unemployed, received training in specific literacy programmes and assessments. These teacher aides then provided specialist in-class literacy support to students requiring specific support in oral language, reading and/or writing, throughout the school. Ongoing assessments consistently confirmed the benefits to students in the programme. Interestingly, these schools also consistently found that up to 40 per cent of their tutors reported a greater sense of personal efficacy and also used their tutoring experiences as the springboard for further training opportunities and employment, many becoming teachers (Open University, 2002a).

The principle of ensuring that the content of lessons is meaningful and salient is crucial if we assume that students have active agency in learning. 'The only good learning is that which is in advance of development' (Vygotsky, 1978, p. 89). Learning that leads to development in literacy arises from interactions oriented towards the individual learner's zone of proximal development. It is important, therefore, that professional development and training for classroom assistants and teacher aides includes an understanding of sociocultural theory, particularly with respect to the zone of proximal development, responsive social contexts for learning, reciprocal teaching and peer tutoring. In the 1970s and early 1980s, withdrawal group work which focused on the teaching of specific skills to pupils who experienced difficulties in certain areas was common practice. Lewis (1995) notes that this has now largely fallen into disfavour because:

- Apparent gains made in the small group situation could not be sustained and/or generalized in the context of the classroom. In other words, the interactions did not lead to accomplishments that the learner could perform alone.
- Students lost the continuity of classroom activity and instruction.
- The teaching methods used in the withdrawal groups might conflict with those in the main classroom.
- Class teachers had less incentive to take an interest in examining how teaching for all pupils, including those with difficulties in literacy, might be improved.

The particular forms of support offered in mainstream classrooms can be important factors in maintaining, or undermining, individual student self-efficacy. As Davies (2004) comments, participation in a community is 'transformative' both for participants and for the group. Non-participation in the activities of the regular classroom that results from the kind of support on offer is also transformative. Within an institution, both educators and students are defined by that institution's social practices. As Bruner (1996) notes, one of the prime responsibilities of schools is to support the construction of a student's sense of self through an acknowledgement of agency and the development of self-esteem.

One important factor that contributes to the development of poor self-efficacy is the visibility of assessment information relating to how a child performs relative to his or her peers. There are many adults who can recall being humiliated by public demonstrations of their lack of achievement in literacy in comparison with peers (Wearmouth, 2004). However unintentional this may have been on the part of those professionals concerned, the fact remains that many have had similarly upsetting experiences which they still remember vividly. Research conducted in mainstream classrooms suggests that children who experience difficulty in learning are more likely to evaluate their abilities as poor when information of this sort is highly visible (Ames and Archer, 1988). Public comparison with higher-achieving peers can be very damaging to individual learners, but so, also, can be withdrawal from the classroom situation, unless withdrawal work occurs for a variety of reasons, and not only for 'remedial' support.

An interview held with 22-year-old James (not his real name) about his educational experience illustrates some of the issues surrounding support for literacy difficulties (Wearmouth, 2004, pp. 60–7). On account of serious difficulties in literacy acquisition, in his primary school 'James' was placed in the lowest ability groups for reading and writing in his class and withdrawn for special lessons. Separation from the community of competent learners and from literacy practices in the classroom, together with tuition in literacy activities that he felt were irrelevant and meaningless, resulted in feelings of hopelessness, helplessness and frustration. Intense feelings of anger and defiance resulted from the conflict between the provision made by the school, what he felt he needed, and by his own impotence in the situation:

> I think I felt very excluded. But the way that manifested it in my character was, I was really defiant. I thought that everyone else was stupid, and I was very frustrated . . . I must have been as awful to them as they were to me, but I felt so separated from them, and the teachers, I didn't respect my teachers. I thought that because of the situations that they'd put me in, I felt like, you know, you won't sit here and listen to me so why should I listen to you?

His new conception of himself as one labelled and stigmatized as slow-learning was reinforced by the empirical evidence of separation from peers and placement in a group where the work was different and, he felt, too easy:

> . . . the lessons that they gave seemed very simple. They were like obvious repetitive stuff, going over stuff that I found simple . . . I think the type of work that it was, was perhaps, writing out a page of like, a hundred, you know a full page worth of say a letter at a time, say D, repeating it over and over again and although my handwriting

wasn't fantastic, I could write the letter D, but then that seemed to bear no relation to me writing a word.

This statement indicates both the degrading of a communicative literacy activity into a repetitious technical task that sometimes occurs in the name of 'remedial help', as well as James's complete awareness of this and its impact on his own learning and his concept of himself. James needed to feel a sense of belonging and a sense of agency over his own learning. The category of slow learner, created in order to manage special literacy provision in the school, hovered in the air ready to 'gobble up' likely candidates (Mehan, 1996):

> . . . first of all, when I went to the lessons, I was called out in front of the class, and they were referred to as special lessons, and politically correct as the teacher thought that was, it really wasn't. Kids are cruel, and I felt really targeted and singled out . . .

Fortunately for James, his experiences at secondary school were very different. Teachers responded to his difficulties in a way that suited his individual learning needs and he was encouraged to see himself as an active agent in his own learning, capable of making sense of his own world and learning needs:

> In secondary school things were different . . . they were still . . . tough because I still obviously had problems, but the teachers' handling of it was so different. For one I didn't ever feel excluded from anything and it wasn't ever made a big thing of at all. . . . I can remember some things that really helped were, if I'd be taking notes, and obviously I'd be a lot slower than everyone else, it wouldn't take a teacher saying, 'Are you finished James?' and directing attention towards me and the fact that I was slower. But I'd catch every so often a teacher subtly looking over, and checking that I was finished and often I'd acknowledge the fact that they were looking over, and they wouldn't start again until I'd finished.

With the added motivation of an expectation that he could and would learn, despite extreme tiredness every day James began to look for ways to achieve and overcome the difficulties he experienced:

> I was still slow and it was still hard work . . . I'd be in bed by eight thirty, up until fifteen almost. I was exhausted . . . and I felt like I came home and it would take me about twice, three times as long as anyone else to finish the work, homework or whatever, but I was coping.

James's secondary teachers had established a more 'responsive' approach where control was 'shared between James and his teachers' and in which the more skilled participant adopted 'a responsive interactive role, rather than a controlling or custodial role' (Wheldall and Glynn, 1989, p. 97). James portrays himself as beginning to achieve highly, largely by assuming agency over his own learning at this point:

> Well by that time, I'd started to get quite good at coping . . . I did have problems, but my note taking started to become a bit more efficient. I also worked a lot with books, with a [published examination] syllabus. I found that I could use the syllabus to have an advantage. Basically for the sciences, I could get a book, and just work through each point of the syllabus, and if I knew it then that was fine and I didn't almost need the lessons. You know in lessons, I could always cope with the concepts. That was something I was very good at. So, if there was something that I missed in class or couldn't keep up with . . . I basically listed each point of the syllabus, and found the relevant piece of information and picked it out. . . . Basically, I'd know that . . . a question would be awarded five or ten marks, and I know for ten marks they give you five points and I'd cut out the waffle. I became very strategic . . . it was a strategy I worked out for myself, but for me it seemed blatantly obvious. If the course provides a syllabus, and the examiners can only ask you on that syllabus, then why not learn everything in the syllabus, and keep to that?

Self-taught study skills, supported by sensitive, aware teachers who responded effectively to James's initiatives and growing sense of agency, rather than extending a custodial and controlling relationship with him, enabled James to achieve academic success at the General Certificate of Secondary Education level (GCSE):

> . . . before then it was blips, because the rest of my work was terrible. But when I did my GCSEs (General Certificate of Secondary Education), I think all told I took thirteen GCSEs, and I got two A stars, six As five Bs. By then people were like, 'Bloody hell!' and then it got to my A-levels, and in the three sciences I got three B grades which was quite good.

These skills, refined for study at degree level, enabled James to extend responsibility for his own learning until his graduation with an Upper Second Honours degree.

Collaborative learning: Peer support among children

Classroom assistants, teacher aides and support teachers are not the only people capable of helping teachers establish interactive and responsive classrooms. Families and communities can often offer great strength of commitment as well as cultural knowledge and resources to work with teachers to address major literacy difficulties their children experience at school. Successful inclusion and participation in lessons and in the life of the school depends to a large extent on other children. Peer tutoring has been shown to be particularly effective in the teaching of reading, provided the tutor is properly prepared and supported and the pupil is willing to accept such help. Westwood (1997), quoted in Mittler (2000), summarizes four essentials of peer tutoring as:

- clear directions as to what they are to do and how they are to do it;
- a specific teaching task to undertake and appropriate instructional materials;
- a demonstration of effective tutoring behaviours; and
- an opportunity to role play or practise tutoring, with feedback and correction.

Peer tutors, too, can be struggling readers themselves, providing their reading competence is at a level higher than that of their tutee. There is ample evidence (Medcalf and Glynn, 1987; Glynn et al., 1996; Glynn, Berryman, O'Brien and Bishop, 2000) that peers can learn to implement responsive and interactive reading and writing tutoring procedures, and that their own reading and writing skills may be enhanced as a result of engaging in interactions with tutee students around shared literacy tasks.

Establishing a safe, responsive and cooperative classroom environment

Linking the social context and individual learning is an important concept in addressing barriers to students' literacy acquisition. It is important to ensure that classroom practices contribute to a young person's sense of agency and personal esteem and, therefore, to the construction of a positive concept of self, and his or her feelings about being able to cope with the world of school (Bruner, 1996).

> Students feel safe in an environment where they are not put down, where they are confident they will learn what they need to know, and

where they can take a few risks from time to time without the fear of
being embarrassed or ridiculed.

(Brown and Thomson, 2000, p. 52)

A sociocultural approach is applicable to the social context of the classroom because it explains the dynamic of student literacy learning in this interactive context. It makes links between the individual and the social, and
emphasizes the roles of the more competent and experienced 'others' who in
their tutoring role initially offer guided instruction for the learner through a
process of 'scaffolding' (Bruner, 1986; Palincsar, 1986; Stone, 1989). The tutor
then reduces the explicit instruction as the learner gains greater expertise as
a result of internalizing the instructions and self-directed verbalizations and
taking control over his or her learning. A sociocultural approach also explains
how, in a responsive social context, the tutor's own learning is influenced by
the student's participation and shared responsibility and agency.

Cooperative learning strategies offer learners opportunities to model, discuss, share and evaluate their learning as they plan work together, revise, edit
each others' work and discuss the content of texts and the process of reading.
However, cooperative learning does not just happen. Brown and Thomson
identify and describe a number of cooperative strategies crucial to classroom
learning that enable teachers to:

- build relationships and a sense of belonging;
- encourage students to support each other in their learning;
- empower students and foster self-responsibility;
- provide fun and enjoyable learning experiences.

(Brown and Thomson, 2000, p. 54)

At the beginning of the school year it is important for teachers and students to get to know each others' names (and how to pronounce them correctly) and something about each other. It is also important to respect their
peers' individual differences as well as the attributes and experiences they
share. Teachers can do a lot to foster this by displaying their interest in the
different experiences and backgrounds of their students and by sharing information about their own experiences and backgrounds. Effective learning conversations are never one-sided. Shared information and shared experiences
help to construct the kind of positive interpersonal relationships between
teachers and students that engender natural trust and respect. Shared literacy
activities, and reciprocal learning, can then follow, as is clearly shown in the
effects of responsive written feedback on students' writing (see Chapter 5).

In society, individuals are often required to work on their own as well as to
work collaboratively. There is an interesting paradox that autonomous and
independent literacy skills are developed and maintained in social contexts

that are responsive and interactive. Students in many classroom contexts may be quite unused to the idea of shared learning. Where this is the case, teachers are challenged to introduce their students to a range of cooperative and inclusive learning strategies. They might begin by introducing reciprocal learning within informal pairs. 'It is easy later to pyramid the pairs into teams of four when the students are ready' (Brown and Thomson, 2000, p. 55). 'Think-Pair-Share' is a simple strategy that can be used at any level to initiate a class into, or foster, cooperative learning.

Steps:

- The teacher poses a problem or asks a question to which there could be a range of answers.
- The teacher gives the students time to think about the question.
- Students turn to a partner and work together, sharing ideas, discussing, asking, clarifying questions and challenging.
- The pair share ideas with another pair or with the whole class. Students have to be able to share their partner's ideas as well as their own.

(Brown and Thomson, 2000, p. 147)

Useful variations of this activity include 'Question-Pair-Share' and 'Precis-Pair-Share'. These variations are particularly useful when students with literacy difficulties need to process information. For students such as these, the task can be more successfully achieved in the context of responsive peer tutoring.

Fostering more shared and collaborative responsibility between teachers and students creates opportunities for shared decision-making. This could involve, for example, formulating classroom rules and setting consequences for following them or not following them. Collaborative responsibility is more likely to ensure that, while each student has the right to be safe, s/he also has a responsibility not to destroy the safety of others. The right to be respected carries a responsibility to respect others. The right to learn means a responsibility to support others' learning.

Interacting with others around genuinely shared tasks and activities often leads to fun and enjoyment in learning. In cooperative learning activities, each member of the group is required to participate actively in the group's activities. Assigning specific learning support roles to individuals within groups is one way to make sure that groups work well together, that everyone has a role to perform, and upon whom others can depend. Some of the many roles that have been found useful in group work include: noise monitor, time keeper, materials manager, on-task manager, general manager/organizer, recorder, reader, checker to ensure that everyone understands the material, participation checker, agreement checker, summarizer and challenger (Brown and Thomson, 2000). However, each of these roles needs to be modelled and learned. Effective cooperative learning will not result from merely assigning different roles to students, and expecting them to understand and perform them correctly. Regular feedback needs to be provided on the accurate implementation of roles, as well as on task achievement.

Pickens, Glynn and Whitehead (2004) carried out a study of the effects of reciprocal teaching on students' reading comprehension. This study addressed the growing gap in literacy achievement between many students from non-English-speaking ethnic and cultural backgrounds, and students from homes where English is the mother tongue. The study was carried out in a low-decile South Auckland school that has a large multi-ethnic student population. Schools such as this face major challenges in delivering literacy programmes that address not just strategies for decoding English reading texts but strategies that also foster comprehension and cognitive processing of information within those texts. This study introduced a modified reciprocal teaching programme within a peer-tutored reading context, involving triads of students such that each triad comprised a higher, middle and low achieving reader. The study was conducted over two school terms, in a two-group repeated measures cross-over research design. The reciprocal teaching strategies were introduced to half the students for three 40-minute sessions per week for eight weeks, and subsequently to the second half of the students for a further eight weeks. The design involved pre, mid, and post measures on a range of standardized reading achievement measures, as well as weekly comprehension measures to assess the effect of the reciprocal peer-tutoring strategies taught within the programme, and surveys of teacher and student opinion of the procedures in action.

Pickens et al. (2004) report that their overall findings indicated clear benefits in terms of text comprehension from engaging students in the modified reciprocal teaching programme. Findings were consistent across different standardized measures and across measures of strategy knowledge. There were clear differences between the two student groups (in favour of the programme group) at the critical mid-point assessments, when one group had completed the eight-week programme and the other group had not. Corresponding gains occurred for the second group during the eight weeks when that group was in the programme. There was also evidence of maintenance effects as well as continued gains for the first group on some measures at the post-test assessment point.

The outcomes of a systematic literature review of pedagogical approaches that can effectively include pupils with difficulties in learning in mainstream classrooms serving the 7 to 14 age range (Nind and Wearmouth, 2004) show the importance of peer group interactive approaches to learning. These approaches support not only the progress in literacy acquisition but also the more effective inclusion of students who experience difficulties in learning. Just under a quarter of the studies that met the criteria for inclusion in this review involved peer group interactive approaches. In the cooperative learning groups discussed by these studies, there is a clear view of the need for a careful delineation of the roles of group members. Roles and group interactions were carefully planned, with the students' learning at the centre of the planning process.

A total of 2095 potentially relevant reports were identified for the review. The premise was that to 'effectively include' students with difficulties in mainstream classroom activities, a teaching approach needed to address both learning and participation. Early efforts at integration have been criticized on the grounds that pupils with difficulties in learning may be present in mainstream classrooms but not participating and not learning (Mittler, 2000). Underpinning the studies and the interventions identified as potentially the most useful to teachers was the model of student as learner who has active agency in the construction of personal knowledge. Moreover, all students were conceptualized as capable of learning.

Two particular studies by Stevens and Slavin (1995a, 1995b) stand out for their overall clarity of design and the weight of evidence to be attributed to them. These studies both focus on the way in which the Cooperative Integrated Reading and Composition (CIRC) programme is used in schools to support the learning of 'academically handicapped students' (Stevens and Slavin, 1995a, p. 241) through participation in cooperative learning team activities. CIRC is a research-informed cooperative learning approach to teaching elementary reading and language arts. It consists of three main elements: story-related activities that allow for input from all students while minimizing the risk of being wrong; direct instruction in comprehension strategies shown to facilitate deeper comprehension of texts; and integrated writing and language arts that ensure specific skills are applied and undertaken in wider literacy contexts. The cycle of instruction uses a 'cooperative learning type of cognitive apprenticeship' (1995a, p. 243).

The first study was intended to 'extend previous research on the effectiveness of the CIRC program' (1995a, p. 247) by investigating the effects of long-term implementation over two years, extending coverage of grades and investigating more fully the 'academic and social outcomes of using CIRC as an approach to mainstreaming academically handicapped students' (p. 248). Using a case-controlled trial, progress in reading and writing of 1299 students in 31 experimental classes using the CIRC programme was compared with progress in 32 control classes using traditional approaches. The schools were matched on socioeconomic and ethnic composition and on measures of prior achievement in literacy levels. The classes all included students with difficulties in learning, whose progress was measured and compared separately.

Findings showed that students in classrooms where teachers provide explicit instruction on reading comprehension strategies and use a writing process approach to teach writing and language arts, and where students are organized in cooperative learning teams on reading and writing activities, made greater progress in reading vocabulary, comprehension, language mechanics and expression than students in traditional classrooms. This was the case for students with and without difficulties in learning.

The second study by Stevens and Slavin (1995b) was conducted in elementary schools in predominantly 'working-class' neighbourhoods. Similar gains in literacy levels were made using the CIRC programme in this study also.

A number of issues arise from these studies. Social and academic inclusion are interconnected and fostering them requires a responsive and integrated approach to learning and teaching. Teachers fostered the co-construction of knowledge through scaffolding by, and dialogue with, peers. Belonging to, and participation in, a learning community has an important effect on young people's learning in schools. Further, involving peers may mean having to make skill development socially meaningful. One consequence of this was a holistic approach to skill development. Teachers worked on (basic) skills in a holistic way, embedded in classroom activity and subject knowledge. This meant that, for example, literacy work at the level of sound-symbol identification was carried out within the context of text that was meaningful to the learner as well as to the tutor. This approach differs from the more usual fragmented or task-analysed, phonics-based approach to literacy instruction for those students identified as having special educational needs.

Implicit in the approaches researched in these studies is a necessity for teachers and students to have a shared understanding of their role in the social context of learning in the classroom, as well as a respect for individuals who experience difficulties.

'Inclusion' of individuals in mainstream classrooms in the sense of participation in the learning community cannot occur without cooperation and collaboration. All members of the school community, both adults and peers, were seen to be involved in knowledge construction through social interactions. Stevens and Slavin (1995b, p. 327), for example, write from a whole-school perspective of the 'cooperative elementary school' where teachers, principals and parents collaborate in instructional planning, decision-making and in coaching one another. As evidenced in Stevens's 'cooperative elementary school', cooperative group work in a cooperative classroom is unlikely to occur consistently and as a regular part of the curriculum unless cooperation, collaboration and negotiation are a hallmark of the school as a whole. The rural school described in Chapter 8 provides some detailed evidence of a principal, teachers, parents and community engaged in collaborative instructional planning, decision-making and construction of literacy activities.

Assessing the classroom learning environment

From a sociocultural view of the student-as-learner, in which the social context is crucial to progress in literacy acquisition, classroom teaching by teachers can be experienced by students as either supporting or inhibiting their literacy learning. As we note in Chapter 7, in a wide-ranging review of the literature on learning environments, Ysseldyke and Christenson (1987) argue that, for those interested in improving literacy levels among all students in classrooms, it is important to focus on features of classroom practice because these can be altered to facilitate learning more effectively. The instructional factors in the classroom identified by these authors as influencing student outcomes in all academic domains are:

- Planning procedures
- Management procedures
- Teaching procedures
- Practice – Related factors

(Ysseldyke and Christenson, 1987, p. 19)

'The Instructional Environment Scale' (TIES) (Ysseldyke and Christenson, 1987) was designed to support the systematic collection of data in classrooms to analyse contextual barriers to pupils' learning and identify starting points for designing interventions for individual students. TIES is discussed further in Chapter 7.

Attributes of successful teachers of literacy

Implied in Ysseldyke and Christenson's work is the need for high levels of teacher expertise to effectively support children's literacy acquisition, especially among those who experience difficulties, a clear focus on student literacy learning, and expert knowledge of collaborative and inclusive reading strategies. These teacher attributes are also among the findings of an important research project by Wragg et al. into the effective teaching of literacy at primary level. There is no single formula for good practice in literacy teaching, however:

> . . . several teachers observed gave prominence to the display of children's work and the celebration of it, as well as to the use of environmental print and the labelling of classroom features. Two teachers whose classes achieved amongst the highest gains in reading proficiency on standardised tests given early and late in the school year,

however, showed little interest in display, and their classroom walls were relatively bare. . . . most teachers managed to secure a very high degree of pupil attentiveness to the task in hand, so that was common. What was different was the manifold means through which they achieved this goal, sometimes by fast-paced enthusiastic interactions prior to reading or written work, in other cases though a more quietly supportive, even private, approach to individuals. . . .

(Wragg et al., 1998, p. 265)

Ten features were identified from observations of classroom practices that characterize successful literacy teachers. These clearly suggest how some teachers, as the more informed and more skilful learners, might mediate and scaffold new literacy learning in the classroom.

. . . The ten features which several teachers manifested, in their different individual forms, were as follows:

A high level of personal enthusiasm for literature, some even supplementing the school's reading resources with their own personal collection of books.

Good professional knowledge of children's authors and teaching strategies.

Literacy being made very important, within a rich literacy environment.

Celebrating progress publicly, and increasing children's confidence.

Being able to individualise and match teaching to pupils, particularly in terms of their reading interests.

Systematic monitoring and assessment, though the form of it varied.

Regular and varied reading activities.

Pupils being encouraged to develop independence and autonomy, attacking unfamiliar words, taking their own reading forward, or backing their own judgement as authors.

A notably high degree of classroom management skill and good-quality personal relationships with pupils, with some of the highest 'on-task' scores we have recorded.

High positive expectations, with children striving to reach a high standard, whatever their circumstances.

(Wragg et al., 1998, pp. 265–6)

As Wragg et al. comment (1998, p. 206), of these ten factors, it is particularly important for teachers to be able to differentiate and match tasks to students with regard to students who are 'less able and more reluctant readers'. 'Intimate knowledge of available reading materials and individual children themselves' is required, 'taking account not only of varying levels of ability, but also of individual personal interests'.

Differentiation

In recognizing that different children respond to different approaches and that children may benefit from individual support, many researchers imply the need for differentiated approaches to meet the individual literacy needs and learning styles of pupils (Visser, 1993; Phillips, 1999). Differentiation of teaching to meet individual needs is the very cornerstone of inclusion. In the *Special Educational Needs Code of Practice* in England (DfES, 2001, 5:18; 6:18) differentiation is claimed to support the learning of all students, including those who experience difficulties in literacy:

> Differentiation of learning activities within the . . . curriculum frame-work will help schools to meet the learning needs of all children.

In Northern Ireland, the *Code of Practice for the Identification and Assessment of Special Educational Needs* (DENI, 1998) claims that 'differentiation of class-work within a common curriculum framework will help the school to meet the learning needs of all pupils'. This statement, however, begs a number of questions. Among these are:

- How can some teachers make special provision for individual students whilst maintaining overall curriculum coherence?
- How can special provision be provided without risking marginalizing and stigmatizing some pupils?

Responding to these issues requires a great deal of reflection on the part of teachers in schools, and discussion with students and their families. There is a particular dilemma accompanying the choice of appropriate differentiated curricula. On the one hand, students sharing identical learning aims and working at the same curricula may be deprived of the opportunity to develop competencies appropriate to their needs. On the other hand, these students may be made to feel inferior, if their curriculum is seen to be different. What-ever alterations teachers make to enable pupils who experience difficulties with literacy to engage more fully in any aspect of the curriculum might solve some problems but create others (Norwich, 1994). Solutions commonly adopted include:

- reducing the content coverage of the curriculum to release more time for literacy development;
- enabling some pupils to access the curriculum through alternative means, for example through the use of information and communications technology;
- providing different pedagogy, materials or specialist teaching for some pupils.

The issue of the readability of text is also linked to that of differentiation in that it is a major concern in considering the appropriateness of reading materials for all students. There are at least three major factors to take into account when considering how easily students can read text (Lunzer and Gardner, 1986):

- The interest level of the text – and/or prior knowledge of the subject matter. If pupils are interested in, or already understand, the ideas and events that they are reading about, they can cope with more difficult text.
- Sentence length and complexity, word length and familiarity.
- Conciseness of explanation of concepts. More pupils can understand higher-level concepts if ideas are expanded and explained step by step.

There are numerical formulae to work out the difficult levels and hence the recommended reading age of a text. However, these are largely technical in the sense that they only take word/sentence length into account, and not meaning or interest level. The Flesch Formula (1994) is an example of such a technical understanding of readability.

There are, however, ways of modifying texts to reduce reading and/or conceptual difficulty. Lunzer and Gardner (1986), for example, offer the following suggestion:

- Shorten sentences.
- Use easier, shorter, more familiar words. Cut out technical vocabulary, unless it is absolutely essential.
- Spread out the text so that there are fewer words per page.
- Simplify sentence structure.
- Turn passive verbs ('He was bitten by the dog.') into active verbs ('The dog bit him.').
- Give a step-by-step explanation of concepts.

Motivational strategies

Another challenge regularly facing teachers of students experiencing literacy difficulties is lack of motivation for reading. Most motivational theories propose that students tend to take an active approach to learning if they believe their effort will succeed. 'Locus of control' theorists (for example, Crandall, Katkovsky and Crandall, 1965) propose that, to succeed in academic learning, it is important to believe that academic successes and failures result from one's own efforts and skills, that is to 'internal' factors, rather than to 'external' factors, such as luck or the fairness of the task. One very important motivational factor for literacy development is students' increasing sense of control over their own level of achievement. 'Attributional' theorists (for example, Weiner, 1979; Dweck and Licht, 1980) propose that willingness to try hard is more likely where previous academic difficulties have been attributed to factors within the learner's control, such as lack of effort. 'Self-efficacy' theorists (for example, Bandura, 1982; Schunk, 1989) stress that, if a learner is to succeed, it is important for her/him to believe that s/he has the ability to perform well. Encouraging pupils to set specific, 'proximal' goals (for example, by indicating the number of tasks they aim to complete in one lesson) leads to higher self-efficacy and greater achievement than setting 'distal' goals (for example, by indicating how many sessions it takes to complete an entire learning programme) (Bandura and Schunk, 1981).

Motivational interventions, however, are likely to be effective only if they are integrated with good teaching programmes and are certainly no substitute for them. Many pupils with difficulties in the literacy area, for example, cannot read, write or spell better simply by trying harder. Indeed, it is quite unrealistic and harmful to increase pressure on students to improve performance on tasks which they do not understand, or for which they do not have the necessary experience and skills. These students therefore do not need further motivation, but need strategies to help them improve their literacy level (Palincsar and Brown, 1984). Later studies have integrated 'attribution retraining' with training in strategies for improving literacy, for example strategy training in improving reading comprehension (Borkowski, Weyhing and Carr, 1988). Borkowski et al. concluded that students who receive both attribution retraining and training in literacy strategies are more likely to use the literacy strategies than students who receive the strategy training alone.

To ensure that students continue to believe that increasing their efforts will help them to succeed, responsive classrooms must ensure that these students experience early success. However, tasks set must not be so easy that they do not require much effort (Dweck, 1975; Schunk, 1989). They need to be set at a level of difficulty at which the learners can achieve if they try hard. Also, as noted earlier, tasks and activities should not be so fragmented that they lose their meaning for students. For example, excessive practice in matching letters to sounds may result in some students 'losing the plot' and not learning how these tasks connect with reading and writing interesting stories.

The comments teachers make about students' learning and performance have also been shown to affect pupil motivation. For example, feedback that sets out specific information about what the learner did well and what could be done differently, and how this could be achieved, as well as comments about how the pupil's current level of achievement compared with past achievement, have been shown to enhance pupils' self-perceptions of success, and lead to improved levels of achievement when compared with grades or comments that compare students with peers (Krampen, 1987).

From a sociocultural view, tutoring of students' reading, or responding to the messages that they write, by offering scaffolded support within the learner's zone of proximal development, requires feedback that is responsive to the student's current stage of development, and that is positive, and respectful and not overpowering or controlling. The effectiveness of feedback that meets these criteria is shown clearly in a research project in five mainstream New Zealand schools (Bishop et al., 2003) which sought to identify how teacher responsiveness and the experiences and understandings of Māori students at Years 9 and 10 could lead to more effective educational outcomes. The research project carefully monitored any changes in Māori students' participation and achievement levels that might have occurred as a result of interventions instigated by these researchers.

Researchers used narrative inquiry and discourse analysis of student narratives to identify and explore solutions. Focus group interviews were held with separate groups of Māori students identified by the school as either engaged or non-engaged with classroom learning activities. Interviews were also conducted with students' families. Despite the five schools in this research varying widely in size, socioeconomic circumstances, location, teacher experiences and student composition, student narratives from the five schools and from other groups interviewed were extraordinarily consistent. Both engaged and non-engaged Māori students identified relationships between teachers and students as key to engagement with curriculum learning. Above all, they asked to be treated fairly:

> Don't yell at kids. . . . If you don't like something we're doing tell us quietly. Talk to us about where we sit. Give us a chance to sit with our mates. If we muck up then warn us and if we are too thick to listen [to the warning] then move us. . . . We won't nick if you don't think we will. Expect us to do well and to be good. Don't rave on about how you don't want to be here. Don't put us down and don't let us put our friends down. Be fair.
>
> (Bishop et al., 2003, pp. 240–1)

Respect from their teachers was extremely important to these students:

> Look pleased to see us. Treat us respectfully. Look like you want to be here. Say 'hi' to us when we come in. . . . Mark our work often. Tell us when we're doing good. Better still tell our family.
>
> (Bishop et al., 2003, pp. 240–1)

These Year 9 and 10 Māori students wanted their teachers to have expert knowledge in their subject, be well prepared and focus on high achievement in the classroom:

> Don't start thinking about what you are going to teach us when we walk in the room. Get prepared. . . . Be keen about your subject so we want to come. . . . Just 'cause we are a 'C' class, don't expect us to be dumb. We might be there because we were naughty at Intermediate (Year 7 and 8).
>
> (Bishop et al., 2003, pp. 240–1)

These students also talked about the kind of pedagogy teachers needed to use if they were to engage students with curriculum learning. This reflects very closely the outcomes of the systematic literature review outlined earlier in relation to cooperative learning:

> Don't have us writing all the time and being quiet. Let us talk to each other about what we're doing. We know we have to be quiet sometimes, like tests. Give us fun things to do like quizzes in groups, discussions, debates, art activities, practical maths, solving problems in groups. . . . Let us cooperate about the work. Yeah we have good ideas, good sensible ideas about how to do things. Just ask us.
>
> (Bishop et al., 2003, pp. 240–1)

This research focused specifically on the personal understandings and school experiences of Māori students, and therefore conclusions reached were reported in relation to this cultural group only. However, the 'effective teaching profile' for Māori students that was drawn up by the researchers reflects much of what has been discussed already by Wragg et al. (1998) concerning teacher attributes, effective pedagogy and concern for taking the views of students seriously.

The effective teaching profile requires teachers to:

- reject deficit theorizing about the performance and achievement of Māori students, and demonstrate that they care for students as culturally located individuals;

- encourage students to bring their own prior cultural experiences into the classroom as the basis for new learning experiences;
- care for the performance of their students, assessing their work in a range of ways and providing regular and timely feedback and 'feed-forward' (an example, in reading, when the student comes to an unknown word, would be: 'Leave the word and read on. As you do that, think about what word might make sense in that space');
- have sound pedagogical knowledge that is used to create secure well-managed responsive and interactive learning environments;
- engage students in a range of effective teaching interactions, including peer interactive approaches and co-construction of knowledge.

A number of teachers agreed to pilot the use of this profile. The researchers found that these teachers were able to position themselves to focus more closely on improving relationships and interactions within their classrooms. Detailed teacher observations, feedback, co-construction meetings and in-class shadow coaching revealed that when teachers received sufficient in-school support to maintain these new pedagogies, corresponding improvements were found in Māori students' attendance, attitude, engagement, behaviour and academic achievement. These teachers also reported greater job satisfaction, with a renewed focus on teaching and student learning rather than on managing behaviour.

Literacy learning in responsive classrooms

Across the world there have been a number of attempts to design a whole literacy curriculum in classrooms from a view of knowledge as co-constructed between teacher and learner. This view proceeds from a belief that every child can make progress in literacy within the responsive social contexts created in classrooms. An example of this approach is to be found in the KEEP (Kamehameha Elementary Education Program) Demonstration Classroom Project in Hawaii (Au and Carroll, 1997). The original KEEP project was designed to improve the literacy achievement of students of Native Hawaiian ancestry who, as a group 'in public schools in Hawaii tend to score in the lowest quartile on standardized reading tests (Kamehameha Schools, 1993)' (Au and Carroll, 1997, p. 204).

A whole-literacy curriculum was introduced based on the assumption that teaching should move from wider conceptual understandings of literacy to targeting specific knowledge and skills, 'whole to part'. The overall goal of the programme was student ownership of literacy. The curriculum emphasized reading and writing more than speaking and listening. Ability grouping for reading was used for part of the time to facilitate the learning of beginning reading skills. Grade-level benchmarks were designed 'to focus instruction and facilitate program evaluation' (Au and Carroll, 1997, pp. 204–5). Two blocks of time were set aside for literacy learning through the writers' and readers' workshops. Typically, writers' workshop:

> began with a mini-lesson and teacher and student discussion of writing issues, followed by a period when students selected their own topics and wrote using a process approach (Calkins, 1991; Graves, 1983). Teacher and peer conferences occurred during this time. Near the end of the workshop, the teacher generally gathered the students together for the author's chair (Graves & Hansen, 1983), a time when one or two students read their drafts or published books aloud to the class and received feedback about their pieces.
>
> (Au and Carroll, 1997, p. 205)

The teacher began the readers' workshop by reading aloud or running a mini-lesson.

> The teacher met with students in small groups to discuss works of literature. Generally, teachers selected three to four book titles ... Teachers used different approaches to grouping. In the primary grades, students were grouped by ability about half the time and by interest (e.g. in reading a particular book or in doing research on a particular topic) the rest of the time. In the upper grades, students were usually grouped by interest. Small-group discussion generally began with students sharing their writing in response to literature. When not meeting with the teacher, students read independently or with a partner, wrote in their literature response logs, and worked on individual and small-group projects. Time was allotted for sustained silent reading, sometimes during a different part of the day.
>
> (Au and Carroll, 1997, p. 205)

Both of these workshops incorporated literacy contexts that were responsive, interactive and social.

When the project was first introduced, student outcomes for ownership, voluntary reading and strategies for word reading were seen as 'promising' (Au, 1994). However, outcomes for writing, comprehension and knowledge of language and vocabulary remained 'poor', with around two-thirds of students achieving below-average scores. Three issues appeared to contribute to this initial lack of success, and all have implications for teacher workload and the need for professional development programmes:

1   The shift in teachers' roles of the readers' and writers' workshops meant that 'teachers had to become expert at highly responsive, interactive forms of instruction (for example in writing conferences)'.
2   In trying to achieve the balance between guidance and increasing student choice and responsibility, teachers needed to share in the same literacy processes as students, for example in writing their own pieces.
3   Portfolio assessment also meant a new approach to evaluation of students' work. Support for teachers was focused on teachers new to the profession or to KEEP. Experienced teachers also required support from external consultants.

Deciding what a good writers' or readers' workshop should look like was difficult. This meant that teachers and consultants were not sure how the workshops should be evaluated or of the next steps to be taken. Outcomes suggested that even with much goodwill on the part of teachers, they needed a great deal more support in learning how to introduce more responsive pedagogies. Undoubtedly, it is extremely challenging to shift the teaching pedagogies and practices of some teachers. In research presented earlier, Bishop et al. (2003) found that one effective way to do this was to share with teachers the direct experiences of students through narratives as an objective window into students' reality. Teachers were then able to co-construct more effective in-class responses.

A further initiative, the Demonstration Classroom Project (Au and Carroll, 1997), was devised to take account of these issues. Each consultant in this project identified one teacher who was able, before the end of the year, to fully implement the writers' or readers' workshops and focused his/her efforts on supporting this. A classroom implementation checklist was drawn up for these workshops. Included in the checklist for writing were:

> *Classroom organisation*
> • Clarity and consistency in workshop rules and procedures
> • References and resources accessible to students
> • Regular location for promoting collaboration
> *Student opportunities for learning*
> • Students show confidence and pride in own writing
> • Students have knowledge of writing process: revision
> • Students have knowledge of writing process: sharing
> *Instructional practices*
> • Teacher as a writer: shares own writing
> • Teacher conducts whole-class mini-lessons
> • Teacher makes connections between literature and student writing

Assessment
- Portfolios contain writing samples
- Students set goals for learning
- Students meet with teacher about portfolios

(Au and Carroll, 1997, p. 219)

Thirteen teachers from seven schools took part in the project during year 1, eleven focusing on writing and two on reading. An additional twenty teachers joined in year 2, eighteen focusing on writing and two on reading. Over half the students were of Native Hawaiian ancestry, almost all speaking Hawaii Creole English as their first language, and coming from low-income families.

The results of students who had been present in the classroom for either reading or writing workshops, as appropriate to the class, were included in the analyses of portfolio data if they had been in the school for more than half the school year. Sample students were observed monthly, and progress against benchmarks was monitored and teaching approaches adjusted as needed. Throughout the whole workshop sessions monthly classroom observations of teachers and students were made. The degree of programme implementation was measured using the classroom implementation checklist.

Data showed a high level of implementation of individual programme items by the end of the project. Classroom organization items were the most readily implemented. Instructional practices were harder to implement. Some teachers felt uncomfortable about sharing their writing with their students. However, students responded positively to those who took the risk, and by the end of the project there was a high level of implementation of these items. Portfolio assessment, including record keeping, review meetings with students, discussion of benchmarks and moving towards student self-assessment of progress proved complex and time-consuming to develop. In terms of students' achievements, prior to the project KEEP teachers had not been able 'to move student achievement from below grade level to average and above levels in the writing process' (Au and Carroll, 1997, p. 217). Sixty per cent of student achievement in the writing process was below grade level and 40 per cent was at grade level. After one year the pattern of student achievement was reversed, with 68 per cent achieving above or at grade level, and 32 per cent below. There were similar results in the second year. Au and Carroll identify two tools as instrumental in KEEP's success:

- The classroom checklist, which created a framework/structure for collaboratively evaluating and planning implementation items between teachers and consultants, providing a basis both for self-assessment for veteran teachers and for teacher in-service sessions.
- The grade-level benchmarks which focused attention on all aspects of the programme. These led to careful planning of instruction based on

students' learning needs and facilitated the sharing of a vision of literacy learning between teachers and students who were a party to them.

Au and Carroll (1997) conclude that, to be effective, constructivist approaches must be implemented fully to be effective. However, there was still a great need for teacher development centred on knowledge about literacy, as well as on skills in classroom management.

The failure of KEEP to raise achievement in the writing process during the first two years, and its subsequent success following incorporation of focused and targeted advice and moral support from consultants for teachers, highlights the high degree of expertise needed to make collaborative, constructivist approaches work. 'Teachers without institutional support or a strong background in constructivist curricula may be able to achieve only part of this plan' (Au and Carroll, 1997, p. 217). Similar conclusions were reached in the systematic literature review described earlier (Nind and Wearmouth, 2004).

Conclusion

A sociocultural position on learning underpins the view that classroom contexts that can support all student literacy learning needs, and in particular the needs of those who experience difficulties, should be responsive. This position assumes that, for the individual learner, everything is perceived, mediated and recontextualized by what is salient, socially, culturally and personally, for him or through her as an individual. Students are seen as active agents in their own learning, while teachers, other adults and peers may act to mediate learning through scaffolding within the zone of proximal development, or guiding participation in new learning activities. The implication here is that teachers and others should share control, while offering sufficient support to enable learners to progress and begin to manage their own learning. Sharing control requires a great deal of reflection and sensitivity to young people's learning needs on the part of teachers, and a great deal of openness and collaboration on the part of all those involved in students' classroom learning. This kind of reflective practice, as Schön (1983) notes, allows new understandings of learners' literacy difficulties in schools and opens up new possibilities for pedagogy.

It is probably at classroom level that the most important interactions occur between teachers and learners. It is important to ensure that, whatever pedagogies are employed and whichever activities are organized, participation in classroom practices contribute to students' sense of self-efficacy and identity as literacy learners. With feelings of self-efficacy and a strong identity as literacy learners, students will be better able to cope with the world of school (Bruner, 1996).

3   Responsive oral contexts for literacy

Introduction

This chapter explores the nature of social interactions that serve to increase students' oral language competence in the context of learning to read and write, and outlines a number of facilitative strategies and activities.

There are many students whose reading level is consistently assessed as several years below what might be expected, and whose writing is poor given their chronological age, or given the length of time they have participated in school literacy programmes. Often, these students are drafted into 'remedial' reading contexts in order to address this problem. However, this may seriously limit opportunities for them to engage with meaningful and interesting texts, by increasing the amount of time and effort spent engaging in letter-sound recognition skills, in recognizing individual words in isolation, and in analysis of sounds within individual words. There are also many students who are learning to read and write in a second language, but whose initial fast progress through a series of graded texts is halted when their reading accuracy soon outstrips their comprehension. This chapter explores strategies for building up students' oral language skills, by supporting them to talk about what they have been reading, to re-tell those stories, and to talk about how the reading material connects with what they already know.

Low performance on measures of comprehension of written texts may also reflect students' limited vocabulary, and/or limited experience in talking about characters and events within stories, and relating these to their own knowledge and experience. The potential of a meaningful 'talk to expand literacy' approach that goes beyond studying letters and words is supported in this chapter by a number of research studies. Some of these relate to students who are learning a second language and who are often required to engage with written texts whose language structure and complexity is well beyond that of their current oral language competence.

Thinking and talking

Talking is an essential intellectual and social skill that is shaped by how we think, and forms part of how we communicate with others and make sense of the world. From birth, children appear to learn and use their first language in a natural and easy way from their immersion in oral language contexts. Babies are able to communicate their emotions and have their needs satisfied long before they can talk. Vygotsky (1962) contends that all mental processes have social origins. The sense of words is rooted in experience with others. From what they hear and see, and how others respond to them, babies actively begin to construct language and to communicate their own ideas with those around them. People they know talk to them, talk about them and talk to each other. Sounds from music, rhymes and words are often a part of their very first intellectual and social experiences.

Young children first experience an activity with others, then internalize the experience through symbolizing it in words:

> Any function in the child's development appears twice, on two planes. First it appears on the social plane, and then on the psychological plane. First it appears between people as an interpsychological category, and then within the child as an intrapsychological category. This is equally true with regard to voluntary attention, logical memory, the formation of concepts, and the development of volition.
> (Vygotsky, 1981, p. 163)

The young child's thought development begins through interpersonal negotiation with others, caregivers, teachers and peers at school, and this is internalized into intrapersonal understanding. Vygotsky (1962) further suggests that:

> . . . at about the age of two the curves of development of thought and speech, till then separate, meet and join to initiate a new form of behaviour.
> (p. 43)

Learning to read and write, when interpreted as the ability to perceive and reproduce graphic symbols and make sound-symbol links, is often considered an individual, *intrapersonal* process. However, if learning to read and write are seen, in their broadest sense, as understanding and communicating meaning in the form of text, then the *interpersonal* dimension is crucial, that is the understanding of the reading and writing tasks in company with caregivers, teachers, peers and others.

High expectations and responsive learning contexts

Parents and caregivers expect their children will learn to talk. Children's talk is likely to develop more easily where adults respond positively to the message that a child is trying to communicate, and use all manner of cues to help interpret this meaningfully. Responsive feedback, involving a parent reacting to the messages of a child, is seldom expressed in words alone. Facial expressions and other body language may support the message, or serve alone to convey the message. Whatever the case, parent or caregiver attention is usually directed at responding to the message rather than being concerned with its grammatical correctness. Genuine interest, and honest and positive responsive feedback such as this, encourages children to continue using the language that they have and to take risks with their use of new language and ideas, for example by trying out a successful way of gaining attention, learned in one context, in a new and different context.

An example of the linkages between thoughts and oral language occurring in a responsive childcare context comes from the experience of one of the authors of this book. She is a grandmother with an almost 2-year-old grandchild, Karamea, who is just beginning to combine the use of thoughts with the formation and combination of groups of words. On one occasion they had been waiting for people to join them at a *pōwhiri* (a formal Māori ceremony at which guests are acknowledged and welcomed to the meeting house by locals). A car pulled up and out stepped two elders whom Karamea knew well, liked very much, and had been learning to call 'Nanny' because of their age and position in the local community.

> 'Nannies' she smiled.
> 'Yes', her grandmother agreed, 'Nanny Mate and Nanny Kaa'.

A look of confusion on Karamea's face was followed by a kick on the wheel of the car as she firmly pointed out to her grandmother that this was the 'car'. Understanding Karamea's logic, and not quite knowing how to respond at that point, the grandmother agreed that it was a car and wondered how the confusion between the elder's name 'Kaa' and 'car' as a vehicle could be resolved. The resolution occurred, however, quite soon after the formality of the welcoming rituals had ended and the group had entered the meeting house. Another woman entered the room, asking for 'Kaa'. Karamea was immediately alerted to the woman's request. She watched as the woman approached Kaa and again used her name. Karamea then turned to her grandmother and asked, 'Nanny Kaa?'

> 'Yes', agreed her grandmother, 'Nanny Kaa'.

Karamea nodded her head and smiled and her grandmother knew that the word 'Kaa' had just taken on new meaning. From this shared experience, Karamea was actively learning to learn. Vygotsky (1962) refers to 'inner speech', describing thought as 'a dynamic, unstable thing, fluttering between word and thought' (p. 149). Karamea had been able to process the events, reflect on the exchange between herself and her grandmother, and internalize understanding of two similar-sounding words, 'car' and 'Kaa'. 'From such brief tussles in moments of not quite understanding, the child learns more about language' (Clay, 1991, p. 68).

Culture

Even while we are very young, the cultural contexts within which we grow up and the people with whom we engage begin to shape our ability to organize meaning in ways that we can communicate with others. 'Thought development is determined by language' (Vygotsky, 1962, p. 51) and in turn, this is developed by linguistic skills and sociocultural experiences (Smith and Elley, 1997). Bruner (1996) also contends that cognitive development such as this steadily evolves within a society where the 'reality' of individual experience is represented by symbolism that is shared among people, such as verbal or written language, and where the community's way of life is organized and understood through that shared symbolism. The interpretive system within which human intentional states are situated imposes patterns that are rooted in history and inherent in language and discourse, logic and narrative.

> . . . it is culture, not biology, that shapes human life and the human mind, that gives meaning to action by situating its underlying intentional states in an interpretive system. It does this by imposing the patterns inherent in the culture's symbolic systems – its language and discourse modes, the forms of logical and narrative explication, and the patterns of mutually dependent communal life.
>
> (Bruner, 1990, p. 34)

Kawagley (1995), of the Yupiaq nation, further maintains that the principles and shared symbolism that we acquire throughout our lifetime in order to make sense of the world around us contribute to the formation of our worldview. We learn these principles from birth from the values, traditions, customs, myths, legends and other stories shared and modelled, first by our own immediate family and/or caregivers, then by the community in general.

Learning from experience

Meaning-making, as well as being situated in a cultural context, also comes from the prior conceptions that learners bring with them into new situations (Bruner, 1996). These prior conceptions result from previous learning in other contexts. New learning or our ability to make sense of these new experiences in new contexts is a product of the 'interplay' between contexts and is continuous and recursive. This often involves the learner having the confidence and support to problem solve and take risks. An example of this was observed when Karamea, mentioned above, came across a pair of bright, fluffy slippers that she had never seen before. With the heel of one slipper placed inside the toe of the other, the slippers sat looking like a multi-coloured fluffy toy. Karamea picked them up, turned them upside down, and for a moment looked quite confused. She then found that they could come apart and that there were, in fact, two objects. In so doing, she realized what they were, dropped them on the floor, put her feet in them and proudly explained to everyone around, 'hoos' (her version of 'shoes'). She had clear expectations that her efforts would be affirmed, so paraded forth in the 'hoos' to receive the attention and kudos she felt was due. The nannies responded accordingly.

Sociocultural perspectives on human learning emphasize the importance of responsive social and cultural contexts as key components of successful learning (Vygotsky, 1978; McNaughton, 1995; Gregory, 1996; Rogoff, 2003). Hohepa, Smith, Smith and McNaughton (1992) maintain also that the acquisition of linguistic knowledge and the acquisition of cultural knowledge are interdependent. Participation in structured social activities within a cultural context, where the users are active rather than passive participants in the process, enables the learner to acquire both linguistic and sociocultural knowledge. Ensuring that there are participants within the learning setting who have more expert linguistic and sociocultural knowledge will predispose or 'prime' a learning environment to promote meaningful social and cultural outcome for all (Hohepa et al., 1992; Rogoff, 2003).

Powerful reciprocal learning can occur between parent and child, or in peer interactions. Such learning contexts are often characterized by opportunities for children to initiate learning interaction and reciprocal skill gains between the teacher and the learner (Glynn, 1995). Barnard (2003, p. 1) cites a term coined by Agar (1994) '*languaculture*' to indicate the inseparability of language and learning from culture: 'Language is the cultural tool by which common knowledge is sought and mutual understanding is reached . . . the connection between children's language and their cognitive and cultural development is so close as to be indivisible.'

Framework for language learning

The conditions under which young children learn to use their oral language and their other emergent literacy skills at home also provide a framework for conditions that would be beneficial in classroom literacy programmes (Cambourne, 1988). Cambourne suggests that for oral language learning to be effective, teachers should:

- immerse students in language and literacy;
- demonstrate a range of literacy strategies and in a range of different contexts;
- ensure learners are actively engaged in the language and the demonstrations;
- set high expectations;
- help learners to take responsibility for their learning;
- support learners to make approximations;
- provide learners with ample opportunities to practise language; and
- respond to the learners' language.

As previously noted, the first important responsive social and cultural context in which language learning takes place is within the home, and this begins with the language models and the responses to language provided by parents and caregivers. The different forms of language and social interaction learned first will affect the way that students communicate with others, at home, at school and in the wider community. In the UK, Jack (not his real name), a white, working-class adult inmate in a prison, describes how he was bringing up his child to speak Standard English (Wearmouth, 1999, pp. 15–13):

> I take him down the shops with me and I point out things to him – car, bus.
> We speak to him properly – 'It's a bus, a blue car'. We don't say: 'Car, car', or things like that.

Very difficult home circumstances had resulted in Jack's own education being chaotic and frustrating. What he had come to value and what he wanted for his children, in order that they should be fully included in society, was what he had not had himself: a traditional, structured, disciplined mainstream education:

> I want them to go to a Catholic school because Catholic schools are a higher education. A lot better than these modern comprehensives

where they teach them Hindu and stuff like that, and they come home speaking some kind of foreign language, and stuff like that.

Jack had spent a long time in a residential school for 'maladjusted' young people. His hopes for a good education at the mainstream school to which he was finally sent were dashed when he encountered an English teacher born of an ethnic minority family. Jack made an immediate assumption that a teacher whom he construed as 'foreign' would not have command of the English language, and withdrew himself from the lesson. A teacher of English from a minority ethnic group violated Jack's sense of what was 'normal' and 'good'. According to Jack, 'proper' English was taught by the English:

> I went to a school in L where they had an English teacher who was a P*** (minority ethnic), and I didn't even understand what he said. I was only there for about two weeks . . . I got kicked out of there because I didn't want a P*** (minority ethnic) English teacher. Totally disgusting that a P*** (minority ethnic teacher) who couldn't even speak my language was trying to teach me English. I walked out, half the class followed me, and I got expelled.

Jack construed this teacher as 'bad' because he was supposed to teach English but he could not speak it with an English accent. Therefore, in Jack's view, he did not have command of his own subject and was presenting students with 'rubbish' of the sort that Jack had been subjected to in his secondary boarding school. The teacher did not have long enough to show whether he was good or bad in any other terms before Jack walked out of the classroom.

A similar view to Jack's was held by a group of Year 9 and 10 Māori students interviewed as part of a New Zealand study that looked for ways to engage Māori students with their learning (Bishop et al., 2003). These students expressed frustration with teachers who had strong 'foreign' accents. They reported these teachers as frustrating because they were so difficult to understand. Such teachers need to be aware of these frustrations. Otherwise they may have difficulty forming responsive, social relationships with their students, and so be unable to engage all students effectively with curriculum tasks.

The examples of Jack and the Māori students provide powerful illustrations of what can happen when the language and cultural expectations of students and their families are different from the language of the curriculum and/or the language or culture of the teacher or school. If teachers are to engage students positively in learning then they need to know how to be responsive to the experiences of their students (Bishop et al., 2003). Challenges to oral language learning and subsequent literacy learning certainly occur when students cannot understand their teachers. The language and culture in many schools and classrooms, albeit unwittingly, can overpower and marginalize the language and culture of groups of minority students (Bishop et al., 2003). For students who come from language and cultural backgrounds other than those embodied in the curriculum delivery, it is particularly important to acknowledge and build on the years of accumulated social and cultural experience that these students come with. These students typically include those for whom English is a second language. In some countries this group also includes those who are taught in immersion classrooms as second language learners of their own indigenous language. This is the case for many Maori students in New Zealand.

Although complete bilingualism and biculturalism in all teachers in bilingual and immersion programmes is an important goal, it is a long way from the reality in many schools. Tharp (1994) addressed this situation in the United States and proposed basic teaching and learning principles for supporting other language groups. These were:

- Developing competence and mastery in the language of instruction as the basis for academic achievement should mean that language development is a goal across the entire curriculum.
- The school, the curriculum, and teaching itself should provide language contexts that are embedded in the experiences, skills and values of the community. When this is not occurring, schools are teaching through language that for many students is disconnected from their lives and communities. Such a context ignores and belittles the initial language learning that was acquired in responsive social contexts reflecting the values and practices of the students' own families (Glynn, 1987).
- Teaching and learning should occur in contexts that promote joint productive activity between peers and their teachers.
- The basic form of teaching should occur through instructional conversations or dialogue between teacher and learners. Goldenberg (1991) describes instructional conversations as discussions based on lessons geared towards creating rich opportunities for students' conceptual and linguistic development. These conversations balance the power between 'teacher' and 'learner' in initiating and controlling language learning (Glynn, 1987).

Tharp's four principles provide a solid foundation of culturally responsive teaching and learning methods, for all learners, both those whose first language is the language of instruction as well as those who are second language learners of the language of instruction. The years of accumulated experience of language and sociocultural knowledge that students bring with them into the classroom is recognized, valued and affirmed through the interpersonal relationships teachers have with their students and through the interactions that take place in classrooms.

To reach this position, teachers need to build relationships with their students on the basis of a shared understanding of prior experiences, to set high expectations and develop mutual respect in much the same way as parents learn to relate to their own children.

Where students are able to bring their own prior experiences into the classroom learning context, the purpose of the activity is more likely to make sense to them. This is especially important when the cultural values and practices of the students are different from those of their teachers. Language learning needs to be experience-based and supported by opportunities for students to talk and engage with their peers and teachers. This can be achieved through the use of collaborative interactions and strategies (Bishop et al., 2003) such as story and song, modelling, providing supportive conversational scaffolds or frameworks, co-construction, and problem solving.

The significance of story and song

Orally told stories, rhymes, songs, prayers and routines for meeting and greeting people all have an important role in literacy acquisition, and children participate in these activities within many cultures long before they begin any form of formal education. In making the links between literacy and language, some researchers have defined literacy as a 'specific oral language register' (Jones, 2003, p. 166) which shares many of the elements of the language used in early reading texts (Heath, 1983; Gregory, 1996; Greenhalgh and Strong, 2001), and hence has been labelled 'literate language' (Jones, 2003). One of the differences between text and spoken conversation is that written stories have a different structure, for example Lüthi's (1970) 'story grammar', whereas, for the most part, spoken conversations do not. Features of story grammar can enhance the quality of children's story-telling and create a mental picture of the plot. Familiarity with story language often enables children to retell their own story, verbally or in writing. In reading also, they are able to recall 'chunks' of language that help them later to predict written versions of the same story (Dombey, 1988; Fox, 1988).

In many cultures, stories and songs contain genealogical information, historical interpretations of events and geographical knowledge (oral maps) that are central to maintaining the integrity of the culture. Strong oral traditions and the practice of keeping history and genealogy alive through stories in chants and songs have helped to ensure that traditional practices and understandings of many cultural groups continue, to various degrees, to this day (Dewes, 1977; Karetu, 1977). Dewes (1977), for example, contends that these oral traditions, extending continuously from the past to the present, ensure that an indigenous Māori person in New Zealand can be seen as, 'master of his [sic] environment with a brain, heart and soul; with a religion, a philosophy of life and of nature; who had (has) highly sophisticated educational institutions and agencies of culture transmission to preserve and perpetuate knowledge' (p. 53).

Sarbin (1986) notes that it is through story that children learn to become functioning members of the society into which they are born:

> It is through hearing stories . . . that children learn or mislearn both what a child and what a parent is, what the cast of characters may be in the drama into which they have been born and what the ways of the world are. Deprive children of stories and you leave them unscripted, anxious stutterers in their actions as in their words. Hence there is no way to give us an understanding of any society . . . except through the stock of stories which constitute its initial dramatic resources.
>
> (Sarbin, 1986, p. 201)

From the time children first begin to understand the world, they appear to do so by means of story:

> . . . it is a 'push' to construct narrative that determines the order of priority in which grammatical forms are mastered by the young child.
>
> (Bruner, 1990, p. 77)

They are born into a world of culturally contrived meanings:

> We do not hear the story as separately constituted beings who can scrutinise it from a position of safe separation. We are in the story and the story is in us. . . . Any understanding we have of reality is in terms of our stories and our story-creating possibilities.
>
> (Mair, 1988, p. 128)

The stories themselves, as well as the purpose for which story-telling is used and the manner of their telling, can vary across cultures. Familiarity with the language of story implies a need for familiarity with the context of stories also, in order to make stories intelligible. Gregory (1996, pp. 100–1), writing from the context of educators in the UK working with children for whom English is an additional language, discusses an approach to classroom literacy learning which makes certain assumptions, among which are:

- That language and experience are inextricably linked (Sapir, 1970). Effective use of semantic clues in reading a text will depend on understanding or 'feeling' for the experiences described in the language in which they are described.

- That learning to read and write promotes a greater consciousness of language structure.
- That the teacher's awareness of the child's home culture and an explicit introduction to the new culture of school are prerequisites for the 'joint culture creation' (Bruner, 1996) important for successful classroom learning.

(Gregory, 1996, p. 100)

Gee (1990) describes an example of a small African-American girl telling a story at the class 'sharing time'. She based her story on an oral discourse which was valued in her community, namely that a story should be a good performance, an entertainment. Her story was full of rhythm, pattern and repetition and held the other children's appreciation. The teacher, however, was looking for a different (unarticulated) discourse, that of being informative, linear and to the point, and did not appreciate the child's own poetic or entertainment discourse. In another school-based situation with other conventions, for example a high school literature or creative writing class, the child's narration would be closer to what was valued. Eventually this child was sent to the school psychologist for telling tall tales.

One of the reasons for this unfortunate incident has undoubtedly been successive attempts to displace the validity of minority culture understandings with that of the dominant culture. As above, Cazden's (1988) analysis of classroom discourses also showed that when teachers were unfamiliar with the language patterns of their students they changed the way in which they responded to students' reading errors. Wood (1988), commenting on teachers' perceptions, said that they:

> . . . perceive children who do not talk using 'received pronunciation' and the 'standard' form of their language as less able or less motivated than children whose talk corresponds more closely to that of the currently 'dominant' dialect. Making (perhaps implicit or unconscious) judgements about children's educational potential on the basis of how they talk, teachers set up self-fulfilling prophesies which lead to the anticipated differences in levels of achievement. Crudely, because teachers expect less of children from social backgrounds, these children are taught and learn less.

(Wood, 1988, p. 112)

The language and sociocultural knowledge that children bring to school should work for them, rather than against them (McNaughton, 2002). For this to happen, collaboration between teachers and home communities is essential.

Literacy achievement and revitalization of indigenous language and culture

In some countries, indigenous communities are dissatisfied with the current levels of achievement by their children in English medium classrooms, as for example the Māori community in New Zealand (Bishop et al., 2003). Many non-indigenous educators also share this concern. One response to these concerns has been a move towards developing student confidence and proficiency in both the indigenous language (for example Māori) and English.

In New Zealand the revival of the Māori language and culture has to a large extent been the result of initiatives such as *Te Kōhanga Reo* (the Language Nest, Māori immersion early childhood centres) and more recently *kura kaupapa Māori* (schools which operate within a Māori worldview and deliver the curriculum through the medium of Māori language). There are also Māori immersion mainstream schools and Māori immersion classes established within mainstream schools. However, as one would expect, difficulties arise when the language being acquired is the students' second language and not the language of the parent community. While it is crucial that students immersed in language programmes should be exposed to the most expert models, many teachers of Māori are themselves second language learners, under pressure to teach through the medium of Māori in all curriculum subjects as well as to develop their own proficiency in the language (Benton, 1993). This situation severely limits schools' ability to connect the 'school' language students experience with the language and sociocultural knowledge of the home.

Despite the strong resurgence to revitalize Māori language, English is still the only language constantly available and is still the majority language spoken and heard in New Zealand communities (Smith, 1995). An experienced, mature junior Māori immersion classroom teacher who is a native speaker of Māori and works in a mainstream New Zealand school commented:

> I find it really sad. Even though the tamariki [children] speak te reo [the Māori language] when they are in my classroom, as soon as they go out the door, all that they hear is te reo Pākehā [the English language]. My kaiarahi i te reo [expert language assistant] and I try to be the best language models we can but it's not enough. When they go out the door it's English. When they go out the school gate it's English. When they go home it's English and when they turn on their TV that's English too.
>
> You know when I was at school we used to get the strap for talking in Māori yet even though we weren't allowed to speak Māori at

school we still heard more Māori in a week than my babies hear, and they're meant to be learning in Māori.

This comment provides a stark illustration of the differences between the responsive social contexts available for first language learners and those available for second language learners, and the dilemmas these differences pose for bilingual educators.

So all-pervading is English in the wider community, it is the language likely to be used by the majority of parents to communicate in the home (Benton, 1993), and it is still also the first language of the majority of children attending education in Māori immersion settings (Hollings, Jefferies and McArdell, 1992; Benton, 1993; Education Review Office, 1995). The benefits of growing a language base from the home and within early childhood facilities are well appreciated and well founded.

Language, literacy and early childhood

The vision of *Kōhanga Reo* is to teach children the language at the side of their elders and other family members, and within the embrace of the extended family and *marae* (traditional cultural meeting places) (Royal Tangaere, 1997a, 1997b). The *Kōhanga Reo* movement initiated a programme that totally immersed pre-school Māori children in the values, traditions, customs and stories of traditional Māori, capitalizing on the relationships and interactions within the family in order to recapture and revitalize Māori language and culture (Smith, 1995). For the first time in over two generations, Māori pre-schoolers were receiving the language, cultural knowledge and life principles that would help them make better sense of their own cultural worldview. The New Zealand Māori Education Commission (1998) identified that intergenerational learning contexts such as this were an important part of the traditional Māori philosophy that underpinned the pedagogy of *Kōhanga Reo*. The Commission reinforced the need to nurture relationships between elders and their grandchildren and identified the language, social, cultural, emotional, cognitive and physical benefits that accrue as a result.

Rangiwhakaehu Walker, a well-respected Māori elder who was instrumental in the initiation and consolidation of the *Kōhanga Reo* movement in her tribal area, explained how some of her peers grew up without the benefits of their own language (Berryman, 2004a, unpublished interview):

> Rangiwhakaehu: Parents were looking for the *Reo* [*Māori* language] for their children. Most of them had missed out on the language as children.

Rangiwhakaehu believed they were afraid that their own grandchildren would be raised equally disadvantaged, and although there had been many challenges, they had welcomed the *Kōhanga Reo* initiative with open arms.

> Rangiwhakaehu: Everything was voluntary. It wasn't until some time down the line that we got any funding. We started in the *wharenui* [Māori meeting house] then we shifted into the garage at the back of the *marae* [meeting area, focal point of settlement, space in front of a meeting house] dining room. We really started with almost no resources. We had nothing so we used all of the resources from the environment.

Māori elders, family members and the Māori community in general took responsibility for modelling the Māori language and preferred cultural practices of their ancestors with these children, using experiences and resources that came from within their own culture (Hohepa, Smith, Smith, and McNaughton, 1992; Ka'ai, 1996). Every opportunity was taken to immerse the children in Māori language and Māori experiences.

> We took the *tamariki* [children] to the sea, to the bush, to places that had been important to our people. When we went to the bush we talked to the *tamariki* about the trees, what they looked like, where they grew, what their leaves looked like. We talked about the birds that lived in the trees. We talked about food from the bush like *piko-piko* [edible asparagus-like fern shoot]. We took them to the farm. The farm belonged to one of the *whānau* [extended family]. We took them to gather *titiko* [winkles] and *pipi* [cockles]. We gathered them, then cooked them and ate them. All the time talking, talking, talking. There was a lot of learning from each of these experiences. Learning for the children and for the parents that came with us. Learning about what to do and how to do it properly and also learning about the language that went with those experiences.
>
> We took them to the beach for a swim, to play in the sand, to gather stones and shells. We used to get the shells with the holes in them. There was only one place you could get them, that was at *te akau* [the ocean beach]. These shells we used to thread on *harakeke* [strips of flax]. We took those things back with us, then we would use them to work with our *tamariki*. We would get the *tamariki* to feel them to look at them, to talk about them.

This conversation illustrates the extraordinary lengths to which many Māori elders and educators went in order to create, or re-create, powerful second language learning contexts. These contexts can be seen as genuinely responsive social contexts, centred on shared tasks of cultural importance, within which young children could learn to speak their own language. Rangiwhakaehu talked about how the land and resources from the land linked back to special stories from the area.

> Each of those places had a special story from the old days. Way back in the old times they used to put a net out in front of the *marae* to catch herrings. We talk about those things when we go there, we tell those stories.

Rangiwhakaehu then shared how the resources and stories were often linked to learning through song. Even though it had been almost 20 years ago, she recalled a specific learning experience she and another teacher had provided for their children.

> One time we took our children out to the river. There are lots of river stones there. We gathered them, big ones, small ones, the smooth and rough ones. Why? Because there's a *kōrero* [story] for each of those stones. We used them as teaching tools for our *tamariki*. We made up a song to sing when they were playing with the stones. We taught them the words that go with the smooth ones, *maeneene* [smooth], the rough ones, *taratara* [coarse, jagged]. The *tamariki* would play with the stones and sing along with us.
> *Kohatu nunui* [large stones]
> *Kohatu rikiriki* [small stones]
> *Kohatu maeneene* [smooth stones]
> *Kohatu taratara* [rough stones]
> *Horahia ngā kohatu* [spread the stones out]
> *Tamariki e kori* [children play with the stones]
> *Kia mau ai ngā tauira* [so that you can hold on to what you have learned]
> As they played we'd ask them questions. *Kei hea te kohatu nunui?* [Where is the large stone?]

Rangiwhakaehu recalled that this had been one of the ways that she had learned the language as a child:

> When we did this it reminded me of my own mother when we used to sort the potatoes out after we had harvested them. We would sort them according to their various sizes for storage. You identify the ones to eat straight away, the ones that will be put into storage and the very little ones that you couldn't eat. They were *ponaho* [useless] and they were fed to the pigs.

> This was how me and my brothers and sisters learned the lan-
> guage. We learned the language, and we learned what the language
> meant as we did the activities. So that is why we taught in *Kōhanga* in
> this way.

The shared tasks in both of these examples, labelling and categorizing
stones and potatoes, were tasks of genuine significance to the survival and
well-being of the community. Smooth stones were selected as *hāngi* stones
(suitable for heating and used for cooking in an oven in the ground) and
the selection of potatoes for eating and for keeping as seeds ensured the
continuity of supply of an important food source as well as avoiding any
waste.

Rangiwhakaehu shared another learning context:

> An important resource was the *harakeke* [flax] plant. We would cut it
> and let the *tamariki* taste the juice. We would talk about that. Then
> we would strip the flax and plait it. Teach them how to plait it and
> then for the older ones teach them how to make it into a headband.
> Some of them were crooked and didn't work properly. But that was
> all right. It was not about the finished thing, its about what you learn
> on the way. Sometimes you've got to make a few mistakes before you
> get it right.

This piece of advice from Rangiwhakaehu speaks of the importance of children
being able to experience and trial activities in contexts where they are supported and where new learning can continue to build upon existing knowledge and experience. She finished with a reflection on one of the changes that
have taken place in the last 20 years.

> Nowadays they have got their resources, their books, so they don't go
> out so often. I think we had more fun with the natural resources than
> from the plastic toys they have nowadays.

Many of the activities described by Rangiwhakaehu incorporate features
of 'literate language', for example 'story grammar' (see above, Jones, 2003),
and connect oral language with children's entry into reading and writing.
Particularly important here is a sense of the close link between 'literate language' and the children's lived experiences. Other teachers in *kōhanga reo* in
this area also used a combination of story-telling, song and the local *marae*
complex as contexts for learning. They capitalized on the strengths provided
by people from the local *marae*, including family, even though many may
have had little Māori language proficiency. The granddaughter of one such
teacher shared how her grandmother used the stories, told in the stylized

carvings, weavings and paintings in the *wharenui* (the main *marae* building) as the context for learning for both her students and their parents. Each part of the *wharenui* represented traditional stories about the genealogy of the people and/or their local environment.

First, the teacher encouraged other family members, her granddaughter included, to develop resources to support the re-telling of these stories. Resources included recordings of the stories themselves, artwork to represent the events, characters and places in the stories, simple repetitive songs and actions that also told the stories (many long and complex traditional songs for use in adult gatherings already existed) and lists of words and phrases. Units of work would then involve the teacher engaging in extended conversations and language interactions with both her pre-school students and their family members. Units began with story-telling, followed by excursions into the wider community to visit the places and participate in the situated language activities pertinent to the story.

Just as Rangiwhakaehu has described, these excursions also included hands-on experiences with traditional resource-growing or food-gathering techniques. From oral language interactions around these stories or experiences, young children acquired important cultural knowledge and practices to do with history and geography of the area, and gender roles and responsibilities. Back inside the *wharenui*, the students and their parents learned about the carvings or other artwork that the stories related to. Simple songs and their actions were incorporated into this exercise, as was the use of the contemporary artwork that family members had prepared. Children were encouraged to use the props to re-tell the stories to their peers and to family members. Given that adults were learning alongside the children, they too were able to assist with these exercises so that everyone benefited.

Responsive interventions

Students' proficiency with spoken language affects the development of all other communication skills. It is especially important to recognize this when students are learning at school in a second language. This situation is faced by many recent immigrants to English-speaking classrooms in different countries. The Education Department of Western Australia (1997) highlights the importance of recognizing and responding to the following when teaching children for whom English is a second language:

- the diversity and richness of experience and expertise that children bring to school
- before cultural values and practices that may be different from those of the teacher

- the need for children to have the freedom to use their own languages and to code-switch when necessary
- the context and purpose of each activity needs to make sense to the learner
- the learning needs to be supported through talk and collaborative peer interaction
- the child may need a range of 'scaffolds' to support learning and that the degree of support needed will vary over time, context and degree of content complexity
- the children will need time and support so that they do not feel pressured
- the supportive attitudes of peers may need to be actively fostered
- there may be difficulties in assessing children's real achievements and the active involvement of parents will make a deal of difference, as will on-going monitoring.

(Education Department of Western Australia, 1997, pp. 4–5)

These principles are compatible with those already advocated in this chapter for all children, including those who are learning in a second language other than English. For these children, sufficient exposure and experiences with oral language prior to school are important if they are to make an easy transition between words used in oral language contexts with those used in written language contexts. Because of the many variables associated with the acquisition of language in a society where the language of instruction is not the dominant community language, some students need a great deal of additional support to develop their oral language base before they can fully participate in classroom literacy practices.

Writing from a UK perspective, and from a wealth of experience of supporting children for whom English is an additional language, Gregory (1996) poses the question: 'What enables learners to take the step from speaking to understanding writing on a page or screen, to realise that knowledge of life and language can help them make sense of words and texts?' (1996, p. 95). Gregory advocates addressing building from the known into new literacy acquisition by explicit scaffolding of children's learning through:

- recognizing children's existing linguistic skills and cultural knowledge, and building these into both teaching content and teaching strategies;
- limiting the size of the reading task by introducing explicitly common new lexis and language 'chunks';
- modelling chunks of language orally and in an idealized way through puppets and/or songs and socio-dramatic play;
- devising home-school reading programmes which recognize the role

of both parent and child as mediator of different languages and cultures and which families feel comfortable with.

(Gregory, 1996, p. 112)

Gregory (1996, p. 110) outlines an example of a reading session that draws on children's oral language and makes use of puppets to mediate learning. This should draw on the child's emotions, for example fear, love, sympathy, hate, and aim to tell an adventure or drama such as 'Dina (a puppet) in hospital following an accident':

- Initially, teachers 'model' the experience through the puppets. Teachers use (sometimes hesitantly and sometimes needing the children's help) essential chunks of the target language which are to be introduced and practised. The chunks (or structures) of language practised will form the basis for early class 'Big Books' for reading together. As the theme is developed together orally, children are encouraged to experiment, and the language used is less controlled.
- After the scene has been enacted by the puppets, the children offer their own parallel experiences and key words are noted by the teacher. They then re-enact the scene shown by the puppets. Sometimes, the teacher will use a song she has found or invented which practises these particular language chunks. The children will act out the song.
- During the early stages, one or two sentences (later more) are written on strips of card using the language chunks that the teacher wishes to practise and containing the children's key words. Two copies of each sentence are made: one is cut into separate words which fit on to the teacher's word stand or can be attached to the magnet-board; the other remains intact as a sentence and is stored with a collection of past class sentences.
- The class reads the sentence cut into individual words first in chorus after the teacher, and then individually. As the teacher changes children's key words, the child who originally 'owned' the word is given the chance to read the sentence first. During the early stages, one or two replacements are sufficient, but these increase rapidly. The teacher is careful to refer to terms like 'word', 'sentence', 'full stop', 'question mark', and so on as the children work and, where relevant, calls children's attention to letters that recur.
- Finally, the sentence is entered in the class news-book and illustrated by the child whose key word it contains. These big sturdy books, together with the class sentence and past sentences, are freely accessible to the children to practise with each other during free moments.
- At odd moments during the day, take the pile of key words. Choose a word and ask the child to whom it 'belongs' (or any child who

volunteers) to read the word first and then to use the word in a sentence or question.

In a Māori context in New Zealand, Berryman et al. (2002) describe *Hopungia* (pick up the language), a range of interactive oral language activities aimed at getting children to collaborate in small groups. The tutors, the activities and the resources provide a scaffolded and meaningful context for this language learning.

Hopungia activities can utilize classroom or natural resources and be developed around classroom themes or learning areas. One of these activities uses co-construction to produce a group picture and to tell stories. The tutor and group members select a theme for a picture, preferably connected with any of their current learning topics.

On a large sheet of paper or whiteboard, the tutor draws the first image and tells their story pointing at the same time to the image they have drawn. For example, '*he maunga tino teitei*' (this is a very tall mountain). The second person draws another shape that will complement the first image. They then repeat the first story before adding their story, each time pointing to the appropriate image. For example, '*he maunga tino teitei, he awa kōpikopiko*' (this is a very tall mountain, this is a winding river). The third person draws another shape that will complement the first two images and repeats and adds to the story, each time pointing to the appropriate image. For example, '*he maunga tino teitei, he awa kōpikopiko, he tuna kei roto i te awa*' (this is a tall mountain, this is a winding river, there is an eel in the river). The activity continues in this manner until a group picture has been constructed. The tutor could add labels as each picture is added or write each person's story as a group story to be displayed alongside the picture. The pictures can be displayed on the wall and/or shared with other groups by having the students tell stories about the picture they have constructed. Pictures from all of the groups can be stapled together into books for independent reading at other times.

Peer collaboration in developing literate language

Much of the recent research on the development of children's literacy skills emphasizes the crucial importance of the social context in which learning takes place (Pellegrini et al., 1998) and, in so doing, stresses again the crucial link between oral language and literacy acquisition. Included in the construct of social context is classroom pedagogy, in particular interactions between peers and between adults and children. Although the value of peer collaboration has been researched for a number of years in relation to overall improvement of literacy, both for students with and without difficulties in literacy acquisition, research into how peer collaboration supports literacy learning is comparatively recent (Jones, 2003).

Literate language includes 'story grammar', as we have noted earlier. 'We dream, remember, anticipate, hope, despair, love, hate, believe, doubt, plan, construct, gossip and learn in narrative' (Westby, 1991, p. 352). It is important for students to learn to express these feelings in written as well as oral form. Narratives can be seen as an early step towards later expository text since they contain a number of essential elements such as: comparisons, problem-solving, exhortation and persuasion, and so on (Montgomery and Kahn, 2003). Some students who experience difficulties in literacy may need support to reproduce story grammar. Montgomery and Kahn (2003) note an inter-active oral teaching strategy 'scaffolded story writing' that has been used as an interactive group activity to support struggling writers:

> In the scaffolded narrative method, questioning is used to help students build their comprehension, organisation, sequence of ideas, and metacognition. This questioning encourages students to become 'meaning makers'.
>
> (Montgomery and Kahn, 2003, p. 145)

The learning support teacher introduces the concept of an author, what s/he does and why students might want to be one. The students are taught five elements of an effective narrative: interesting character(s), context, a credible problem, possible solutions to the problem, good ending (Apel and Masterton, 1998). The support teacher sets up a series of questions to support the students in thinking about the stories they want to write and the students discuss possible approaches with each other. The approach comprises five steps:

> **Step 1: Draw a sequence story.** The [teacher] divides an 8″ × 11″ blank sheet of paper into six sections and asks the students to draw their stories on the paper in correct sequence, using as many sheets as are necessary ... The students may use stick figures and simple drawings ... Some students need help in sequencing their stories properly
>
> **Step 2: Describe the main characters..** Students should list descriptive details for the main characters, including age, height, weight, body build, hair color and style, eye color, clothes, family, favourite foods, things they like to do ...
>
> **Step 3: Begin writing the narrative.** The students begin their narratives with an interesting opening sentence or two to catch the reader's interest. The teacher might read to the students opening paragraphs from stories he or she has enjoyed. Students should follow

their picture sequence when writing their narratives. They should also incorporate the information they compiled before they started writing the story, including the character descriptions.

The teacher uses a questioning technique throughout this intervention. She or he must facilitate the student's ability to come up with creative, independent ideas . . .

The dialogue between the student and the teacher continues until the student is certain about what he or she wants to write. . . . The teacher needs to ask questions until a coherent story emerges, which sometimes occurs in stages. The teacher may get the first part down and then move on to the next part. Some stories change in the process as better ideas occur and the student revises his or her initial thoughts. It is best to get a first draft completed and then rewrite.

Step 4: Write the story. From the beginning, the teacher reinforces the idea that the story belongs to the student, and changes are never made without consulting the student. . . .

Step 5: Rewrite and correct. Some students require corrections and help throughout the writing process. They need words to be spelled for them, or they want to try out a sentence or two orally before they write. . . . Grammar is often incorrect, and syntax is sometimes awkward. Editing the final draft is the point at which these areas must be addressed.

Many students approach the editing process with trepidation . . . suggestions for change must be given diplomatically. When the teacher suggests a possibility and the student does not like it, the change should not be made.

(Montgomery and Kahn, 2003, pp. 146–7)

Montgomery and Kahn suggest that punctuation and spelling should be taught within the context of such stories:

The editing process is an ideal point at which to teach language structure to students who want to learn, because it pertains to their stories. They want to make their stories the best that they can be. It is nice to have a final product of which they can be proud.

(Montgomery and Kahn, 2003, p. 148)

As well as story grammar, literate language also includes metacognitive and metalinguistic talk that helps to support children in thinking about both how to track their own understanding of what is going on, and how stories fit together. Jones gives two examples of this:

This type of language . . . includes talk about linguistic processes (e.g. 'Let's read this part again') as well as talk about cognitive processes (e.g. 'I think this goes here').

(Jones, 2003, p. 166)

There is increasing interest in sociocultural frameworks based on Vygotskian theory (Vygotsky,1978) to investigate the influence of interactions with peers on student's use of literate language. Cognitive development is able to progress only 'when the child is interacting with people in his environment and in cooperation with his [sic] peers' (Vygotsky, 1978, p. 90). The language that is exchanged facilitates whatever joint activity is being undertaken and also the internalization of new skills and new knowledge construction. Collaborative reading and writing activities can provide children with the opportunity to scaffold peers' learning in the zone of proximal development through observing, guiding or offering assistance, while the less skilled learner is motivated to respond to and initiate language interactions, as well as respond to peer questions and challenges. Metacognitive and literate language as described above can be seen to have their origins in interactions of this sort with peers and adults as shown by Jones's (2003) sequential analysis of the language interactions of young children during collaborative writing. In a seminal study of 'comprehension-fostering and comprehension-monitoring activities', Palincsar and Brown (1984) showed that reciprocal oral language exchanges between learner and 'tutee' (more experienced other) has a positive impact on reading comprehension. Six elements were identified as contributing to comprehension:

1   Understanding both explicit and implicit purposes of reading.
2   Accessing relevant background knowledge.
3   Focusing attention on the major content of text.
4   Evaluation of the content of the text for consistency and compatibility with the learner's prior knowledge.
5   Self monitoring of understanding of the text as the reading proceeds.
6   Drawing and testing a range of inferences: interpretations, predictions and conclusions.

The researchers selected four specific language activities in which to train learners and tutors, which embodied the six elements above. These are 'self-directed summarizing (review), questioning, clarifying and predicting' (Palincsar and Brown, 1984, p. 121). These activities were embedded in the context of dialogue between tutor and tutee that took place during the reading of text:

The basic procedure was that an adult teacher, working individually with a seventh-grade poor reader, assigned a segment of the passage to be read and either indicated that it was her turn to be the teacher or assigned the student to teach that segment. The adult teacher and the student then read the assigned segment silently. After reading the text, the teacher (student or adult) for that segment asked a question that a teacher or test might ask on the segment, summarized the content, discussed and clarified any difficulties, and finally made a prediction about future content. All of these activities were embedded in as natural a dialogue as possible, with the teacher and student giving feedback to each other. . . .

Gradually, the students became much more capable of assuming their role as dialogue leader and by the end of ten sessions were providing paraphrases of some sophistication.

(Palincsar and Brown, 1984, pp. 124–5)

The success of that initial research project has been replicated many times with pairs of tutors and tutees and within small groups, for example by Pickens, Glynn, and Whitehead (2004). Several syntheses of research (Mastropieri et al., 1996; Swanson et al., 1999; Fuchs et al., 2000) have been conducted which demonstrate a number of critical elements common to each other and to the initial work of Palincsar and Brown. These elements relate both to the social context of interactive classroom activity, in which oral exchanges of language are embedded, and also to a commonality of understanding and respect between learner and tutor. Among them are:

a   Making instruction visible and explicit
b   Implementing procedural facilitators or strategies to facilitate learning
c   Using interactive groups or partners
d   Providing opportunities for interactive dialogue between students, and between teachers and students

(Klinger et al., 2004, p. 291)

Conclusion

This chapter discusses the crucial role that oral language plays in literacy, and how it is acquired through guided participation with more-skilled speakers in learning contexts that are responsive, social and interactive. Most children readily learn to speak through social interaction with parents, family members, peers, and other mediators around shared activities that are important to both parties. Within these activities, mediators both model appropriate language usage, and, more importantly, respond to the messages children are striving to communicate. By learning to initiate language interactions, as well as responding to instructions and questions from others, children acquire a share in the topic focus and the direction of these interactions.

However, when students enter school, the oral language contexts they experience may not be so responsive and interactive, and students may have less agency within them. Among the three intersecting school literacy domains of oral language, reading and writing, oral language is the domain that is often undervalued and under-represented in classroom literacy pro-grammes. A major theme in this chapter is the need for teachers to expand the opportunities for students experiencing difficulties with literacy to elaborate their oral language structure by using it in a variety of different literacy contexts in order to improve their reading and writing achievement. These students need to be supported to talk more about what they have been doing at home and at school, to re-tell stories and experiences and to talk about what they are going to write. This strategy may be a more effective way of improving students' reading and writing achievement than increasing the time they spend in practising mechanical production skills that reflect an understanding of literacy as a largely technical, rather than a communicative, activity.

The chapter also draws attention to the many communities of oral literacy practice in which students successfully participate prior to entering school, and the extent of the knowledge and experience with oral literacy they bring with them. This is particularly true for students who are second language learners, and students who come from language and cultural backgrounds that are different from those of their teachers, especially indigenous students. Such students may be highly competent in song, dance, chants and rituals of greeting, and in the stories of their home communities. Teachers need to understand that these are important literacy achievements to be built upon in classroom reading and writing activities, and not construed as barriers to literacy learning. The chapter outlines a number of evolving strategies that some teachers are exploring in order to expand students' oral language use in their classrooms. Some of these activities are stand-alone oral language activities, while others are activities that build more opportunities for oral language interaction within reading and writing programmes.

4 Responsive contexts for reading

Introduction

From the perspective of sociocultural understandings of human development and learning, children are construed as active agents who come to know the world in terms of their own operations upon it, and as being in control of their own learning. One important way children exercise this control is by seeking out opportunities for regular and sustained interaction with more-skilled individuals around genuinely shared activities. For young children, these individuals may include parents and other family members as well as other significant adults and peers. Regular interaction around these shared activities with a more-skilled person leads to children developing and refining their knowledge and skills within specific domains, such as reading.

For reading, as well as for writing and oral language, the responsive, social features of effective learning contexts need to be emphasized. Students need opportunities to talk about what they are reading, and to talk about what other people understand from reading the same text. Teachers and other adults need to build and deepen their relationships with students through the medium of the literacy tasks they select and engage in. We examine the need to establish authentic opportunities for students' learning, through the provision of reading texts and writing and speaking activities that connect with students' own family and community experiences, as well as those of the school and its teachers (Berryman, 2000a, 2000b; Au, 2002; Glynn, 2003). Difficulty or complexity of reading texts should be appropriate to the nature of the task. For example, texts taken home for 'demonstration' reading to one's family or for reading alone for leisure and pleasure may be at an 'easy' level for the reader. However, texts selected for one-to-one tutoring within the context of extra support and scaffolding by a skilful tutor may be at a more demanding or challenging level. Students themselves need to have a real choice of texts to read to ensure that what they read is of real interest to them.

Regular interaction around shared reading activities also leads to affirming and extending the interdependence and positive social relationships between both participants. These important learning interactions have been identified as responsive, social contexts (Glynn, 1985). This type of social and interactive context is seen by developmental psychologists as fundamental to the acquisition of intellectual knowledge and skills (Wood, Bruner and Ross, 1976; Bronfenbrenner, 1979; Vygotsky, 1981; Bruner, 1996; McNaughton, 1987, 2002). However, the knowledge and skills acquired in particular responsive social contexts are not simply those that are specific to particular tasks and situations, but also those that provide generic knowledge about how to exercise a measure of autonomy and independence in learning.

In this chapter, we discuss different interpretations of 'literacy', different models of the reading process and their implications for pedagogy to scaffold reading development. We discuss how some contexts for learning to read (particularly 'remedial' contexts for students experiencing reading difficulties) can lead to learning that is dependent on the continued control and direction of a more-skilled person and may actually promote 'learned helplessness', while other contexts appear to lead to learning that becomes more and more autonomous and independent of such control and direction. We consider how adults and peers can support and scaffold reading within the zone of proximal development. In particular, we focus on one reading intervention, 'Pause Prompt Praise', which has evolved and developed in response to the literacy learning needs of students who experience difficulties. We analyse the extent to which this intervention may be seen to address the implications of changing views of what constitutes 'literacy' as well as the implications for teaching practices of different models of the reading process.

Literacy as an individual attribute or a social practice

Conventionally, literacy has been seen as an individual attribute – the individual's ability to read, write and spell competently. More recently, however, there has been a recognition that literacy can also be seen to lie within the social practices of a group. There is a link 'between the activities of reading and writing and the social structures within which they are embedded and which they help to shape' (Barton, 1995, p. 6). These different conceptualizations of literacy have particular implications for the teaching of reading in schools. The first implies that reading competence is discrete to the cognitive processes of the individual learner and can be addressed as such in the classroom. The other implies that the social context in which reading is developed is crucial. Reading should most appropriately be acquired in a responsive partnership with more informed others who can support the sense-making process and help to establish the links between the text itself and the wider world and cultural practices in which it is situated.

Reading as an individual attribute: contrasting models

The skills involved in reading can be quite complex, and different views exist on how children read, and on the relative importance of each of these skills and processes in reading. These models can offer conflicting and diverse understandings of the process of becoming literate, and therefore offer differing and possibly conflicting notions of what might cause difficulties with literacy. Differences and conflicts can arise because many models of reading are derived from a psychological base, which focuses upon the individual and from a view of literacy as an endeavour associated primarily with reading and the decoding of text.

If we take a view of reading as an individual endeavour, then understanding of different models of reading is essential in order for the teacher to make decisions about appropriate strategies for facilitating individual success in learning to read. Reading programmes and interventions for individual learners are underpinned by different models of reading, and it is crucial to know what these are before deciding which programme or intervention to implement to address any student's specific difficulty.

'Bottom-up' (phonics), 'top-down' (whole book/whole language) and interactive approaches

As Gregory (1996) notes, the traditional debate about the reading process revolves around two principal models:

- the 'bottom-up', data-driven model that suggests fluent readers look first at the visual information, that is the component features of the letters in the words, before they move on to consider the meaning of the print;
- the 'top-down', concept-driven model which assumes that fluent readers first anticipate the meaning of text before checking the available syntactic and graphic cues.

In addition, there is a third, interactive approach which assumes a reciprocal relationship and interaction between these two models.

These contrasting theoretical perspectives on reading each lead to different approaches to the teaching of reading to students who experience difficulty.

'Bottom-up' approaches

From the bottom-up perspective, the reconstruction of the author's meaning is achieved through the process of decoding the abstract and complicated alphabetic code. Learning to read progresses from the particular to the general in a series of small steps, to be learned one by one, in sequence. Children must first learn the letters of the alphabet, establish the principle of symbol to sound identification and then apply this in order to decode words. Bottom-up skills teaching emphasizes the mastery of phonics and word recognition. The bottom-up approach was the earliest method of teaching reading (Adams, 1994, p. 21). There was little need to be concerned about constructing meaning, since the Bible, whose text meaning was predetermined, constituted most reading matter for children.

Adams (1994, p. 108), in a major US report commissioned by the Center for the Study of Reading in Champaign, Illinois, designed to review all aspects of phonics and early reading instruction, argues that skilful readers of English thoroughly process the individual letters of words easily and quickly because they are well acquainted with the sequences of letters they are likely to see. Good readers are distinguished from poor readers by their ability to visually recognize frequent spelling patterns and to make visual-sound correspondences automatically.

'Top-down' approaches

In contrast, Goodman (1986) advocates a top-down approach to reading. This perspective views reading as the active *construction* of meaning. It is influenced by psycholinguistics, with its emphasis on how we make sense of our world through the use of language. Goodman (1996, pp. 110–11) likens the way in which the human mind makes sense of print to the way in which it makes sense of any other aspect of the world. The strategies that the mind uses for making sense of print are called psycholinguistic because thought and language continuously interact in this process. Beginning with written text, the mind constructs meaning drawing on cues 'from the various language levels' (Goodman, 1996, p. 111). He calls the process a 'psycholinguistic guessing game' (Goodman, 1967) because the reader has a hypothesis of what a text might be about, and then tests this hypothesis and confirms or rejects it as s/he reads through the text.

A number of other researchers, for example Adams's colleagues Strickland and Cullinan (1994), follow a similar top-down model of reading and criticize the use of terms such as 'pre-readers', 'reading readiness' and 'prerequisite skills' as implying that children acquire literacy skills suddenly and as a result of formal instruction in phonics. Strickland and Cullinan feel that the emphasis should be on providing literacy-rich environments for early literacy acquisition rather than direct instruction in phonics. Instruction in reading should include phonics but should begin from an emphasis on meaning.

Interactive approaches

Despite her advocacy of the importance of phonics in initial reading instruction, it should be noted that Adams (1994) also acknowledges the importance of semantic cues in reading and other 'critical sources of information':

In the reading situation, as in any effective communication situation, the message or text provides but one of the critical sources of information. Other information must come from the readers' own prior knowledge. Further, in the reading situation as in any other learning situation, the learnability of a pattern depends critically on the prior knowledge and higher-order relationships that it evokes. In both fluent reading and its acquisition, the reader's knowledge must be aroused interactively and in parallel. Neither understanding nor learning can proceed hierarchically from the bottom up even if instruction is organised and presented in that way. Phonological awareness, letter recognition facility, familiarity with spelling patterns, spelling-sound relations, and individual words must be developed in concert with real reading and real writing and with deliberate reflection on the forms, functions and meanings of texts.

(Adams, 1994, p. 422)

Stanovich (1988) suggests that both top-down and bottom-up methods have limitations because readers draw on both processes when reading. He suggests that readers use information simultaneously from different levels and do not necessarily begin at either the graphic (bottom-up) or the context (top-down) level. During the development of reading skills some readers may rely more heavily on some levels than others. In the interactive view of reading, three processes interact:

- Sound – the sound pattern of the letters or word. This is called the *phonic* aspect of the reading process.
- Sight – the visual characteristics of the word are focused on, or a word is read as an entity. The *whole word* method of teaching reading was designed to reinforce this process.
- Meaning – context, both *semantic* (meaning) and *syntactic* (grammar) aspects of text.

This model of the reading system highlights the interactive relationship between content, meaning, orthography (print) and phonology (speech). Processing at the level of orthography includes sequencing the letters in a word, whilst at the phonological level, it encompasses matching those letters to the letter sound. Processing of meaning relates not just to the reader's knowledge of meaning at word level, but at the context level, it also provides a framework for understanding the text. These processes combine to make up the practice of reading. This is the model of reading assumed by the UK National Literacy Strategy (NLS) (DfEE, 1997):

All teachers know that pupils become successful readers by learning to use a range of strategies to get at the meaning of a text. This principle is at the heart of the National Curriculum for English and has formed the basis of successful literacy teaching for many years. The range of strategies can be depicted as a series of searchlights, each of which sheds light on the text. Successful readers use as many of these strategies as possible.

- phonic (sound and spelling)
- knowledge of context
- grammatical knowledge
- word recognition and graphic knowledge

(NLS Framework for Teaching, YR to Y6, Introduction, DfEE, 1997)

The view taken in the NLS is that, in the first few years of school, there should be a particular emphasis on phonics teaching:

> Most teachers know about all these [aspects considered above], but have often been over-cautious about the teaching of phonics – sounds and spelling. It is vital that pupils are taught to use these word level strategies effectively. Research evidence shows that pupils do not learn to distinguish between the different sounds of words simply by being exposed to books. They need to be taught to do this. When they begin to read, most pupils tend to see words as images, with a particular shape and pattern. They tend not to understand that words are made up of letters used in particular combinations that correspond with spoken sounds. It is essential that pupils are taught these basic decoding and spelling skills from the onset.
>
> (NLS Framework for Teaching, YR to Y6, Introduction, DfEE, 1997)

Stanovich (1986) argues for an interactive compensatory model in which the various processes interact and the reader can compensate for weaknesses in one area by relying on strengths in the other aspects. The argument is that readers who are not proficient in the phonological sub-skills of reading rely on context to compensate for their difficulties in processing the individual sounds of words. However, in Stanovich's view, this is not an argument against encouraging these sub-skills. Because such children do not have easy access to reading text in situations where the context is unclear, they will not have the opportunity to acquire these skills, the so-called 'Matthew effect'. This is a view that is taken also in the NLS:

> When pupils read familiar and predictable texts, they can easily become over-reliant on their knowledge of context and grammar. They may pay too little attention to how words sound and how they are spelt. But if pupils cannot decode individual words through

their knowledge of sounds and spellings, they find it difficult to get at the meanings of more complex, less familiar texts. They are likely to have problems in dealing with more extended texts and information books used across the curriculum at Key Stage 2, and with spelling. As they learn these basic decoding skills they should also be taught to check their reading for sense by reference to the grammar and meaning of the text. This helps them to identify and correct their reading errors. At Key Stage 1, there should be a strong and systematic emphasis on the teaching of phonics and other word level skills.

(NLS Framework for Teaching, YR to Y6, Introduction, DfEE, 1997)

Because English is a highly irregular language phonemically, mastering all of the different letter sound combinations can be very challenging. However, in a phonemically regular language such as the Māori language in New Zealand problems can arise when grapho-phonic skills are overly relied upon. Māori is a language in which the relationship between letters and sounds is highly regular, and in which only 15 letters of the English alphabet are utilized. Hence, children can readily achieve a high level of accuracy in oral reading from written texts. However, this level of accuracy can often mask a more limited level of comprehension of texts. This has been an important lesson in Māori language immersion settings from which others can also learn (Berryman et al., 2002).

Literacy as a social practice

'Like all human activity, literacy is essentially social, and it is located in the interaction between people' (Barton and Hamilton, 1998, p. 3). Human action is mediated by tools and signs, including language and writing (Vygotsky, 1981). Writing, for example, facilitates the co-construction of knowledge between writer and reader. There are different forms of language which can result in a wide variety of texts using a variety of genres. 'Some genres are more precise and well-written than others . . . nevertheless, once anything is written it becomes a text which can be referred to' (Barton, 1995, p. 58). Society contains a wide range of texts: books, bank statements, crosswords, graffiti, prayers, and so on. Individuals read text, but they are also positioned by the text:

In any text the reader is constructed. There is only a range of possible options which the reader can take up; a newspaper article or a love letter assumes certain knowledge, values and beliefs in the reader.

(Barton, 1995, p. 60)

Barton refers to an article on dieting and points out the limited number of 'subject positions' for the reader who is:

> . . . positioned as being an unhealthy, overweight adult. The reader is also assumed to drink regularly and, elsewhere in the article, to eat meat, to have eaten too much over the holidays, to be in employment, and to have too little will-power.
>
> (Barton, 1995, p. 60)

In a newspaper, 'the small ads and the legal notices position people in different ways . . . All these texts can function to include – and to exclude – people' (Barton, 1995, p. 61). Some texts become 'fixed points' in people's lives, such as religious books or the paraphernalia associated with particular sports teams or personalities. 'People can structure their identity around a text' (Barton, 1995, p. 61). Some texts are more for communication with the self, for example drafts and personal reminder notes. Behind all texts are people: the people writing them and those using them. Texts cannot be separated from social practices. 'Understanding literacy involves analysing practices as well as analysing texts' (Barton, 1995, p. 64). Taking meaning from a text does not simply involve knowing the meaning of words. Different communities read texts differently according to their own conventions and practices. This involves bringing personal meaning to the text and interacting with it.

Implications

If literacy is seen as an individual enterprise, it follows that the barriers to literacy exist within the individual and we need to develop programmes to overcome them at individual student level. If, however, literacy is conceptualized as a more complex cultural and social process, then the barriers to literacy may be seen to exist beyond the individual and they can be reduced by policies to change pedagogies in order to focus on the social contexts of learning and the interactions that take place within them.

The implementation of programmes designed to cater for individual cognitive difficulties associated with either sound-symbol identification, or with comprehension, is not entirely compatible with that of programmes designed to address the social nature of literacy practices through changing the pedagogical structures of literacy teaching. From a bottom-up view of the reading process, phonics is assumed to play a crucial role in competent reading (Adams, 1994). Beginning readers should first learn to recognize individual letters quickly in order to optimize their ability to recognize whole words. They also need to pay attention to the sequence of letters in a word, not simply the whole word. The implication of this view is to highlight the significance of: 'synthetic' phonics, writing and spelling of whole words, 'exercise with frequent blends and digraphs, practice with word families' and attention to every letter of the word, in left-to-right order (Adams, 1994, p. 131).

This implies a view of reading as neutral and technical. From a view of literacy as a social process, written language cannot be seen as neutral and technical, however (Barton, 1995). Literacy is 'always contextualized' (Barton, 1995, p. 91):

> With a text, the shared knowledge, which all human understanding depends upon, is part of the context. This is knowledge concerned with the content of the text; it is also knowledge of the genre, the conventions of the discourse.
>
> (Barton, 1995, p. 92)

The reference to 'shared knowledge' necessarily implies that literacy cannot simply be an individual attribute. Phonically based programmes of the sort advocated by Adams (see above) are often divorced from an understanding of the social practice within which text is situated, and will remain so unless the phonological aspects of literacy learning are taught specifically *within* the context of meaningful text. In the UK, guidance from the National Literacy Strategy (DfEE, 1997) advises teachers responsible for the progress in reading of young children that pupils should be taught to:

- discriminate between the separate sounds in words;
- learn the letters and letter combinations most commonly used to spell those sounds;
- read words by sounding out and blending their separate parts;
- write words by combining the spelling patterns of their sounds.

In the early stages, pupils should have a carefully balanced programme of guided reading from books of graded difficulty, matched to their independent reading levels. These guided reading books should have a cumulative vocabulary, sensible grammatical structure and a lively and interesting content. Through shared reading, pupils should also be given a rich experience of more challenging texts.

This Framework organises teaching objectives at three different levels: word, sentence and text. This underlines the importance of teaching pupils to use the full range of searchlights – to tackle texts from individual words upwards and from the text downwards. While all searchlights are important, the balance between them should vary at different stages of learning to read.

As pupils gain fluency the forms of teaching should shift to emphasise advanced reading and composition skills at text level. The sequence needs to be right for effective teaching and learning of reading.

(NLS Framework for Teaching, YR to Y6, Introduction, DfEE, 1997)

The heavy emphasis on phonics in this guidance may appear to reflect a view of literacy as a neutral technical skill and a personal attribute of the individual child, more than as an integral part of social practice.

In New Zealand, the Ministry of Education Literacy Experts Report (1999) comments that a key to effective teaching is for teachers to have clear strategies for gaining knowledge about children's literacy and language skills, particularly when children bring widely differing literacy experiences to school. This is especially important when the experiences and prior knowledge of the students are different from those of their teachers (McNaughton, 2002). The challenge for teachers is one of recognizing, accepting and building on the diverse skills brought by children from different cultural backgrounds.

The New Zealand Literacy Experts' Report (1999) stresses the importance of schools addressing each of the speaking, reading and writing dimensions of literacy, as well as recognizing their close interdependence. The report emphasizes that understanding the interdependence of the reading, writing and speaking dimensions of literacy is especially important when students in New Zealand schools come from non-English-speaking backgrounds (NESB). Such students may face the extremely challenging task of reading from English texts that take them beyond the limits of their current competence in speaking English. For NESB students, this difficulty is usually addressed through additional teaching effort being applied to developing both oral and written English skills that will support or scaffold their reading of English texts. The Literacy Experts Group included oral language as a basis for defining the goal for success in literacy learning. This expert group concluded that successful reading for children at age 9 meant comprehending in print much of what they were expected to comprehend when listening to spoken language, while successful writing meant expressing in print much of what they were expected to express when speaking (Ministry of Education, 1999). The goal for reading and writing for success have proven to be an effective platform for the subsequent development of literacy.

The Literacy Taskforce agreed that reading and writing for success as defined above were essential for further progress both in school and in the community. However, they saw that further progress was dependent upon two things. First, pedagogy needed to be effective; and second there needed to be ongoing practice that extended beyond the classroom setting.

Linking strategies that develop individuals' comprehension of text with notions of literacy as social practice is less problematic than phonically based interventions, however, since comprehension implies moving beyond a sense that any text is completely free-standing. To comprehend a text fully means understanding the genre, the purpose it serves, the context it fits, and so on. One of the current authors has memories, as a teacher of English in a school in Cameroon, West Africa, of watching students struggling to understand a piece of poetry about Guy Fawkes and fireworks that was set as part of an English Literature examination by an examining board in England. The students could read the words, but there was no possibility of understanding the metaphorical language relating to the guy rising like a phoenix from the flames, and fireworks exploding like flowers. Reading comprehension is a particular area of difficulty for many students.

Using a social constructivist framework, Palincsar et al. (1993) report a research study into the successful use of reciprocal teaching to enhance reading comprehension with pupils who experience difficulties in literacy development. Reciprocal teaching emphasizes collaboration between teachers and learners to apply four specific strategies to the task of reading comprehension. Teachers and students take turns to lead a small group discussion about the meaning of a section of text that they are jointly trying to understand and memorize. The four strategies in the reciprocal teaching technique to assist understanding of the text and joint construction of its meaning are: generating questions from the text, summarizing its content, clarifying areas of difficulty, and predicting the content of subsequent sections of text based on the content and structure of the current portion. Learners are taught the terminology of reciprocal teaching through direct instruction in each of the four strategies prior to the start of the procedure. This technique emphasizes the role of the teacher in modelling expert performance and the role of the learner as active participant in his/her learning in addition to the function of social interactions in learning. Assessment of learners' progress is ongoing and judged through their developing contributions to discussion of the texts.

It is the experience of one of the authors of this book that, where students have severe difficulties understanding text, it is useful to shorten the amount read before questions are raised. This may mean a page by page reading, or even a paragraph by paragraph reading. Close consideration must be given to the composition of the groups in this case. However, as students pay more attention to the messages conveyed by text, the amount of text read before questions are asked can be lengthened. One of the authors found this technique very worthwhile when used with older fluent readers reading novels. However, she also found it just as effective when working with older low-progress readers reading much shorter stories. This technique was particularly effective when stories related to the interest of the students, whether because of topic, genre or author. Groups formed on the basis of interest in the topic meant that a wider ability range could support or be supported by this reciprocal technique. Shared interest and prior experience resulted in messages conveyed in the text being fully explored and well understood.

Inducting children into school literacy practices

For those children newly coping with life in school, or for those students who experience difficulties in literacy, well-chosen stories told in the classroom by the teacher can 'provide a valuable set of "recipes" for coping with school literacy practices', through acting 'as unique "scaffolds" to children's learning in a way that conversation cannot' (Gregory, 1996, p. 142). In the same article Gregory discusses a number of stages for introducing beginning readers to story-reading sessions through explicit modelling of what fluent readers do. This includes making clear what is actually written and what is teacher/student commentary:

- setting the context for the story through discussion of place, one or more of the characters and the main theme as it relates to real life and/or the children's lives;
- reading the story slowly, clearly, with 'lively intonation' and without interruption;
- discussing the story, relating the themes to life, talking about the characters;
- re-reading the story, if appropriate.

For all students, but particularly for those who experience difficulty with understanding text, 'reciprocal teaching', as noted above by Palincsar, Brown and Campione (1993), provides focused practice for discussing text and improving comprehension.

Choosing books for class reading

As Gregory (1996, p. 142) comments, where teachers are setting out to use texts to bathe children 'in a magic where story and text intertwine and understanding comes somewhere in-between', the choice of books for class story-reading is crucial. Although the points she makes are specifically related to the literacy learning of emergent bilingual children, nevertheless they have salience for all children, including those who experience difficulties in literacy acquisition. She compares two examples of books found in infant and primary classrooms. The first, 'The Clay Flute' by Mats Rehnman, is set in the Arabian desert and tells the story of a poor boy who suffers many misfortunes but finally 'makes good'. For young children the text is complex, yet has proven to be very popular. Gregory identifies a number of reasons why this might be the case:

- It portrays universal values of courage and kindness. Children may identify with the little grey monkey or the kind child (two characters in the story).

- It shows the victory of good over evil.
- It shows a world far from present reality, yet with everyday feelings children may experience anywhere.
- Although the language is difficult, it is rich in imagery and uses many words which might be personal 'key words' for children (witch, horrible, grab, scream, kiss, tear, sword, heart, etc.).
- The story moves purposefully and clearly.
- The illustrations are inspiring.

(Gregory, 1996, p. 120)

The second story is, superficially, simpler: 'Don't Blame Me!' by Paul Rogers. It is intended to make children laugh as it tells the tale of a series of events triggered off by paint from a pub sign dripping on to a man's suit. Everyone blames everyone else for the sequence of events that follows. Gregory comments that the story does not hold the attention of those new to the culture because:

- It is very culture-specific (the pub).
- The language is very colloquial and the humour rests upon understanding the finer nuances of the language. There is very little sign of any really important words which might form children's personal 'key words'.
- It relies upon humour itself for success as the story is not memorable, nor does it follow a clear path of events.
- The illustrations are not clear from a distance.

(Gregory, 1996, p. 121)

Gregory's (1996, p. 122) point that choice of books for beginning reading should include 'memorable stories and texts from all times and places', perhaps containing 'universal truths, values and morals, fear and security' pertains to students of all levels and ages. One of the authors of the current text remembers supporting an 11-year-old non-reader in a secondary school learn to read by preparing for him audiotapes of *A Hitch Hiker's Guide to the Galaxy* (Adams, 1995). She taped 30 minutes' worth of text every evening with the agreement that he would follow it through twice the following day. All his friends had read it and he wanted to be able to join in their discussions. Using this approach through a number of texts, he progressed from non-reader to reader, able in six months to read the (English) *Daily Mirror* newspaper independently at home.

It is interesting that the NLS Framework for Teaching YR to Y6 does not place a similar emphasis on ensuring that schools and students have a wide range of freely accessible, quality literacy texts and materials, sufficient to engage the interests of their increasingly diverse student populations. When texts are written by leading writers from different ethnic communities and are made easily accessible to all schools, students from increasingly diverse backgrounds are likely to benefit from seeing their home languages, stories, songs and cultural values represented and affirmed within their school reading programmes. Other cultures can also benefit from seeing another's culture in an authentic context. The motivational properties of such texts means that students want to find out what the stories are about, and how they connect with their lives outside of school. Having texts written by community writers with community artists illustrating the texts may well result in reading materials that offer a way of leading students, from different cultural backgrounds and who are experiencing learning difficulties, into the literacy practices of the classroom and school. Such materials may enable teachers and students to engage in more interactive and top-down strategies, in addition to bottom-up strategies.

In New Zealand all schools receive a wide range of such text materials commissioned and supplied by the Ministry of Education. Effective reading depends on teachers' access to a wide range of interesting, high-quality, appropriate materials that reflect the authentic yet diverse backgrounds of their students, while also exposing them to contexts that they may not yet have encountered. As well as being able to purchase a wide range of published reading materials and teaching resources, the Ministry of Education commissions widely acclaimed authors of books and stories, for both children and adults, to write reading materials that are interesting, contemporary and attractive to young readers. These books and stories are accompanied by teaching resources, for students at all levels of the compulsory sector and for both English and Māori medium classrooms. The main sets of reading materials available for English medium classrooms are the 'Ready to Read' series, published by Learning Media since 1963, for junior class students and the 'School Journals', a series of four levels of miscellaneous collections of short stories and other genres. These have been published in attractive format at least twice yearly since the early 1900s for older, more fluent readers (Years 3 to Years 7). The 'School Journals', published from Part 1 to Part 4, come with identified reading ages that cover an age range beginning before age 7 and extending to 12 to 14 years.

The English medium series are paralleled for students in Māori medium classrooms by the *He Purapura* (meaning 'the seeds') and *Ngā Kete Kōrero* (meaning 'the baskets of knowledge') readers for junior class teachers, and four series of miscellaneous collections for older, more fluent Māori language readers. As well as increasing the number of resources since the re-emergence of Māori medium education in the early 1980s, they have now begun to be placed into a framework of increasing levels of difficulty. In both cases (English and Māori languages), the resources that are available cover a wide genre range. When these journals were first published, they largely reflected the stories of a Eurocentric, mono-cultural society, but journal stories now reflect the stories and cultures of bicultural and multicultural New Zealanders. Consequently, students are now more likely to find a range of meaningful stories to which they can bring their own experiences and relate on a more personal level. They are more likely to see their home and community languages and cultures affirmed in the 'official' reading texts used in classrooms and schools.

If choice of reading books in the classroom is important, so, too, is listening to children read. In order that meaningful interactions can take place between reader and listener, classroom conditions must predispose to attentive listening. The adult or peer should be responsive to the learner's understanding of, and interest in, the text, and any difficulties that are experienced in reading and understanding. Wragg et al. (1998, pp. 264–5) highlight research findings, which are important in listening to children's reading in the classroom:

> . . . we concluded, in the light of observations of what seemed to be successful practice, that there were six ingredients that were needed if teachers were to derive maximum benefit from hearing children read and conversing about the book. These were:
> - Orderliness – disruptive behaviour by other pupils can be a powerful distractor.
> - Focus – a strong focus on reading as the major activity of the moment, so that maths or other problems do not take the teacher away from the principal domain.
> - Independence – children reading alone need to be able to make their own decisions, so they are not too dependent on the teacher; equally, those reading with the teacher need independence, so they can guess intelligently at unfamiliar words.
> - Priority – the child being heard needs to have top priority, except in emergencies.
> - Importance – reading must be made important, so that interruptions are frowned upon.
> - Worthwhileness – the book needs to be engaging and worth talking about.

Wragg goes on to note 'striking instances' of particular efforts by teachers or parents to scaffold the literacy development of pupils:

> These tended to reflect themes that have recurred more than once in this research, like matching books to pupils' individual interests, offering praise and encouragement, giving confidence, or helping children to become autonomous as well as offering them a degree

of direction and structure. When these factors operated together they formed a powerful combination, especially if combined with children's personal qualities, like persistence and determination, sociability, concentration and independence of mind.

(Wragg et al., 1998, p. 268)

Wragg et al., illustrate practices of some of these 'successful' teachers who were accustomed to:

> . . . using the half-hour daily ERIC (everyone reads in class) session when the rest of the class were fully occupied with reading, and by reinforcing her rule that she was not to be interrupted while with a child, she was able to give each one an individualised and focused reading experience. She also ensured that when the classroom assist-ant or parent helpers read with a child they were seated away from other children and not interrupted.
>
> Infant-age children were likely to read more regularly to the teacher than those in junior schools, where it was generally only the less able readers who did so. Several teachers mentioned that it was better to hear children less often but in a more concentrated fashion, diagnosing their mistakes and discussing their progress with them. Many kept quite detailed records of the child's progress, and these were filled in by whichever adult heard the child. Two teachers had found that they were not hearing the better readers and so arranged to give children a special day when they would guarantee to hear them. Most children knew which book to read, or could easily find an appropriate one, but occasionally children in some classes would pick something way beyond them,, or others would pick the easiest one they could find.

(Wragg et al., 1998, p. 152)

Attributes of successful mediators of literacy learning

Within a tutor-learner reading partnership, particularly when the learner has experienced considerable difficulties in literacy development, it is important that support for literacy learning is offered in ways that are responsive and productive. In a UK study of the school experiences of students identified as 'dyslexic', Riddick (1996) noted the very strong views expressed about which teachers were best able to help them. The key qualities of the 'best' teachers were a propensity to offer praise and encouragement linked with understand-ing of the difficulties experienced by the child. Riddick reported that the 'best' teachers were able to enter the student's world and would:

- encourage and praise;
- help students, adapt work and explain clearly;
- understand students and would not attempt to humiliate them;
- not shout;
- have a sense of humour;
- know if students are dyslexic;
- treat all students as if they are intelligent.

The worst teachers, on the other hand:

- are cross, impatient and shout;
- criticize and humiliate students;
- are not helpful, and are negative about students' efforts;
- ignore some students and show they consider some students 'useless';
- do not understand the problems faced by students with difficulties in literacy and are insensitive;
- blame students for their problems and call them 'lazy';
- put red lines through students' work.

School reading policies and difficulties in literacy

Smith (1999, pp. 25–6) notes that it is especially important to consider published reading schemes within school policy on literacy acquisition and provides some points to consider when selecting a reading scheme for a school:

- Who is the scheme for?
- Why has it been written?
- How does it fit in with other reading material used within the school?
- Is there a handbook providing its rationale and giving helpful information?
- Can parents work through the scheme?
- Is there information about the reading books inside the children's books for parents?
- How are the books sequenced or grouped?
- Is there a range of styles or genres?
- Is the language close to speech patterns or is it stilted and unnatural?
- Is the language too simple or does it appear to be complex?
- Is the scheme a sight word scheme, using repetitive words and phrases?

- Does the scheme use a language approach where high interest words can be guessed through contextual cues?
- Is the scheme phonic using a sequence of phonic features or letter strings?
- Is the scheme a mix of all reading strategies?
- Does the scheme have back up materials and activities?
- Are the books well illustrated, colourful, attractive and well printed?
- Is the size of print suitable for the intended age levels?
- Which age group will enjoy the scheme?
- Have gender and racial issues been considered?
- Are there any special features which might make them particularly interesting?
- Are the books durable?
- Do the books give value for money?

'Pause Prompt Praise' and literacy development in a social context

As we have outlined in Chapter 1, effective, responsive social contexts provide opportunities for:

- learners to assume some control over, and not simply respond to, interactions;
- regular interaction between more-skilled and less-skilled learners around genuinely shared tasks;
- reciprocity and mutual influence between learner and teacher;
- learning that is scaffolded within the zone of proximal development;
- feedback that is responsive to the learner's current level of understanding and competence, and is not simply corrective or evaluative.

These characteristics are particularly important within the area of tutor–tutee oral interactions around learning to read.

Different understandings of the process of becoming literate offer differing notions of what might cause difficulties with literacy and, therefore, different approaches to designing effective interventions. Below we describe the genesis and development of a set of reading tutoring procedures known as 'Pause Prompt Praise', which have been adapted over nearly thirty years to suit a wide diversity of contexts and learners and to respond to changing perceptions of what constitutes 'literacy'. Given the evolution of 'Pause Prompt Praise' over this period of time, it is interesting to analyse the extent to which, in its current form, 'Pause Prompt Praise' can be seen as able to address the competing tensions of views of literacy. These views stress the social nature of literacy and the need for a responsive social context in which to support literacy development, together with the need to focus on the cognitive processes through which the technical skill of reading develops.

The 'Pause Prompt Praise' procedures were developed in South Auckland, New Zealand, in the late 1970s. A team of researchers worked intensively with parents of a group of 10- to 12-year-old low-progress readers to produce a training booklet and video: *Remedial Reading at Home: Helping You to Help Your Child*. The booklet (Glynn, McNaughton, Robinson and Quinn, 1979) and accompanying research monograph (McNaughton, Glynn and Robinson, 1987) were first published by the New Zealand Council for Educational Research, and the 'Pause Prompt Praise' procedures have been continually researched to the present day.

'Pause Prompt Praise' was developed to support students of middle to upper primary school age who were making very slow progress in learning to read, and whose reading achievement was two to five years below their chronological age. The procedures were designed to be consistent with applied behaviour analysis perspectives that stress the collection of continuing data on reader and tutor behaviour, through the employment of repeated observational measures (Wheldall and Glynn, 1989). They were also designed to be consistent with pedagogical approaches that construe learning to read as learning to 'make sense' of a coherent text. The procedures focus reader and tutor attention on all sources of information available to access the meaning of a particular text and, within that, the meaning of unknown words. These sources include personal knowledge and experience of text themes, information inherent in understanding the whole story context, information inherent in the language structure of the text sentences, information from familiarity with the structure of oral language, as well as information from the knowledge of specific letters and sounds. At the time that the 'Pause Prompt Praise' procedures were constructed (in the late 1970s), the researchers were aware that many students experiencing difficulties in reading text material, instead of being given additional support to help them engage with that text material, were removed from text reading and given a 'diet' consisting almost entirely of word study and practice in recognizing letters and the sounds they made, individually and in combinations. It seemed to the researchers at the time that such a diet was unlikely to provide poorer readers with the range of strategies that would assist them to become competent. The focus of research across the world had not yet shifted into the area of literacy as a social practice when the 'Pause Prompt Praise' procedures were piloted. However, in retrospect, it is clear that from their inception, 'Pause Prompt Praise' enabled account to be taken of a view of literacy in the way in which learners were encouraged to view texts as situated and to make the links with the world beyond in a variety of ways.

'Pause Prompt Praise' aims to break into the cycle of instructional dependence which entraps many low-progress readers into an over-dependency on their tutors, be they peers, teachers, teaching assistants, parents of family or community members, who in turn may become entrapped in a 'transmission of knowledge' mode. This is frequently illustrated when low-progress readers, on encountering an unknown word in the text they are reading, learn to 'cue' their tutor to help them out by immediately telling them the correct word. When supplied with the correct word, these readers will typically imitate the tutor's response, and then receive praise for correct reading. However, what is more likely to have happened is that the reader has been reinforced by tutor praise for the whole cycle of dependent responding, for looking into the tutors eyes to cue the tutor's help, and for simply repeating the word given (without any attempt to fit this word into its sentence or story context). This is a clear example of a 'positive reinforcement trap', which can readily lead to maintained instructional dependence where both reader and tutor are entrapped in a spiral of mutually dependent interaction.

In contrast, the specific responsive tutoring behaviours in the 'Pause Prompt Praise' procedures are designed to prompt and reinforce readers for attempting to draw on all information available to them to solve unknown words. Active agency in learning is thus acknowledged and promoted in readers. Tutor prompts might focus on the reader's background knowledge of the story theme or context, the reader's familiarity with the language structure of the text, the meaning contained within the context of each sentence or paragraph, as well as the letter-sound information carried within words. Tutors are trained to take particular note of current levels of competence and understanding in reading, and give priority to prompts that focus the reader on understanding word and text meaning, and on developing reading strategies that will enable them to manage their own learning. Hence, a 'Pause Prompt Praise' tutor's first response to a reader's error will be to pause, that is, to delay attending to that error, for up to five seconds. This allows time and space (free from tutor intervention) for the reader to 'take in' all the meaning of the sentence, but particularly the meaning in the remaining words following the error, and then to attempt some response. When a reader's response indicates that the reader does already have some understanding of the meaning of the unknown word (for example the reader reads 'engine' for 'locomotive') only then does the tutor scaffold new learning by focusing the reader's attention onto letter and sound information. For example, the tutor might say: 'Yes, that word does mean a railway engine, but this is another word that means the same – what do you think that other word might be?' [Pause] 'Have a look at how the word starts.'

Tutors using 'Pause Prompt Praise' may choose to ignore some minor errors that do not greatly alter the meaning of the text, in the interest of not interrupting the flow of the story being read. For example, a reader might read

'. . . she went in the house' instead of '. . . she went into the home'. Tutors are instructed to supply ('tell') the reader the correct word only as a last resort, and only after two prompts have been tried, thus scaffolding the reading which is beyond the reader's current level of development. Tutors are instructed not to respond with more than two prompts for any error, so as to encourage them to pause and think carefully of an appropriate type of prompt *before* they intervene, so as to keep the reader-tutor interaction around any particular error as brief, but as responsive, as possible.

The 'Pause Prompt Praise' procedures are built upon regular and brief oral interactions between a tutor and tutee around a written text that is of high interest to the reader and the tutor, but at an appropriate instructional level beyond what the reader could manage alone, within his/her zone of proximal development. Selecting a text at an 'appropriate' instructional level is a challenging professional task. Apart from clearly being of high interest to the reader, the text should not be so difficult that a large number of unknown words will destroy the reader's flow and disrupt the reader from accessing the meaning of the text. However, the text should also not be so easy that the reader will make too few errors for the tutor to respond in ways that will connect the reader more closely with the text and with salient sources of information. The difficulty level of text that students can handle when scaffolded by 'Pause Prompt Praise' tutoring will be clearly well in advance of the difficulty level of text they can handle on their own. Hence, effective 'Pause Prompt Praise' tutoring involves a tutor working with a student within their zone of proximal development, and helping them acquire additional strategies that will make them independent readers of texts of increasing difficulty and challenge. Thus, students may take home 'easy' texts in order to increase their fluency in reading from safe and familiar materials and, perhaps, to show their parents and families how well they can read on their own. Paradoxically, autonomous, independent and self-managing reading strategies, for example self-correction of errors, are learned in social and interactive learning contexts.

'Pause Prompt Praise' tutoring interaction with the tutee around the text (that is, centred on specific errors) is also strongly linked with and supported by the few minutes of 'preview' or conversation between reader and tutor about the story theme before reading commences. Links can be made at this point with other, similar, themes found in stories, or with any other aspect of the reader's world beyond the text itself. It is also linked with a further few minutes 'review' conversation at the end of the reading session. All of these contexts are interactive and conversational, and the skilled tutor will ensure that key new words or potentially difficult words are introduced into the conversations. This occurs in the context of a guided rather than a formal or systematic 'word study' approach (Glynn, 1985).

The initial 'Pause Prompt Praise' research project (formerly known as the Mangere Home and School Project) involved intensive observation and training in home settings with a group of older students (10 to 12 years) experiencing reading difficulties and included careful collaboration with their parents. The project required close involvement of the researchers in both school and home settings, allowing access to information not readily access-ible to teachers. Teachers of children both in the original project (Glynn et al., 1979) as well as in a subsequent parallel study in Birmingham, England, reported in McNaughton, Glynn and Robinson (1987), perceived parents of these low-achieving readers as apathetic towards their children's learning at school. Yet there was little evidence in either study that teachers had had contact with the children's homes. Researchers in these studies found other-wise – that parents cared deeply about their children's reading difficulties at school, and were highly motivated to do something about it. They all volun-teered to participate in learning to implement the 'Pause Prompt Praise' reading tutoring procedures with their own children at home, and they maintained their commitment to the programme, successfully implementing the pro-cedures two or three times a week over 12 weeks. With the assistance of the 'Pause Prompt Praise' procedures, parents were readily able to create and sus-tain responsive social contexts for their children's reading development, which was then situated in the child's own world. The strength of these par-ents' motivation and commitment to helping their children learn to read at home was extraordinary and successful.

The strength of parent motivation to help their own children learn to read, and the way in which reading development can be situated in family and community interactions, is further illustrated in a study of six refugee Khmer-speaking mothers of 6- to 7-year-old migrant children, using a modified form of the 'Pause Prompt Praise' procedures (Glynn and Glynn, 1986). Despite having very little English language, and having had little or no schooling in Cambodia, these mothers were able to implement the modified 'Pause Prompt Praise' procedures with their own children at home. This intervention improved their children's rate of reading progress at school over and above that resulting from participation in the school programme alone. In this study mothers and children were invited to work together, using either Khmer or English to 'work out' the meaning of the stories in the reading texts sent home from the school, following usual classroom practice. Mothers appeared to draw on children's new knowledge and recall of English words learnt at school, and children appeared to draw on the mother's first-language skills (Khmer) and life experience to discuss the pictures and events portrayed in the stories. Important additional outcomes from this study were clear gains in emergent English reading skills measured for mothers as well as for their children. An important side effect was a marked increase in the mothers' self-esteem.

The following example shows how these same direct observation strat-egies have contributed to the reporting of data on reading progress of students in a home and school literacy programme in nine urban primary schools

(Glynn, Berryman and Glynn, 2000). Pre and post measures were taken of the reading performance of two groups of 6- to 7-year-old students learning to read in English and some learning to read in Māori. Group 1 participated in a 20-week home and school literacy programme in addition to the literacy programme implemented at school. Group 2 participated only in the school's literacy programme. Students in the home and school programme reading in English advanced four book levels, while those participating only in the school's programme advanced two book levels. Further, students in the home and school group increased their scores on a cloze comprehension measure from 53 per cent to 65 per cent (while reading texts four levels in advance of their pre-programme levels). In contrast, students in the school-only group showed a decrease on this measure from 65 per cent to 52 per cent (while reading texts two levels in advance of their pre-programme levels). There were only minor changes in correct and incorrect reading rates, with no appreciable differences between groups. Students were not increasing their reading rate (speed of reading) at the expense of accuracy. Students reading in Māori shared similar positive gains.

In more recent years 'Pause Prompt Praise' has also been able to contribute in quite a different arena, that of the revitalization of indigenous language and culture. 'Pause Prompt Praise' has been implemented also within the context of assisting learning to read Māori as a second language in both primary and intermediate (middle) school settings (Glynn et al., 1996; Glynn et al., 1998).

'Pause Prompt Praise' data on reader-tutor interaction have proved invaluable in helping tutors or teachers to change their teaching behaviour. Presenting teachers and tutors with such specific and focused information on their own teaching behaviour supports them in reflecting on ways to create responsive social learning contexts for students experiencing difficulties in learning to read. Guided discussions of reader and tutor interactions around a small sample of reader errors provides a powerful contribution to teacher professional development in assisting older students with reading difficulties. Guided discussions typically take the form of 'talking through' with teachers their own responses to four or five specific reader errors, from information recorded on the 'Pause Prompt Praise' data sheet (as discussed in Chapter 7). Tutors are invited to reflect on their tutoring behaviour as they follow the line from left to right for each error, and with the benefit of the recorded information, to suggest alternative responses to try on a further occasion.

Teachers as responsive agents

From two separate meta-analyses of large numbers of education research studies, Alton-Lee (2003) and Hattie (1999) identified that the major single influence on student achievement within the education system, accounting for between 16 and 60 per cent of the variance on diverse student achievement, was the quality of the teaching they received. In her synthesis of research findings, Alton-Lee (2003) identified the following ten characteristics of quality teaching:

- Quality teaching is focussed on raising student achievement (including social outcomes) and facilitates high standards of student outcomes for heterogeneous groups of students.
- Pedagogical practices enable classes and other learning groupings to work as caring, inclusive and cohesive learning communities.
- Effective links are created between school and other cultural contexts in which students are socialised to facilitate learning.
- Teaching is responsive to student learning processes.
- Opportunity to learn is effective and sufficient.
- Multiple task contexts support learning cycles.
- Curriculum goals, resources including ICT usage, task design, teaching and school practices are effectively aligned.
- Pedagogy scaffolds and provides appropriate feedback on students' task engagement.
- Pedagogy promotes learning orientations, student self regulation, meta cognitive strategies and thoughtful student discourse.
- Teachers and students engage constructively in goal-orientated assessment.

(Alton-Lee, 2003, pp. vi–x)

Recognition of the role that teachers can play as responsive agents of educational improvement has more recently been prioritized in educational research within New Zealand. Underachievement has been conceptualized by various groups, including educators, in terms of perceived deficiencies residing outside both the school and classroom environment and located within students, their families and communities (Bishop et al., 2003). Much attention therefore has been paid to research that seeks to understand solutions outside the school context. However, the idea that teachers themselves are responsible for the achievement levels of the students they teach has recently impacted upon the professional development of teachers. The Early Childhood Primary Links via Literacy (ECPL) project (Phillips, McNaughton and MacDonald, 2001) is a New Zealand-based project that set out to measure the impact of teacher professional development on literacy learning for children who came largely from Māori and Pacific populations.

The over-riding emphasis in the research was the need for teacher professional development that addressed and challenged three sets of teacher beliefs and associated practices. First, teachers needed to believe in their students' ability to achieve in literacy and to set higher goals and expectations. Second, teachers needed to examine the impact of their own teaching on student learning so that they focused on the teaching/learning relationship and on their own self-efficacy in this role. Third, the research emphasized that teachers' ability to increase literacy levels within their classrooms was greatly enhanced when they developed new domain knowledge in the form of redefining literacy tasks and how to teach them. This research showed that when teachers were supported to respond positively to these challenges, the usual gap that occurred between those students who were achieving in literacy at 6 years of age, and those students who were not, did not occur.

Timperley and Phillips (2003) identified key factors that contribute to high-level teacher expectation in literacy development. They proposed the following factors as being influential in developing teacher high expectation:

- increased knowledge, both in procedural definition and teacher pedagogy;
- unanticipated student improvement;
- feeling capable to make the changes.

These results suggest that teachers' high expectations derive from successful attempts to utilize new knowledge about literacy and put it into practice. A lack of opportunities to build theory into practice, and embed practice within theory, may perpetuate teacher low expectation and consequently low student achievement. The importance of a student strength-based model and accurate assessments of individual student strengths were also identified in the ECPL project (Phillips et al., 2001). Teachers need to be able to recognize diverse knowledge and skill levels within their classrooms as a foundation on which to build the strengths of each individual.

Both Phillips et al. (2001) and McNaughton (2002) demonstrate that teachers' understanding and ability to accommodate mismatches between knowledge bases for ethnic minority groups is crucial to the literacy development of these groups. Effective teachers viewed knowledge base inconsistencies as challenges to be overcome rather than as problems outside of their expertise. This outcome aligns with international literature on working with minority students and also with New Zealand research that looked at effective Māori medium literacy teachers (Bishop, Berryman and Richardson, 2001, 2002). Teachers in this project (*Te Toi Huarewa* – the name given to an evaluation of effective literacy teachers from Māori immersion junior classrooms) went to great lengths to ensure that resources incorporating local customs, local dialects and local stories were gathered from community experts (*kaumātua* elders) and prepared for incorporation into their own classroom literacy programmes. This outcome also aligns with the most effective mainstream teachers working with Year 9 and 10 Māori students who encouraged Māori students themselves to bring their own experiences into the classroom and to build from those experiences. Māori students in these classrooms were also encouraged to engage with teachers in co-constructing their own learning pathways (Bishop et al., 2003). Rattray (1999) asserts that contrasting belief systems can present real difficulties for indigenous students as they try to make sense of the world. He further suggests that positive interactions with indigenous students require teachers to understand this mismatch and plan interactions and practices accordingly.

Bishop and Glynn (1999) identify the denial of cultural diversity as a feature of power imbalances within classroom relationships and practices. They suggest the need for classroom teachers to move from traditional teaching interactions to more discursive (interactive and conversational style) teaching interactions. They assert that teachers who use a knowledge transmission model often merely pose the questions, evaluate student responses and explain conceptual relationships, resulting in the learner remaining a largely passive recipient of knowledge. Teachers such as these continue to perpetuate traditional pedagogy that maintains unequal power relationships in classrooms. These interactions result in learners rarely being given opportunities to ask questions beyond seeking clarification of instructions. Discursive interactions ensure opportunities for knowledge to be reciprocally developed and co-constructed. Learners ask their own questions. They are co-participants in the learning process and, as such, motivation is intrinsically focused. The teacher acts as a guide, facilitating the student's theorizing and explanations. In the context of literacy, this means teachers and students, or students and peers, should collaborate in order to co-construct the meanings of different types of texts. For students who are experiencing literacy difficulties, and who come from diverse cultural home backgrounds, it is particularly important to include texts that have aspects of familiarity. In this context, the roles of the teacher and learner are more likely to be exchangeable and mutually beneficial, as is understood in the Māori concept of *ako* (Pere, 1982). Learning is co-constructed and can be built on from students' prior knowledge and experiences (Bishop and Glynn, 1999; Bishop et al., 2003). Furthermore, these interactions between teachers and students are greatly enhanced when mutually acceptable goals are clearly set and when a relationship of respect for the students' prior experiences has been laid down as the foundation for their future learning. Such relationships ensure that teachers continue to hold high expectations of their students and provide well-managed learning environments for them (Bishop et al., 2003).

Conclusion

This chapter has examined the importance of establishing responsive social contexts for students experiencing reading difficulties. It is important for these students to have a sense of agency over their own learning and, with the support of effective mediators, to be able to co-construct the meaning of coherent texts. Viewing learning to read as an individual psychological process leads to pedagogical approaches that assume knowledge or skill deficits within the individual and that emphasize the provision of increased practice of specific decoding skills, often fragmented and isolated from meaningful textual contexts. Viewing learning to read as a collaborative social process leads to teaching strategies that emphasize the need for more effective interactions between student and mediator, and careful guided participation in working with texts that are salient for both.

In this chapter, two contrasting national literacy policies are described which differ markedly in the way that literacy is defined and understood, and in their relative emphases on decoding and meaning-making skills, for students experiencing literacy difficulties. The chapter argues for the need for classroom and school programmes to provide students who are experiencing difficulties with access to a wide range of rich literacy texts and activities, including those from their own homes and communities as well as those originating in the classroom. Providing teachers and students with high-quality reading materials, representing a variety of genres, and written and illustrated by writers from students' home communities, is seen as crucial for engaging students experiencing literacy difficulties. In order to improve literacy outcomes for students experiencing difficulties, it is also crucial to provide teachers with effective professional development to help them extend their pedagogical practices from traditional and technical skill-based approaches to include pedagogies that are more responsive, interactive and discursive.

5 Responsive contexts for writing

Introduction

The understanding of human development and literacy learning adopted throughout this book is founded on sociocultural theory originating in the work of Vygotsky (1896–1934), and further developed by Bronfenbrenner (1979), Lave and Wenger (1991, 1999), Rogoff (2003), Bruner (1996), and McNaughton(1995, 1996, 2002). Intellectual development occurs primarily through the use of language in social interaction with significant others. The processes of interpersonal and intellectual learning are tightly interwoven from birth and continue to remain so throughout life.

Young children interact with more competent adults, siblings or peers in ways that enable them to achieve a higher level of skill and understanding than they could achieve on their own. Effective support for learning occurs within what Vygotsky calls the 'zone of proximal development' (Vygotsky, 1981, p. 163). This concept is fundamental to an understanding of learning in a social context, but has particular application to conceptualizing ways of supporting students experiencing difficulties in writing.

This chapter examines responsive social contexts for facilitating students' writing, where more-skilled partners (parents, peers or teachers) act as a responsive, interactive audience for the messages students are trying to write (Glynn, 1985a, 1985b; Wheldall and Glynn 1989). These are powerful inter-active learning contexts that can occur between less-skilled and more-skilled participants. Responsive social contexts are characterized by a balance of con-trol over initiating and continuing learning interactions, such that the more-skilled participant takes on a range of responsive, interactive roles rather than instructional, custodial or managerial roles. They are characterized also by reciprocal intellectual and social benefits for each participant that result from their language interaction around shared tasks. These contexts may be charac-terized, too, by frequent reversal of the traditional learner and teacher roles, and by feedback that is responsive rather than evaluative. Such reciprocal interchanging of learning and teaching roles is well understood in pedagogies that construe students as active agents sharing in the construction of their own learning, from effective co-constructive teaching practice (Bishop et al., 2003), cooperative learning (Johnson and Johnson, 1992; Brown and Thomson, 2000), peer tutoring (Glynn et al., 1996; Medcalf et al., 2004), and reciprocal teaching (Westera, 1995, 2002; Lederer, 2000; Pickens, Glynn and Whitehead, 2004). Within a responsive social learning context, each partner supports, and is supported by, the other. Indigenous pedagogies, in particular, recognize the interdependence of the learning and teaching roles. Pere (1982), for example, describes how in the Māori language the root word *ako* forms part of both the word for teacher (*kaiako*) and the word for learner (*akonga*).

The place of formal grammar

One factor believed by many teachers, editors and members of the wider community to contribute strongly to students' writing difficulties is their lack of understanding of syntax, and lack of formal grammar teaching. Smith and Elley (1997) point out that traditional pedagogy in many countries has insisted on a major allocation of time to the teaching of formal grammar. The UK National Literacy Strategy, for example, has a very clear focus on syntax and the formal teaching of phonics and spelling. This strategy arose in the context of increasing public concern over declining standards in basic and functional literacy in England and other Western countries such as Australia, New Zealand and the United States. This concern over 'literacy standards' encouraged policy-makers to assume a view of literacy as a set of technical skills that can be identified, quantified and evaluated, and to adopt 'literacy benchmarks' and the nationwide introduction of pedagogical approaches such as the UK Literacy Hour. The Literacy Hour, with its whole-class approach, focuses on raising standards through changing pedagogical approaches at the classroom, school and national level rather than through focusing on providing programmes and resources which encourage teachers to adjust their pedagogies to the needs of individual students.

The Framework describes its model for the teaching of literacy as making use of 'a series of searchlights' each of which 'sheds light on the text' (DfEE, 1998, p. 3). Riley analyses this 'searchlight model' as follows:

Structure of the Framework for Teaching
- The organizational basis of the Framework for Teaching adopts a subdivision of written language which reflects its visual features. Distinction at the level of words/sentences/texts provide points of reference for teachers and pupils to use when talking about the processes and products of literacy experiences and learning.

These organizational distinctions are compatible with models used by Crystal (1995) and Perera (1979). The teaching objectives of the content at the three levels encompass:

- the word which is the smallest free-standing unit of linguistic description – the teaching at this level covers vocabulary which includes phonics and spelling and also morphology (the within-word rules, e.g. prefixes, roots, suffixes);
- the sentence is the largest linguistic unit within which grammatical rules systematically operate – the teaching at this level covers between-word rules (syntax) and punctuation (the main function of punctuation being to separate units of grammar or to indicate contractions, e.g. Jeni's . . .
- a text (or discourse) is a collection of one or more sentences that display a coherent theme and with the appropriate cohesion. The teaching at this level deals with the structures of discourse as well as with both the comprehension and composition of the meanings which texts can convey.

(Riley, 2001, p. 33)

Outcomes of a series of reviews of research, spread over 80 years, however, indicate little evidence of positive benefits to students' writing from the effects of teaching formal grammar (Smith and Elley, 1997). The amount of attention needed to establish lower-level skills (spelling, punctuation and basic grammar structures) for writers experiencing difficulties may be counter-productive to their learning of higher-order skills of planning and the generation of content (MacArthur and Graham, 1987). Time and energy spent in teaching and monitoring basic grammatical structures may come at the expense of providing opportunities for beginning writers to learn to express their ideas and feelings and communicate with those who might read their writing. Child development research shows that children internalize the conventions of grammar incidentally through the many thousands of language events that take place in their lives from early childhood, and without formal instruction (Smith and Elley, 1997, p. 98). If, in learning to speak a language, learners received only corrective feedback on grammar conventions, they would soon lose enthusiasm and motivation. If we asked which platform our train leaves from, and instead of getting a simple answer, we received corrective feedback on our pronunciation, our inappropriate choice of vocabulary, and our incorrect sentence structure, our train might have arrived and departed, and we may still not know the right platform.

Similarly, in writing contexts where accuracy of spelling, punctuation and grammar is deemed paramount, there is a danger that feedback on structural accuracy may come at the expense of feedback on the written message. How writers present their message may come to be valued above the message itself

(Jerram, Glynn and Tuck, 1988). Excessive, and sometimes exclusive, teacher use of this type of corrective feedback for writing may result in students limiting their choice of sentence structures and genres to those in which they feel 'safe', that is where they know they can avoid or minimize errors. This is particularly true for students from minority language backgrounds who are learning to write in English. In New Zealand, Māori educators and researchers at the Poutama Pounamu Education Research Centre note further that many students learning to write in Māori also choose to limit themselves to a single 'safe' genre, typically that of personal narrative.

In the UK, a recent major systematic review of 4566 research papers reporting on the effect of grammar teaching on the quality or accuracy of the writing of 5-to 15-year-old students found the evidence base that such teaching had any positive influence on writing outcomes to be very small (Andrews et al., 2004). The authors conclude that the clear implication of this review is that:

> . . . the teaching of syntax in English to 5- to 16-year-olds in order to improve writing should cease to be part of the curriculum, unless in the context of rigorous evaluative research.
>
> (Andrews et al., 2004, p. 55)

The early evaluations of the UK National Literacy Strategy, which indicate that the standard of children's writing has not improved to the same degree as reading, also lend some support to this view (Fisher, Lewis and Davis, 2000).

Early development of writing

How students initiate writing and how teachers and others respond to that writing are critical determinants of students' writing progress. Vargas (1978) contends that the method by which students are taught to write may be one reason why we do not learn to write very well. She notes that many children learning to write are seldom given the opportunity of seeing the impact that their writing has upon another person, of learning that what they write can make someone happy, sad, interested or excited, or want to share in their experiences and feelings.

When young children attempt to initiate writing at home, parents and older siblings typically act as responsive and interactive partners rather than as language assessors. For example, 4-year-old Sarah draws a picture of a person standing next to a car. She manages to write a word that looks something like 'Dad'. Her mother, having seen Sarah and her father washing the family car earlier in the day, 'reads' Sarah's message and says: 'Oh, Dad is washing the car'. She has correctly interpreted Sarah's written message. Sarah is delighted that her attempt at communicating in writing has 'worked'. As Sarah improves in writing messages, so does her mother improve in interpreting and responding to her messages. This is a mutually rewarding and powerful social learning context, likely to result in continuing gains in skill for both Sarah and her mother.

We may pose the question of whether it is possible to create responsive social contexts for children's writing that are as effective as the responsive social contexts we create for conversation. Indeed, young children's emergent writing at home does occur in responsive social contexts, as the above example with Sarah illustrates. Such responsive social contexts for writing may occur more naturally at home than at school, in the same way that responsive social contexts for oral language occur more naturally at home (Glynn, 1985). Smith and Elley (1997) note the many ways in which young children attempt to communicate in writing at home, including making marks on paper, books, walls, concrete paths, using any of the various tools readily available, pencils, pens, crayons, felt-tip markers. They note also that children expect others to respond to these marks and make sense of them. A scribbled mark on a coloured 'post-it' on the fridge may be correctly understood, within the context of a specific household, as an item to be placed on a parent's shopping list, perhaps a child's instruction to the parent to buy more of a favourite breakfast cereal. In effect, children who are emergent writers expect others to answer the question: 'What did I write?' (Clay, 1975).

Within responsive social contexts at home, young children soon learn to attempt more than merely making marks. In a study of 79 children experiencing difficulty in learning to read at school, researchers found that 60 of these children made regular attempts to write something at home (Glynn, Bethune, Crooks, Ballard and Smith, 1992). Nineteen of them were reported by their parents as trying to write something every day. Writing tasks these children engaged in included writing names (80 per cent), copying specific alphabet letters and words (72 per cent), writing stories (55 per cent), greeting cards (55 per cent), letters (50 per cent). However, children do not simply initiate these writing activities in a vacuum. Fortunately, in many homes, there is at least one interested adult or older family member who enjoys spending some quality time in responding to young children's attempts to initiate writing. These people act as mediators and seem to enjoy interacting in the zone of proximal development with children who are making their first moves at learning to write. Like Sarah's mother, they very quickly develop expertise in understanding and interpreting the messages the child is attempting to write, and in responding in ways that affirm the communicative intent of the writing.

Support for writing within the ZPD

There is a major challenge facing teachers adopting a sociocultural approach to supporting students learning to write. That is how to utilize Vygotsky's concept of the zone of proximal development to create authentic responsive social contexts for writing at school that are as effective as those that occur at home. Beyond initial attempts at communicating simple messages, effective writing is an even more challenging and complex cognitive task. Flower and Hayes (1980) conceptualize writing as incorporating a hierarchical series of goals that writers achieve through engaging in the cognitive processes of planning, translating and revising. Planning involves generating information to be included in the script, selecting and organizing what is relevant, and deciding on criteria for judging successful completion of the script. Translation involves converting the plan into the script. Revising includes editing for both grammatical errors and structural coherence. These processes overlap, and competent writers revisit each of them many times before the writing task is complete. Competent writers can also switch their attention between these processes according to their perception of what is required for successful task completion (Scardamalia and Bereiter, 1986).

In contrast, students experiencing difficulties in literacy often find it very difficult to learn to write clearly and effectively. According to Graham and Harris (1993), cited in Meltzer (1993), writing difficulties may, in large part, be the result of three factors:

- lack of proficiency in text production skills, that is, frequent errors in spelling, the use of upper and lower case, and punctuation;
- lack of knowledge relating to the subject content of the script to be written, and/or of the conventions and characteristics of different writing genres;
- lack of effective strategies in planning or revising text.

Graham and Harris (1993) adopt a cognitive approach to supporting students experiencing writing difficulties because this approach emphasizes the component processes of writing production which can then be focused upon individually. They report that the area researched most thoroughly in relation to pupils with difficulties in literacy development is the use of strategies intended to improve planning processes. These include, for example, self-directed techniques for generating words relevant to the content of the script (Harris and Graham, 1985), the use of writing frames to generate and organize ideas (Englert and Raphael, 1988; Graves, Montague and Wong, 1989), and articulating process goals for establishing the way in which the end product is to be achieved (Graham, MacArthur, Schwartz and Voth, 1989).

Even though these cognitively demanding writing processes are seemingly internal and personal to the individual writer, paradoxically they may be effectively learned in responsive social contexts which provide structured interaction with more skilled writers (Berryman, Reweti, O'Brien, Langdon and Glynn, 2001; Medcalf, Glynn and Moore, 2004). From a sociocultural perspective, it is literacy that drives cognition, rather than the reverse. What may be needed to facilitate effective writing is therefore not so much formal instruction in grammar and conventions of spelling and punctuation, but many opportunities to communicate with others through the medium of writing, that is to write and receive feedback in writing from people who are more skilled at writing. Responsive social contexts for writing may help to address these requirements.

Writing from a UK perspective, Topping has piloted a 'Paired Writing' technique and recommends its use with students who experience difficulties in expressing themselves in writing to work with more informed and experienced partners for three sessions of 20 minutes per week for six weeks. This technique 'is intended to ease the dysfunctional anxiety of some individuals when confronted with a blank piece of paper' (Topping, 2000, p. 1). 'Paired Writing' embodies the practices of constant in-built feedback and cross-checking, to ensure that what is written makes sense to both partners and also to address the issue of the fear of failure and anxiety about spelling or punctuation. 'Paired Writing' is targeted for use with writing tasks slightly beyond the learner's current level of achievement but within the zone of proximal development. It is intended to provide:

> A structured framework to support interactive collaborative behaviours through all stages of the writing process. There is clear role division of labour at every stage ... the emphasis is on thinking, planning, intelligent questioning, self-disclosure and discussion, reorganization and restructuring – to counterbalance the traditional focus on mechanics and the final tangible product. A sense of participant ownership of a learner-managed process is considered important, not least to avoid feelings of helplessness and dependency.
>
> (Topping, 2000, p. 2)

Topping (2001) lays out a clear method for the system which consists of six steps:

- Step 1 is Ideas Generation. The helper stimulates ideas by using given questions (Who? What? To? With? Where? When? How? Why?) and inventing other relevant ones. The helper makes one-word notes on the writer's responses.
- Step 2 is Drafting. The notes then form the basis for drafting, which

ignores spelling and punctuation. Lined paper and double spaced writing is recommended. The writer composes the text and scribing occurs either by the helper alone, or by the writer alone, or by the writer with whatever help for spelling s/he requests from the helper. If there is a hitch, the helper gives more support.

- In Step 3 the pair look at the text together while the helper reads the Draft out loud with expression. The writer then reads the text out loud, with the helper correcting any reading errors.
- Step 4 is Editing. First the writer considers where s/he thinks improvements are necessary, marking this with a coloured pen, pencil or highlighter. The most important improvement is where the meaning is unclear. The second most important is to do with the organization of ideas or the order in which meanings are presented. The next consideration is whether spellings are correct and the last whether punctuation is helpful and correct. The helper praises the writer then marks points the writer has 'missed'. The pair then discuss and agree improvements.
- In Step 5 the writer (usually) copies out a 'neat' or 'best' version. Sometimes the helper may write or type or word-process it. However, making the final copy is the least important step.
- Step 6 is Evaluation. The pair should self-assess their own best copy, but peer assessment by another pair is very useful. The list of edit levels: meaning, order, spelling and punctuation provide a checklist for this.

Topping (2000) describes three interventions in primary schools in England where paired writing has been shown to have a significant effect on improving children's writing relative to controls. For example, the 'Yarrow Project':

> ... involved same-age, cross-ability tutoring within a behaviourally difficult class of 10-year-olds. Children were assigned randomly to Pairs Writing (interaction) or Writing Individually (no interaction) conditions. Both paired and individual writers received the Paired Writing training. The metacognitive content of this, together with an increased rate of practice in writing during the project, led to improvements for all the children. However, Paired Writers (whether tutees or tutors) showed significantly greater gains than children who wrote alone.
>
> (Topping, 2000, p. 5)

Studies investigating responsive feedback

It is certainly more challenging for teachers to construct responsive social contexts for writing at school, given the number and diversity of students in their classrooms, and given schools' use of pedagogies that often cast the teacher in instructional and managerial roles rather than in responsive and interactive roles. Nevertheless, as seen in paired writing examples and the three research studies that follow, teachers can establish effective responsive social contexts for writing at school. They can achieve this through building collaborative writing partnerships, in which teachers themselves, or older students, parents or others, provide young writers with regular responsive written feedback on their writing at school.

Effective pedagogies for students who experience literacy difficulties may be usefully informed by studies of the performance of competent students. It may be that students who experience difficulties need more support in the zone of proximal development with the technical aspects of text production in the context of conveying meaningful messages, rather than the focus of literacy instruction being on the technical aspects themselves.

In the first study to be discussed, Jerram, Glynn and Tuck (1988) explored, over two school terms, the effect of a teacher supplying feedback in writing on the expressive writing of 8-year-old students in a primary classroom. This teacher, after reading each child's writing from a given session, wrote an individual personal response, reaction, or comment focused on what the child had written. Typically these comments took up four or five lines in which the teacher shared her own experiences, feelings, thoughts and ideas as stimulated or triggered by each writing sample. However, this written feedback made no reference to the accuracy of spelling, punctuation or grammar. Nor did she comment orally to students on any of these features. Specifically, the themes the teacher developed within her written feedback comments were:

- identifying with the writer's theme;
- personalizing the response;
- identifying with any of the characters in the writing;
- conversing with the writer;
- empathizing with the writer;
- enjoying the content of the writing;
- sharing an experience with the writer;
- anticipating the development of a theme.

Three 15-minute sessions were provided each week when students were invited to write, but not compelled to do so. If they chose not to write, they engaged in any other quiet activity that did not disturb others who were writing. Students were free to select their own writing topics, whether factual or imaginative, and to decide, session by session, whether to continue writing on an existing topic or to begin a new one.

This study employed a within-subject repeated-measures reversal research design (Hersen and Barlow, 1977). The first sixteen writing sessions were baseline sessions and students wrote under the above conditions. The teacher next introduced the written content feedback procedure for the following nine sessions, after which she withdrew the procedure for three sessions as part of the planned withdrawal phase in this within-subject research design. However, this phase was curtailed after three sessions because both teacher and children had come to value and enjoy the responsive feedback process so much that they did not want to continue this withdrawal phase. The teacher re-introduced written content feedback for a further twenty sessions, over a further six school weeks.

Data from this study showed that across the sixteen baseline days, the number of words students wrote decreased considerably. It was clear that the provision of a regular, quiet and unforced opportunity to write on any topic of the students' own choosing proved in itself to be insufficient to maintain these children's writing rate and their enthusiasm for writing. In contrast, when the teacher introduced responsive written feedback, students greatly increased the amount they wrote, well above their baseline levels. During the three-session withdrawal period, students' writing rate dropped dramatically. They strongly requested the teacher to provide further feedback. When the procedure was re-introduced, students again displayed major gains in their writing rate.

While students' quantitative gains in writing rate under conditions of responsive written feedback were important, because they demonstrated that they would write more when they had a responsive audience than when they did not, there were also important qualitative changes in their writing. Over the period of the study, children wrote an increasing number of imaginative, rather than factual, stories, and they increasingly chose to continue a story over several sessions, rather than start a new story every session. This suggested that having a responsive audience encouraged them to expand and elaborate their writing on a given topic as the teacher's feedback indicated that she was interested in their experiences and shared some of their feelings.

Qualitative changes in these students' writing were noticed by independent readers of their stories. Reading a random selection of writing samples, selected from sessions right across the study, three sets of independent raters (educators, parents and students) provided a qualitative rating on a seven-point scale of the overall quality and perceived interest of the writing. Raters were blind as to the writers' identities and as to whether a particular writing sample was written during baseline, withdrawal, or during the responsive written feedback conditions. All three sets of raters gave their highest ratings to stories written under conditions of written content feedback, and their lowest ratings to stories written under the baseline and the withdrawal conditions, with stories written during withdrawal receiving the lowest ratings of all. In terms of writing quality, the study found that students attempted more 'adventurous' words (words beyond their current spelling levels) during responsive written feedback conditions than they did under baseline or withdrawal conditions. Interestingly, despite students increasing the rate and quality of their writing, their spelling accuracy on those words within their current individual spelling levels remained close to 100 per cent throughout the entire study.

In discussing the results of this study, Wheldall and Glynn (1989) concluded:

> In this study, the teacher adopted the role of a responsive interacting audience, and not the role of a controlling or corrective one. Through the provision of individual personal feedback in writing, this was able to provide beginning writers with an effective means of influencing an interested and responsive audience. The changes in rate and quality of children's writing, and the increased sharing of experiences and feelings between teacher and children that resulted from their writing, support our claim that writing can be usefully viewed as both an interactive and a social process.
>
> (p. 153)

Throughout the responsive written feedback phases of the study, students were highly motivated to read in their writing books their teacher's feedback from the previous session before they began to write. They wanted to respond to the comments, shared experiences and shared feelings expressed by their teacher, who had become by now more of a conversational writing partner than an evaluator or critic. These students came to regard their writing books as highly prized possessions:

> In many ways, the books recorded the development of a growing positive relationship with the teacher as much as they recorded changes in children's writing.
>
> (Wheldall and Glynn, 1989, p. 153).

The study clearly demonstrated that this teacher had developed a successful responsive social context for writing for her class of 8-year-old students, and that her personal relationship with them strengthened and deepened over time. She was able to work as a mediator with her students within their zone of proximal development for expressive and communicative writing.

However, there may be greater challenges facing other teachers wanting to work in this way to improve their students' writing. This may be especially true for teachers of students whose home language and culture differs from the language and culture of the school (McNaughton, 2002). First, these teachers will find it difficult to enter into the zone of proximal development of their students. They may be unable, or unwilling, to share in the language, values and cultural experiences of their students' homes, and hence unlikely to be able to make sense of and respond to children's attempts to initiate writing that emerge from these language and cultural experiences. Secondly, and conversely, parents and others at home may be unable to share in the language, values and cultural experiences of the school and hence be unable to make sense of, and respond to, children's attempts to initiate writing that emerge from language and cultural experiences at school. However, with these students also the use of responsive writing partnerships may offer an effective way to address this challenge, as is illustrated in the following research study.

In recent years, there has been rapid growth in immersion and bilingual education with the intended outcome of bilingualism in some countries. For example, in New Zealand, the two official languages are Māori and English. In the case of New Zealand, there are extraordinary demands made on the time and energies of teachers in Māori immersion education. In addition to their full-time teaching loads, many are also heavily involved in designing and developing Māori curriculum materials and teaching resources, maintaining their crucial support networks with their tribal communities and furthering their own Māori language and cultural competence, in order to be better equipped to assist students' language and cultural learning (Bishop et al., 2001). Providing regular responsive written feedback for each student's writing in a Māori immersion classroom is not feasible for many of these teachers. In addition, many Māori parents who have chosen to place their children in Māori immersion schooling do not themselves have sufficient language proficiency or cultural knowledge to provide written feedback for their children's writing in Māori. Undoubtedly, they strongly wish their children to acquire the language and cultural knowledge and experience of which their own generation has missed out. One solution to this issue in New Zealand has been offered in terms of building on the cultural traditions of the *tuakana-teina* (peer support) relationship, so that more experienced older members of the extended family (*whānau*) have a specific responsibility for sharing their learning with younger and less experienced members. The roles and responsibilities embedded in this relationship extend beyond the immediate context, beyond the extended family structure, and can operate even at the sub-tribal (*hapū*) and tribal (*iwi*) levels.

The *tuakana-teina* relationship was utilized in the second study to be discussed, in which students in Māori immersion education were learning to write in Māori (Glynn, Berryman, O'Brien and Bishop, 2000). The more experienced tuakana *students* provided an alternative to the teacher having to enter the zone of proximal development and provide written feedback for all students. This 12-week study addressed the questions:

- Could *tuakana* (older siblings, cousins or friends) who were initially not known to the less experienced *teina* (younger siblings, cousins or friends), but whose skills in writing in Māori were somewhat in advance of those of the *teina* students, provide an effective responsive social context that would assist *teina* students to improve their writing?
- What effect would this process have on the writing of the *tuakana* students?
- Would the relationship between *tuakana* and *teina* students deepen and grow as it did between the teacher and her students in the previous study?

In this study, Glynn et al. (2000) employed a within-subject repeated-measures multiple-baseline research design (Hersen and Barlow, 1977). Three separate year groups, Years 3, 4 and 5, each with four *tuakana-teina* pairs, were matched across the two schools. The teacher of the *tuakana* students had completed teacher training as a mature student and had several years of Māori medium teaching experience. She was a fluent native speaker of Māori. She was assisted by an experienced language assistant (*kaiarahi i te reo*) who was also a native Māori speaker. The teacher of the *teina* students was younger but had a similar amount of teaching experience. He was a second language learner who could speak, read and write Māori with competence and confidence.

Teina (tutee) students were then given opportunities at their school to choose their own topics and write stories in Māori for their *tuakana* (tutor) partners. *Tuakana* learned to respond in writing to the stories written by their *teina*. They implemented the responsive written feedback procedure (known in Māori as '*tuhi atu tuhi mai*' – write away, write back) to focus on what they understood of their *teina*'s messages as was done by the teacher in the previous study (Jerram, Glynn and Tuck, 1988) rather than on language structure or corrective feedback on errors. *Tuakana* responsive written feedback was introduced in a step-wise sequence, with each of the three year groups starting at successive four-week intervals.

Analysis of *tuakana* responsive written feedback showed that every sample contained four or more of the eight responsive written feedback components. The first six components (personalizing the response, identifying with the theme or with characters, talking or empathizing with the writer, enjoying the content) were found in at least 70 per cent of the samples, while sharing an experience occurred in 63 per cent and anticipating a theme occurred in only 23 per cent. In addition, 70 per cent of the samples showed evidence of *tuakana* support for their *teina* learning to write in Māori. *Tuakana* were sharing quite complex messages in writing with their *teina*. In some cases a story theme developed over a series of two or more exchanges. A close relationship developed between *tuakana* and *teina* through the exchange of writing. Over time, there were increases in personal disclosures and sharing information about families and events. Both *tuakana* and *teina* looked forward to receiving the next writing sample and there was always instantaneous chatter on the arrival of the writing samples in each school. Writing the response to be returned to the other party was never a problem and was always done enthusiastically and independently.

Teina students gained considerable benefit from participating in this study. Quantitative data from the baseline to the responsive written feedback phases of the study showed that their fluency (correct writing rate) increased from 3.0 to 4.0 words per minute, while their accuracy (incorrect writing rate) remained less than 1.0 word per minute. *Teina* also received increased qualitative ratings of the 'audience impact' and the overall language quality of their writing from an independent rater who was also a teacher and a native speaker of Māori.

Furthermore, *tuakana* students gained considerable benefit from participating in this study. At first, there was a slight decrease in their own writing rate when they introduced responsive, written feedback. They indicated to the researches that this was because they did not want to 'belittle' or to embarrass or disrespect their *teina* by writing far more than their *teina* were able to. Avoiding displaying one's own individual performance in ways that 'show up' the performance of others in the group is an important cultural value among Māori. However, after several sessions when *teina* students had markedly increased the amount they wrote, *tuakana* went on to increase their own writing rate. In addition, their error rate also decreased in comparison with baseline levels. Further *tuakana* writing samples received higher ratings of audience impact and overall language quality following the introduction of responsive written feedback than those written under baseline conditions.

Taking the time and trouble to assist their *teina* not only had no adverse effects on the writing of the *tuakana*, but instead resulted in positive gains in both rate and quality of their own writing. This finding is consistent with findings from studies of peer tutoring of reading which report measurable gains for both tutors and tutees (Wheldall and Mettem, 1985: Limbrick, McNaughton and Glynn, 1985; Medcalf and Glynn, 1987).

Recurring themes and genres evident throughout both *tuakana* and *teina* writing showed that these students wrote about what was happening in their everyday lives. Most samples were written from their experiences within a Māori cultural context. For example, stories about the sea were likely to be about the gathering of *kai moana* (seafood). Stories about special occasions were likely to be about extended family events celebrated on the *marae* (ancestral tribal community centres) such as birthdays, twenty-firsts or *tangihanga* (gatherings to say farewell to the dead, conducted according to appropriate Māori protocols). Stories about food were likely to include specific references to the importance of providing and preparing food for the many guests at frequent family and tribal gatherings, such as the making of *paraoa rewena* (bread). Few stories represented non-Māori events, with the exception of one special occasion theme, the celebration of Guy Fawkes night.

Teina students appreciated the short waiting time between writing and responsive feedback (turnaround within the week) and the regular and personalized feedback. Writing for these students became an important and authentic task with high credibility. *Teina* students looked forward to their story being returned with their *tuakana* response attached. They reported feeling very positively towards their *tuakana* and felt able to write to them about anything. *Teina* liked not having to re-write or re-format their original story, but that it was accepted and responded to just the way it was. *Tuakana* looked forward to reading what the *teina* story was about. Both *teina* and *tuakana* also enjoyed finding out what was happening in each other's schools and reflecting upon community cultural events that both schools had attended.

Comments from the Māori language assistant (*kaiarahi i te reo*) on the results of this study indicate that responsive written feedback (*tuhi atu tuhi mai*) had made a positive contribution to their Māori language writing programme. For example, she observed:

> I am a *kaiarahi i te reo*, my job is to provide the language so that the language will not be lost. This process is different to how I have been teaching the language and now that I have seen their writing I can tell that it's been very good.
>
> (Glynn, Berryman and Harawira, 1996, videotape)

When asked which students were effective providers of responsive, written feedback, she replied:

> Those who speak the language, those who have a rapport with the children, those who can give new words and those who are able to write.
>
> (Glynn, Berryman and Harawira, 1996, videotape)

When asked about any benefits she had noticed for students, she replied:

> I could see that they were comfortable to sit and talk, it is easy for them to express themselves, their writing is good and that is what is good to me.
>
> (Glynn, Berryman and Harawira, 1996, videotape)

Through the repeated exchanges of writing, not only were there gains in writing rate and quality, but important cultural learning also occurred. Students gained a deeper understanding of their dual commitment and responsibilities within their *tuakana-teina* relationship. Each group learned from working within this relationship as well as learning about the relationship. They learned to value their skill at writing in Māori, and they learned that this skill was valued and affirmed by others.

These important linkages between written language acquisition and cultural learning are consistent with the findings from an observational study of oral language in a *kōhanga reo* (Māori language pre-school) by Hohepa, Smith, Smith and McNaughton (1992). They are also consistent with the findings of an earlier *tuakana-teina* reading tutoring study (Glynn et al., 1996). It is enjoyable and affirming for students to advance their literacy skills in contexts in which their cultural identity is recognized and valued (Glynn, Berryman, Atvars and Harawira, 1998).

The regular exchange of writing between *teina* and *tuakana* students in this study provides a compelling example of the effectivness of creating responsive social contexts for learning that embody Vygotsky's principle of working within the zone of proximal development. This was a learning context where a less-skilled and a more-skilled partner, in this case older and younger students, were able to engage in extended shared writing so that each could exercise a degree of control over the topics written about and the directions their writing could take. There were measured quantitative and qualitative academic gains for both partners.

Educators in New Zealand are continually seeking ways to improve learning outcomes for Māori students that are consistent with the values and beliefs of the culture and that strengthen the relationships between members of the extended family (*whānau*). The students in this study were second language learners who had limited access to fluent models of spoken language at home. Nevertheless, the responsive written feedback procedure was found to be a user-friendly and effective strategy for assisting students learning to improve their writing at school.

The first study demonstrated how successful responsive social contexts for writing at school were developed and extended over time by a class teacher who shared with her students common experiences and understandings of life in the classroom, school and community. The second study demonstrated how successful responsive social contexts for writing were developed and extended also by older students living approximately 20 kilometres away from the school where the emergent writers attended. The older students (*tuakana*) were initially unknown to the emergent writers (*teina*), but connected to them through the links of a common language and culture.

The third study (Glynn, Berryman and Weiss, 2003) formed part of an extensive community and school English literacy transition project in a small rural school. The full project (Berryman and Glynn, 2003) is discussed in Chapter 8. The writing data presented by Glynn, Berryman and Weiss (2003) demonstrate how Solomiga, a young Māori woman who was not a teacher, provided highly effective responsive written feedback for Year 6, 7 and 8 Māori students learning to write in English. She lived 140 kilometres from the school the students attended and was unknown to any of them prior to the study. As was the case for the older student tutors (*tuakana*) in the previous study, Solomiga acted as an interested audience, and responded in writing to the content of the messages in students' stories. Her written feedback included the same components utilized in the previous studies, and did not include corrective feedback on the accuracy of students' writing. However, in this study an additional procedure, a fortnightly 'structured brainstorm', (Whitehead, 1993), was introduced to assist students' writing. This involved the teacher and students collaboratively generating an extensive list of interesting words, next sorting these words into groups of related meaning, and then organizing these word groups by major topics or ideas. The word lists and their groupings were then available to assist students whenever they were writing their stories.

As was the case with the previous study, this study employed an intra-subject, multiple-baseline, repeated-measures research design (Hersen and Barlow, 1977). Across four school terms, the responsive written feedback was introduced sequentially, term by term, to each of three student year groups. Measures were taken of total words written, adventurous words written, as well as qualitative holistic ratings of audience impact and overall language quality.

Before considering the quantitative and qualitative outcome data from this study, it is helpful to examine an example of responsive written feedback. The following writing sample from one student, Huia, illustrates the nature of these transition students' writing in English and the nature of the responsive written feedback provided. In this example, Huia was writing about her experiences in a *kapa haka* (traditional cultural performance) group, and this sample preserves her original spelling, punctuation and sentence structure. This example of student writing and the responsive written feedback personalizes and contextualizes the information represented in the quantitative and qualitative data gathered in this study. The example illustrates how Solomiga was able to identify clearly with the themes in Huia's story, and construct her response to Huia through 'conversing' easily with her in writing, and connecting her own experiences and feelings to Huia's.

Huia's writing sample:

> When you are on the stage you feel so happy and so excited and very proud standing up there on the stage for your family and your hapu and iwi. The *kapa haka* is oright sometimes to me, but to other children it's cool and it's dum . . .
>
> Our tutors are working hard on us for last three or four weeks till

now. They are still working hard on us. They play games with us sometimes. We all like our tutors even though they are hard on us we still like them, and we are very lucky to have them with us. When I was in the little team I was the leader, and the next team it was me and my best friend the two leaders.

(Glynn, Berryman and Weiss, 2003, p. 15)

Solomiga's responsive written feedback:

Kia ora Huia. Thank you for sharing with me your story about why you enjoy *kapa haka* competitions. I agree with you that when you are on stage that it is exciting and you feel so proud. I would get really nervous before we would go on, thinking that I would forget the actions or I would drop my poi but I would manage to do all right.

Like you, our tutors would give us a hard time especially one lady called Mrs M. She would growl you in front of everyone so loudly that you would go red in the face. It was really embarrassing!!! I take it that you have been performing in a *kapa haka* group for quite sometime, am I right? I hope you are still enjoying it in many years to come.

Awesome story, Huia. Your effort for trying is now beginning to pay off. Your writing is improving each time you write. Keep it up and looking forward to your next story.

(Glynn, Berryman and Weiss, 2003, p. 15)

This example also illustrates how Solomiga was able to understand the messages in Huia's writing, and build strong cultural links with her, even though at the outset of the study Solomiga did not know Huia at all. Solomiga identified closely with Huia about feeling excited at being on stage in the *kapa haka* competitions, about still liking your *kapa haka* tutors, even though they may be hard on you. Through the medium of writing, Solomiga soon established a deep and personal relationship with the students that proved highly motivating for them. They became very keen to read their feedback from Solomiga each week, and just as keen to write back to her immediately.

Data were collected to show quantitative and qualitative changes that occurred in the writing samples of students in each of the three year groups.

The findings from this study can be summarized as showing that contingent on each year group entering the responsive written feedback programme, students made gains in writing rate and in the number of adventurous (low-frequency) words they used in their writing. There were also marked improvements in independent ratings of students' writing on the two qualitative measures of audience impact and language quality. These quantitative and qualitative improvements occurred at no cost to the accuracy of students' writing.

There was only one exception to this pattern. Data on some of the writing measures for Year 6 students suggest that these students may have benefited from the writing programme when it was being delivered to the Year 7 students (who were in the same classroom) and before the Year 6 students 'officially' entered the programme. There may have been some 'spill over' effects from this onto the Year 6 students, for example exposing them to seeing and hearing a greater range of English vocabulary. Furthermore, *whānau* members and community tutors of Year 7 students who had already been trained in the reading tutoring procedures may have exchanged advice, information and support with *whānau* members of Year 6 students. Indeed, teachers, parents and other *whānau* and community members were explicitly encouraged by the programme to share such advice, information and support.

While the increases in qualitative ratings of students' writing was very pleasing, the size of these increases typically was limited to one point on a seven-point scale, usually showing movement from 2.0 to 3.0, or from 3.0 to 4.0. There was clearly still considerable room for improvement on these holistic qualitative measures. Nevertheless, the finding that these independent global ratings detected positive shifts in students' writing that corresponded with students' ten-week period in the programme is educationally significant and worthwhile.

All three studies reviewed provide clear evidence that responsive social contexts can be created at school to greatly improve the quantity and quality of students' writing. Teachers, peers, people in the community and parents can readily learn to provide written feedback focused on the content and messages carried in students' writing. Students are highly motivated to read and respond to written feedback that conveys the reader's identification with themes or characters in their stories, and that allows the readers to share their feelings and experiences with the writer. Where this story writing and responsive feedback process operated weekly over ten to twelve weeks, there were positive gains in the rate and quality of students' writing. In addition, there was evidence that through the medium of writing, the personal relationships between writer and readers deepened, and cultural connectedness was strengthened.

Culturally appropriate resources within the literacy curriculum

Supporting the acquisition of literacy, particularly writing, in ways that are relevant to children and their lifestyles is a central concern also to Dyson (1997, 2003). Her interest acknowledges the importance of the responsiveness of the partnership between learner and tutor. Her particular focus, however, is on the cultural resources that children themselves bring into schools and that can be built upon to support literacy learning. She notes the contradictory pressures on teachers serving students from culturally and socioeconomically diverse backgrounds. On the one hand, there is a pressure to 'include' children by incorporating texts and materials which acknowledge the diverse kinds of knowledge and experiences children bring with them to school. On the other, 'the more politically influential "accountability" movement has urged teachers in many countries, for example, in the USA and parts of the UK to narrow the curriculum and concentrate on "basics" like phonics and spelling' (Dyson, 1997, p. 171).

Teachers, as the more experienced others, have the responsibility to scaffold children's literacy learning by ensuring access to cultural resources which are seen as valuable in society generally. They also have a responsibility to pay attention to the cultural resources that are both meaningful to children themselves and supportive of their well-being and self-esteem, in order to build on from the known.

Dyson investigated how young school children in urban American classrooms appropriate superhero figures from popular culture to take on powerful cultural storylines in ways that give rise to both literacy and social learning. Along with other researchers (Heath, 1983; Rogoff, 1990) she depicts learning to write as learning to participate in cultural groups in ways that are socially appropriate. Children's ways of writing are seen as:

> 'shaped, not only by their interaction in adult-guided worlds, but also by their social goals and ideological positioning in peer-governed worlds. Moreover, social identification and social conflicts, not only social interactions, make salient new kinds of writing choices, newly imagined ways of depicting human relationships'
>
> (Dyson, 1997, p. 6)

Thus she shows how children, irrespective of socioeconomic or ethnic background, can build from 'the very social and symbolic stuff of their own childhoods' (Dyson, 2003, p. 328) to enter school literacy practices.

Dyson (2003) has conducted a close examination of the way in which children often recontextualize materials from the media: popular songs, characters from films and so on, in various activities at school, for example in their play and verbal interactions with peers and adults. She illustrates, for example, how, in one particular classroom, children used songs and reflections on characters from the film *Space Jam* for:

> Drawing adventures, making lists of valued knowledge, announcing and reporting the results of sports events, composing and recalling

songs, telling and retelling stories – these were just some of the literacy practices through which children recontextualised popular media texts.

(Dyson, 2003, p. 349)

Manipulating media materials shaped how 'children made sense of and began to participate in school literacy' (Dyson, 2003, p. 328). As they recontextualized media materials from *Space Jam* in their practices at school, the children were able to experience challenges, social expectations and ideological tensions:

> In the 'scary story' event [in a classroom writers' workshop] the girls ... struggled quite vividly with symbolic and social tensions as they negotiated what one had to 'say', 'write' or communicate with gesture in a joint performance for the official sharing time practice. In a nascent way, then, they engaged in the sort of analytic work that furthers the symbolic, social and ideological decision-making involved in text work in varied media.

(Dyson, 2003, p. 349)

These children's writing was thus situated 'within the social and ideological complexity of children's lives and contemporary times' (Dyson, 1997, p. 6). Use of media materials in the literacy curriculum was only possible, however, because the curriculum in the classroom was 'permeable ... that made space for and productively engaged their social and symbolic – their textual – resources' (Dyson, 2003, p. 349).

Dyson comments that a curriculum that allows use of materials from the popular media may be particularly important when children come from economically limited families:

> In Rita's [the teacher's] classroom, media use in official school contexts was much more pervasive among children ... than it was among those from the more affluent neighbourhood. Moreover, certain media sources (like the movie Space Jam) were uniformly and almost exclusively referenced by African American children.

(Dyson, 2003, p. 349)

Dyson (2003) argues that the processes of manipulating media materials to local needs are crucial to the development of written language, to the way children play with issues of identity, and to children's awareness of themselves as individuals with a particular heritage:

> Opening up classrooms to children's textual resources and literate

processes means opening them up as well to the pleasures and challenges of children's everyday lives and to the multimedia of the emerging and ever-changing textual scene

(Dyson, 2003, p. 350)

The New Zealand Curriculum English document (Ministry of Education, 1994) identifies interpersonal language characterized by the direct exchange among people in conversation, debate, or personal letters as being an essential and natural part of the child's language development and of the English language curriculum. This notion is further supported in the New Zealand Māori Curriculum Māori language document (*Te Tahuhu o te Matauranga* [Ministry of Education], 1996). Responsive written feedback, as implemented within the writing partnerships established in the studies examined in this chapter, offers a promising strategy for assisting students to achieve these curriculum objectives, whether writing in English or in their community languages.

Conclusion

Key features in studies of responsive social contexts to support writing development, especially of those students who experience difficulties, include the provision of regular and extended opportunities for a less-skilled writer to engage and interact with a more-skilled writer, around topics of shared interest and concern. They also include an awareness of the balance of power and control over the content and direction of the writing. Sometimes it can flow like a conversation, even though writer and reader live in different places and are initially unknown to each other. As well as marked improvements in writing skill for the writers, positive social relationships can also develop between reader and writer as time goes on.

In the case of older students working with younger students, there can be measured gains in writing rate and quality for both partners. In the studies reviewed in this chapter, both partners are reported to have enjoyed working together in this context and to be looking forward to continuing their regular shared writing activities. It seems that these responsive social contexts for writing are literacy contexts that create or enhance opportunities for students to operate within their zone of proximal development alongside a caring and responsive and interactive partner.

6 Responsive approaches to spelling

Introduction

This chapter addresses challenging issues in the teaching and learning of spelling. We outline some of these issues and go on to suggest how they might be addressed in ways that are responsive to students' current literacy needs, and supportive of their writing skills.

Often, methods for learning spelling are quite arbitrary and disconnected from students' current writing needs. Some spelling approaches group words to be learned in terms of similar letter-sound patterns within words. Students may spend a great deal of time learning large lists of words, and getting them correct, but may still show little or no generalization of these correct patterns into similar words that they encounter in their writing. Other approaches to spelling may require students to construct personal spelling lists from the errors they make in their written work. In order to reduce errors, and the resulting corrective and often negative feedback from teachers, students may limit themselves to writing short, simple, minimal sentences or phrases, so that their writing is of little interest or stimulation to a reader. This is particularly likely if the feedback provided from teachers for writing is contingent only on surface features such as spelling.

This chapter discusses approaches to spelling that can build on the motivation of students' own interests and needs, methods that have been shown to be effective for students with spelling difficulties, and for providing peer support for learning spellings in the classroom. We discuss the trade-off between accuracy and fluency in producing written texts, which is the dilemma teachers face in whether to identify and mark all spelling errors, or not. We suggest responsive approaches to the development of more accurate spelling.

Responses to the complexity of the English spelling system

The question of how important it is to learn to spell accurately is fraught with controversy. The English language has an alphabetic writing system in which the symbols bear only some relationship to the sounds of the language:

> It is not a direct relationship . . . the symbols (the letters) may best be described as providing a clue to the sounds.'
>
> (Barton, 1995, p. 97)

Some words have clear sound-symbol correspondence – but even then, there is often confusion for speakers whose speech does not conform to Standard English or Received Pronunciation. One of the authors of the current volume recalls being asked by an 11-year-old student in an English lesson at school:

> 'ere, Miss, aah d'ye spell 'parf'?
> It's 'p-a-t-h', Stephen.
> Naa, Miss, 'parf', 'PARF'!
> Do you mean the thing you walk along to your front door?
> Yes, that's the one.
> It's still 'p-a-t-h', Stephen.

English also uses meaning in its spelling system. The similarity of spellings of word parts often indicates meaning: for example, 'sign', 'signature', 'assign' and 'signal' all relate to the Latin word '*signum*'. In addition, as Barton (1995) points out, English contains some logographs where one character is a unit of meaning, for example '&' and 'etc.'. Many spellings are idiosyncratic and the particular combinations of letters serve as logographs, for example 'right', 'rite' and 'write'. In this case, homophones indistinguishable in speech are differentiated in writing by their spellings, and each has to be learned separately:

> . . . we are never sure of the spelling of a new word we hear until we have seen it written down; we are often unsure of how to pronounce a word we come across in reading until we hear it spoken.
>
> (Barton, 1995, p. 100)

Given the complexity of English orthography and the difficulty experienced by many students in learning to spell accurately, it is hardly surprising that there is a diversity of approaches both to teaching spelling and to the need for doing so. Some of the issues that we have already discussed in relation to underlying assumptions about the reading process and their implications for reading instruction also apply to the learning and teaching of spelling. Spelling can be approached from a holistic, top-down, whole-word perspective, or from an analytic attempt at individual letter-sound identification and combinations of letters into words. Choice of words to be spelt can be made on the basis of what the student needs and wishes to spell for the purpose of his/her reading. This approach may require students to construct personal individual spelling lists from the errors they make in their written work. In contrast, choice of words to be learned can be made from any number of pre-constructed word lists. These may be hierarchical, phonically regular combinations of letters and sounds that the learner is already expected to know. This approach may group words to be learned in terms of similar letter-sound patterns within words. The National Literacy Strategy (DfEE, 1997) that operates in parts of the UK, for example, has a strong focus on phonically based approaches to spelling acquisition, for example the summary of the specific phonics and spelling work to be covered in YR to Y2 in term 1 involves:

Reception year
Recognise all initial consonant and short vowel sounds (a-z, ch, sh, th) in speech and in writing; to identify and write correct initial letters in response to the letter sound, word, object or picture.

Recognise and name each letter of the alphabet and to be aware of alphabetical order through rhymes, songs.

Discriminate, write and read final sounds in simple words.

Year 1, (Term 1)
Practise and reinforce work from YR

Discriminate, write and read middle (short vowel) sounds in simple words: 'a' (fat), 'e' (wet), 'i' (pig), 'o' (pot), 'u' (mug).

Year 2 (Term 1)
Practise and reinforce long vowel work from Y1 Term 3.

Discriminate, spell and read the common spelling patterns for the vowel phonemes: 'oo' (short) 'ar' 'oy' 'ow':

oo (short): 'u' (pull), 'oo' (good)
ar: 'ar' (car)

oy: 'oi' (boil), 'oy' (toy)
ow: 'ow' (cow), 'ou' (sound)

(DfEE, 1998)

One of the issues raised by the examples given above is the extent to which the tasks set for young students might appear arbitrary and disconnected from students' lives. It is challenging to see whether and how these tasks might constitute genuinely shared tasks within communities of literacy practice. There is no absolute requirement for students to recognize all the shapes and sounds of the alphabet before they can begin to read and write.

As stated above, students may put a great deal of effort also into learning word lists, but may not be able to generalize the spellings they have learned in their writing. Methods for teaching spelling can often be extremely isolated and disconnected from a student's current writing needs, such as being able to produce a coherent meaningful text. Students may be very discouraged by teachers' feedback that relates only to surface features of their writing such as spelling, and may confine themselves to writing the minimum in order to reduce the number of spelling mistakes. As noted in Chapter 3, it is fortunate that children's learning to speak their first language is not similarly hampered by excessive feedback on incorrect pronunciation of sounds within words.

In a very important study of what primary teachers do to improve literacy learning, Wragg et al. (1998) comment that, in the primary classrooms of effective teachers of literacy whose practices they studied, approaches to teaching spelling varied. Some teachers tried to avoid restricting vocabulary use if they thought their students could not spell a word, and encouraged children to write what they wanted to say and make a 'best guess' for spellings. Some made a conscious attempt to support children in learning spellings of words they wanted or needed to use in their own writing. Others expected all children in the same class to learn the same words in phonic groups. For example, a Year 2 teacher told the children, 'Don't worry about your spelling. I want you to get your ideas down on paper. We can worry about the spellings later' (Wragg et al., 1998, p. 153). Another Year 2 teacher 'initiated "I can try" books in an attempt to increase pupils' confidence in their own ability to spell' (*ibid*). Children were expected to try to spell unknown words before the teacher would write the word correctly in their books. A Year 3 teacher instructed children to, 'Make your best guess now. Then you can check your spellings later for when you're writing up your final copy' (*ibid*).

In contrast, a Year 1 teacher provided a word book divided into three columns for each child. Children wrote their version of a word in the first column, the teacher then ticked the word, if it was correct, or wrote the correct version in column two. Students were then required to cover the correct word and write the word from memory in column three before including it in their own writing. In some classes children took phonically based spelling lists home to learn and were tested on these on set days in the week. For one class, on one weekend the list of words for older children to learn was 'moon, spoon, soon, noon, loop, hoop, shoot, boot' (*ibid*, p. 154). In other classes words to be learned were taken from 'the first 100 key words in the reading scheme' (*ibid*).

Wragg et al. note that, although children's creative writing needs to be allowed to flow freely, unfortunate messages can be relayed to children if they are not encouraged to pay attention to the accuracy of spellings at some point:

> When a Year 2 child in one school, however, was asked by the researcher what he did about spellings he did not know he replied, 'Spellings don't matter in this class.' . . . Teachers of young children in particular should be aware that this attitude could become entrenched and difficult to counter in later years.
>
> (Wragg et al. 1998, p. 154)

These researchers conclude that their observation of the practice of effective literacy teachers in supporting students' spelling acquisition raises two issues:

- Unless there are sufficient opportunities for students' self-management of learning to spell, there are likely to be queues of students needing help with spellings, a high degree of dependency on the teacher and resulting problems of effective classroom management.
- Where they perceive that accuracy is not important, students may learn inaccurate spellings which may be 'extraordinarily difficult' to unlearn.

However, from a sociocultural point of view, this extraordinary difficulty students experience may reflect inappropriate and poorly theorized pedagogies that do not provide the appropriate tasks and support they need to assume agency over their learning to spell.

Writing, spelling and self-identity

Whatever the attitudes of individual teachers to the teaching of spelling, there are some adults at least who did not learn to spell well at school and who come to regret this later in life:

> . . . a 'public audience' will always make harsh judgements about poor spelling . . . good spelling is a vital component of communication through writing.
>
> (Rees/Education Department of Western Australia, 2001, p. 18)

'Katherine', a young adult identified as experiencing literacy difficulties whilst at school, explains in an interview why she decided that for her, at the age of 20, learning to become functionally literate, particularly learning to spell accurately, had become a very high priority (Wearmouth, 2002, in Open University, 2002, appendix). She wanted:

> To prove to myself that I'm as good as anybody else, to get better grades, to be able to stand there and write things down, to write letters – and also, for people in the same situation as myself, to say to them: 'Why don't you go and do something?' Everybody's got a talent. Everybody should have a chance. Dad told me once that you're never too old to stop learning. I thought when you're sixteen you walk out of school and that's that, but now I totally believe it.

She had sought help to address her literacy difficulties six months before the interview. She explained what had been the stimulus for this:

> I was standing in Halford's [a store selling car accessories] and I wrote out a cheque three times. . . . I was totally embarrassed. It was in front of a queue of people and the shop assistant. In the end I just gave her my Switchcard [cashcard] and walked out. I felt everyone was looking at me and thinking: 'What's going on here?' I thought they were all saying behind my back: 'Oh, she's thick.'

Between school and that particular occasion there had not been any other times when she needed to write:

> Cheques were the only thing I was really writing at the time. I had no need to write. I wasn't doing any college work or anything. . . . I was just 'not academic'. Those were the words that were used a lot about me. . . . To me it meant that it was always known that I wouldn't work, I didn't really have the intelligence and the brains. . . . Now I want to learn. I want to catch up on everything I've missed out.

At the time of interview, Katherine was training to be a nursery nurse. Now that she had made the effort to take lessons in spelling and writing, a sense that she was making progress with newly learned literacy skills was improving her sense of self-efficacy. She felt that this was especially important in her training to work with children:

> . . . working with children it's different from adults because they're looking to you for the confidence. When you're working with children

and trying to help them, and you haven't got the confidence yourself, obviously it's hard.

Becoming functionally literate was influencing Katherine's whole identity. It was making her self-reliant and giving her a whole new view of her future:

> I'll be more available to go and do different things. I'll be better able to write reports on children. I'll be in a better position to do it because my handwriting's got neater, my spelling's got better, it's just going to be totally different. If I'd left how I was I would be nowhere the rest of my life. But now I've got different options.

Stages of spelling acquisition

In order to address spelling difficulties such as those Katherine experienced in schools:

> Teachers need to develop their own understandings about spelling and learning to spell so that they have intervention strategies which meet the needs of individual children, leading them towards correct spelling.
>
> (Ministry of Education, undated, p. 64)

A number of researchers have recognized five stages of spelling acquisition: the pre-communicative stage, the semi-phonetic stage, the phonetic stage, the transitional stage and the correct stage (Gentry, 1987; Bentley, 2002):

- *Precommunicative*: the learner represents words with alphabetic symbols. There is little knowledge of sound-symbol identification. Upper and lower case letters are mixed up. Upper case letters often predominate.
- *Semiphonetic*: the learner shows an awareness of sound-symbol relationships, providing a partial phonetic representation of words and using mostly consonants, for example 'Iwf awk': 'I went for a walk' (Ministry of Education, undated, p. 66).
- *Phonetic*: the learner follows the left-right directionality principle. Sound-letter relationships in words are generally clear, with some words spelt correctly, some phonetically, for example 'sed' for 'said', and some semi-phonetically. Words ending with nasals followed by consonants are often spelt in particular ways, for example 'sangk' for 'sank', 'stingk' for 'stink'. Three-letter consonant blends may be

written with one letter missing: 'sring' for 'string'. An example of text written at this stage might be:

> Wen skl was finsd I wnt to the Libee My mmsed to me haree up and I fwnd sum bks.
>
> When school finished, I went to the library. My Mum said to me, 'Hurry up,' and I found some books.

(Ministry of Education, undated, p. 66)

- *Transitional*: at this stage the learner makes the transition from phonetic to visual spelling strategies, 'for example "eightee" instead of "ate" (*ibid*, p. 68). Both vowels and consonants are used in words, not just letter names. Vowel combinations, for example "ee" and "ai", and nasals before consonants, for example "-nd" are used. Words that have been learnt may be spelt correctly, although sometimes letters are reversed, for example "siad" for "said":

> Sanly iS going to the vet today to Hav a neeble and He is going to sta the niet thre and sanly climbs tee and Bits toes.
>
> Stanley is going to the vet today to have a needle and he is going to stay the night there and Stanley climbs trees and bites toes.

(*ibid*, p. 68)

- *Correct*: the learner accumulates a large number of regularly and irregularly spelt words, including some with silent consonants, for example 'dumb', and double consonants, for example 'tripping'. The learner begins to identify when words look incorrect, and there is developing understanding of homophones and increasing skill in using dictionaries.

In practice these stages overlap. It is likely that a given student could be operating at a 'correct' level on some words and at a 'phonetic' level on others. There is a danger that the 'stages' might be used by teachers as a global assessment tool, and used to label the student in a generic way. However, more importantly, from a sociocultural point of view, the significant questions to explore are those that relate to which literacy activities and which learning contexts facilitate the correct recall of spelling. Time spent in spelling activities for students experiencing difficulties should not come at the expense of time spent in practising communicative and expressive writing. At later stages approximations to correct spellings may still be made as learners begin to use complex language to express more complex concepts.

Teaching spelling in context

Learners construct their own knowledge about spelling from a variety of sources: from books, labels, text-based resources of all sorts, listening to and talking with others, and so on. However, in schools it is largely the role of the classroom teacher to identify what students can do in terms of spelling, and plan appropriate responses. Some students need to be shown correct spelling or spelling approaches once only. Others may need to encounter specific words in a wider variety of texts, and in the context of different literacy activities. For others, spelling acquisition is more problematic.

> Learning to spell must be treated as a complex developmental process ... As teachers observe spelling skills unfold, they must engage pupils in the kinds of cognitive activity that lead to spelling competency.
>
> (Gentry, 1987, p. 199)

In the past, teaching spelling has often been through 'the memorising of lists of words often unrelated to the child's own writing' (Ministry of Education, 1992, p. 69). There is evidence, however, that learning is not automatically transferred from formal spelling lists into children's writing unless the words that have been learnt are immediately relevant to what the child wishes or needs to express (Ministry of Education, 1992; Rees/ Education Dept of Western Australia). Children need to progress towards competency from the stage they have reached. As Montgomery and Kahn (2003) point out, a very useful literacy context in which spelling might be taught to students is during the editing of their own writing. This is 'because students want their personal interests to be the center of their learning time' (p. 148).

Diana Rees and the Education Department of Western Australia have developed a *Spelling Developmental Continuum* (2001) to reflect a five-stage model of spelling acquisition which very closely reflects the five-stage model described above. This work is underpinned by social constructivist views of learning and the learner. It is built on assumptions of holistic language learning occurring during interactions in social contexts between more experienced and less experienced learners who are viewed as active agents in the joint construction of meanings. The authors advise that, whatever stage of development of spelling acquisition the student has reached, it is important for teachers to encourage students to 'reflect on their spelling strategies ... their understandings, gradually building a complete picture of the spelling system' and 'to take risks and have-a-go at spelling words they need to write' (Rees/ Education Department of Western Australia, 2001, preliminary overview). A set of 'major teaching emphases' are set out for each stage in the *Spelling*

Developmental Continuum. Effective teachers of spelling can help students at each stage in the following ways:

Phase 1: Preliminary spelling
- Develop an awareness of letter names
- Develop understandings of concepts of print
- Use correct terminology for letters, sounds, words and sentences

Phase 2: Semi-Phonetic Spelling
- Help children develop a stable concept of a word
- Help children to hear different sounds in words
- Help children develop the ability to spell
- Segment spoken words into individual sounds
- Help children to represent sounds heard in words with letters written in the order they are heard
- Select high interest and high frequency words from children's reading and class writing to add to class word lists
- Teach children that letter names are constant but the sounds they represent vary
- Provide many opportunities for children to explore and identify sound-symbol relationships in meaningful contexts

Phase 3: Phonetic spelling
- Teach writers to look for visual patterns and common letter sequences in words
- Teach writers to identify critical features of words (i.e. differentiating characteristics)
- Continue to emphasise the building up of a systematic view of spelling with emphasis on the way letters can represent different sounds depending on context or place in the word
- teach writers that a sound can be represented by more than one letter or letters
- teach writers to think about meaning as a strategy
- continue the development of word banks by incorporating theme, topic, high frequency and interesting words as they arise
- introduce proof-reading strategies

Phase 4: Transitional Spelling
- Continue to emphasise visual patterns, encouraging writers to focus on patterns, and to classify words
- Focus on word meaning and word derivations as a guide to spelling, e.g. sign-signature
- Teach strategies for remembering the correct spelling of difficult words
- Teach strategies for spelling new words

- Encourage writers to generate alternative spellings in order to select the right one
- Encourage writers to hypothesise and generalise, e.g. rules for plurals and syllabification
- Encourage the use of words not previously used to enlarge spelling vocabulary
- Continue the development of Word Banks and class alphabetical lists
- Continue to model and teach proof-reading skills

Phase 5: Independent Spelling

- Focus on meaning as a guide to spelling
- Continue to explore derivations of words – meanings of foreign words as a guide to spelling
- Consolidate and extend proof-reading skills
- Continue to build up a systematic picture of the whole spelling system
- Teach writers to use context as a guide to spelling
- Reinforce strategies for remembering correct spelling of difficult words
- Emphasise social importance of spelling – insist on correct spelling for public audiences, parents, other classes or principal.

(Rees/Education Department of Western Australia, 2001, preliminary overview)

The authors of this *Spelling Developmental Continuum* are insistent that spelling should be taught in the context of reading and writing. It is these contexts that constitute literacy contexts that 'give meaning' to the superficially arbitrary task of spelling words correctly. At every point students need to be immersed in print:

> Reading reinforces children's understandings about the meaning of words and the relationships between them and so fosters their ability to use the semantic and syntactic cuing systems. It helps them develop and extend their knowledge of graphophonics and it exposes them to word models which they can use as referents. Spelling is a writer's tool. As they focus on spelling in the context of writing, children develop a systematic understanding of the way the graphophonic system works. This, in turn, provides children with decoding knowledge which they can use as they read. In itself, spelling has no purpose and no audience, but in the context of writing, spelling becomes very important to both purpose and audience.
>
> (Rees/Education Department of Western Australia, 2001, p. 18)

These authors present a number of contexts, a number of them social contexts, as frameworks for teaching strategies and activities:

- modelled and shared reading to foster awareness and understanding of spelling through talk;
- complementary activities to reinforce learning;
- independent writing to experiment with new understandings about spellings;
- modelled and shared writing to model correct spelling;
- proof-reading and editing of text;
- independent reading to see spellings in context;
- sharing and reflecting, to discuss understandings, and clarify and focus new learning.

One method to model the learning of new spellings is that of Peters (1967), who perceived 'good spellers' as having a good visual perception of word forms, the ability to see words within words and recognize letter sequences and patterns, and sensitivity to the coding system of the orthography of a language:

- LOOK at the word carefully and in such a way that you will remember what you have seen.
- COVER the word so that you cannot see it.
- WRITE the word from memory, saying it to yourself as you are writing.
- CHECK the word. If it is not correct then go back and repeat the steps.

(Peters, 1967, cited in Bentley, 1990, p. 4)

Students should never simply copy words but should always be encouraged to memorize them and then write them down.

Approaches to supporting spelling acquisition from the context of a child's own writing and from an awareness of its developmental nature should lead to a well-planned, responsive literacy curriculum. This is very different from the unplanned, chaotic and frustrating experiences of some students who have left school with literacy difficulties unmet, and find themselves disadvantaged in later life.

Katherine, mentioned above, describes how particular problems with learning to spell properly had influenced her school experiences:

> I remember one time – I must have been about six – I got no spellings right at all, and I just sat there and cried. . . . Everybody else knew about it as well because she [the teacher] read the spellings out. Then

> I got people taking the micky because they thought it was really funny.

Other students were verbally abusive towards her:

> Oh, she's thick, she's stupid. She doesn't know what she's doing. Really cruel things like children say to one another . . .

Nothing was done at school to address her literacy difficulties until she reached secondary age:

> It must have been when I was about 11, when the teacher used to come and take me off for extra spelling. But it never worked. It was not enough. They just used to give me spellings to go away and learn, and then I had a spelling test.. . . . we never used to know when it was going to be.

The spellings never seemed to bear any relation to what she needed to write:

> As much as I remember, they just seemed to be any old words that they thought we should have been able to spell.

By the latter stages of her education she was completely disaffected from school:

> By the age of 13, at upper school I totally and utterly gave up – on school, on teachers. I just thought they were there to give you a hard time. Everyone seemed to be against me, whatever I was doing, and in the end I just mucked around. . . . I never did any homework. I got into trouble, but I just gave up – and they gave up. They just put me in the group of other kids who just mucked around.
>
> . . . I knew what I was doing, but trying to write it down on paper was totally different. . . . I used to write all over the tables because they hated it. I'd take the micky of them by calling them names out loud in class. We knew one teacher's Christian name, so we called it out loud. Whatever you could do to disrupt the class, you'd do it. The French teacher used to go out of the class, so we'd get hairspray and set light to it as it sprayed out. One French lesson, my friend got this little bottle of gin and we just sat there drinking it under the table.

When it came to her final year at school and external examinations:

> I just got through them. I had no intention of doing any revision anyway. When I'd taken dictations into my book and I came to look back at it, I couldn't understand what I'd written. It was so untidy. There were words missing, and it just didn't make sense. I'd think: 'What have I done?' so in the end I just thought there was no point.

As an adult now, Katherine feels:

> . . . angry against so many teachers. It upsets me as well. Everything you've sort of done, you hide. I can't believe what happened. I'm ashamed of what I did. When you've got a teacher there, and you've physically made her cry, it's not clever.
>
> Spelling to me now is very, very important. When you first leave school, if you can't spell you con your way through it somehow. But when you get to my age, you get to thinking that there's not always going to be someone around to help you.

Spelling approaches for students who experience specific difficulties

For some students like Katherine, learning to spell is highly problematic and particular points may have to be modelled many times over, while still writing within the context of genuine reading and writing tasks.

High-frequency word lists

In order to help students to start writing accurate text, one pragmatic approach is to begin with words from a high empirically determined frequency list because, by definition, high-frequency word lists will contain words that students will be using a lot in their own writing. An example of a piece of research that shows how use of word lists can be combined with notions of learning to spell within the context of writing is that of Glynn and Glynn (1980). In this study, two programmes were instituted simultaneously with an intelligent 11-year-old boy, Nigel, who had ceased attending school for a number of reasons including embarrassment at not being able to spell. The amount of writing that he produced at any one time was minimal, so 10-minute 'speed writing' sessions were conducted daily for 57 days. Nigel was:

> required to write as much as he liked on the clear understanding that letter formation, spelling, punctuation and grammar did not matter [in this context].

> (Glynn, 1987, p. 83)

Nigel had been assessed on spelling performance as below the criterion for the level achieved in infant classes. Concurrent with the speed writing programme, a daily spelling programme was instituted which incorporated regular testing and sentence writing, using words selected from Arvidson's (1970) *Alphabetical Spelling List*. The Arvidson spelling list presents seven lists of words, grouped according to their frequency of occurrence within a large sample of students' writing in New Zealand schools. Since that time, the alphabet word list, based on frequency of word usage, has been continually updated and modified by researchers at the New Zealand Council for Educational Research, for example by Croft and Mapa (1998). Students were required to work at level 1 words first, and only when they had passed a mastery test at this level, did they move into learning level 2 words, and so on. This approach proved positively motivating to students because they were set a finite target number of words to learn at each level. Mastery of the most frequently used words (regardless of patterns) made an appreciable difference to the overall accuracy of their writing.

Glynn and Glynn (1980) found that as a result of introducing the two programmes with Nigel:

> not only were there expected gains in spelling and fluency of written expression but the data also showed generalization effects of the spelling programme into the written expression.
>
> (Glynn, 1987, p. 83)

Gains in accuracy of words in Nigel's writing samples occurred for each of Arvidson's first three spelling levels when the spelling programme was focused on each successive level. These gains in accuracy were not made at the expense of fluency because, as the programme progressed, Nigel used proportionately more words from Arvidson's level 4 (less frequent words not yet included in the spelling programme). His spelling of the level 4 words was poor in comparison with his achieved spelling of words from levels 1, 2 and 3. However, and just as importantly, Nigel continued to write as fluently as he had previously. Focusing on one set (level) of spelling words at a time, in order of frequency of occurrence, meant that Nigel was faced with a finite and manageable task, on which success resulted in visible gains in his spelling accuracy within his writing. When last heard of, Nigel had been accepted by a university to study for a degree.

Peer group and family interactive approaches

There are a number of programmes which have been designed to foster interactive approaches with peers or adults in the classroom, or family members at home, in order to improve learning the spelling of words that students who experience difficulties wish or need to spell in their own writing. 'Cued spelling' uses words the student him/herself wishes to spell and relies on principles of praise, modelling, and swift support procedures, 'in the hope of eliminating the fear of failure' (Topping, 1996, p. 50). The basic structure of the technique comprises ten steps:

- (Step 1) The learner chooses words of high interest to him/herself, irrespective of difficulty level. Tutor and learner check the spelling of the word and put a master version in a 'Cued Spelling Diary' (Step 2). The pair read the word out loud together, then the learner reads the word aloud alone (Step 3).
- (Step 4) The learner chooses cues (reminders) to enable him or her to remember the written structure of the word. These may be sounds, letter names, syllables or other fragments of words, or wholly personal mnemonic (memory) devices.
- (Step 5) The pair repeats the cues aloud simultaneously.
- (Step 6) The learner then repeats the cues aloud while the tutor models how to write the word down while it is 'dictated'.
- (Step 7) Roles then reverse, the tutor saying the cues aloud while the learner writes the word down.
- (Step 8) The learner repeats the cues and writes the word simultaneously.
- At Step 9, the learner is required to write the word as fast as possible and may decide for him/herself whether to recite the cues out loud.
- Finally (Step 10), the learner reads the word out loud.

Spelling approaches such as cued spelling, with their clear breakdown into specific steps, would lend themselves to being implemented in either peer-tutoring or cooperative learning contexts, in which teaching and learning roles can be readily exchanged, and where students can learn as much from teaching a list to somebody else as they can get from learning it themselves (Dineen, Clark and Risley, 1977).

Multi-sensory methods

Some students experience a particular difficulty in associating sounds and alphabetic symbols in words, in ordering letters correctly or in letter orientation (Snowling, 2000; Reason, 2002) One way to strengthen new spellings is to take a multi-sensory approach to teaching which emphasizes the spelling of the whole word. Multi-sensory programmes should focus on all modalities – auditory, visual, kinesthetic and tactile. Johnson (2002, p. 275) describes in more detail what is meant by a 'multi-sensory approach':

Multi sensory teaching is teaching done using all the learning pathways in the brain (visual, auditory and kinaesthetic–tactile) in order to
enhance memory and learning. It is crucial that, whatever pathways
are being addressed in a particular exercise, they are directly focused
upon by both teacher and child. For example, they look at, feel, move
and say the names of the wooden letters they are using to compose a
word. When 'writing' a word in the air the left hand holds the right
elbow and the eyes follow the pointing finger. A tray with salt or sand
on it or the reverse side of a piece of hardboard can be used to 'write
on' with a finger. The rough surface maximises the sensory input and
in both cases the letters and the final word are said out loud.

Reason and Boote (1994) describe one multi-sensory approach which,
whilst lengthy at first, can, in their view, be slimmed down as students gain
confidence and competence in spelling. Words should be chosen to reflect
students' current writing needs and interests:

- Look at the word, read it, and pronounce it in syllables or other
  small bits (re-mem-ber; sh-out).
- Try to listen to yourself doing this.
- Still looking at it, spell it out in letter-names.
- Continue to look, and trace out the letters on the table with your
  finger as you spell it out again.
- Look at the word for any 'tricky bits'; for example, gh in right.
  (Different pupils find different parts of a word 'tricky'.)
- Try to get a picture of the word in your mind: take a photograph
  of it in your head!
- Copy the word, peeping at the end of each syllable or letter-string.
- Highlight the tricky bits in colour (or by some other means).
- Visualise the word again.
- Now cover it up and try to write it, spelling it out in letter-names.
- Does it look right?
- Check with the original.
- Are there some tricky bits you didn't spot (i.e. the parts that went
  wrong)?
- Repeat as much of the procedure as necessary to learn the words
  thoroughly.

(Reason and Boote, 1994, p. 138)

A less complex multi-sensory approach that one of the authors of this
book has used with considerable success is that of Bradley (1981). This
approach might well be appropriate to students at the semi-phonetic stage of
development:

The method consists of a series of steps in the following order:

The student proposes the word he [sic] wants to learn.

The word is written correctly for him (or made with plastic script letters).

The student names the word.

He then writes the word himself, saying out loud the alphabetic name of each letter of the word as it is written.

He names the word again. He checks to see that the word has been written correctly; this is important, as less able readers are often inaccurate when they copy . . . Repeat steps 2 to 5 twice more, covering or disregarding the stimulus word as soon as the student feels he can manage without it.

The student practises the word in this way for six consecutive days. The procedure is the same whether or not the student can read or write, and whether or not he is familiar with all the sound/symbol relationships, but it must not deteriorate into rote spelling, which is an entirely different thing.

The student learns to generalise from this word to similar words using the plastic script letters.

(Bentley, 2002, p. 343, adapted from Bradley, 1981)

Spelling approaches for adults

For adults who have tried for many years to learn to spell accurately, but have not succeeded, the issues of self-esteem, motivation and the purpose accurate spelling is to serve, are particularly salient (Riddick, 1996). A variant of the multi-sensory approaches described above which harnesses students' own interests can be illustrated with work with Paula, an adult university student (Glynn, 2004, unpublished). This approach relies on syllabification and is an adaptation of Clay's (1975, 1993) phonological method of representing the syllable sounds of individual words in boxes.

Paula had a history of very poor spelling and separation into special classes for phonics teaching whilst at school. Each year she had stayed in the same special class, or was transferred to another, until she finally left school. As an adult she had fought her way into university admission motivated by the determination to train to teach school students who experience difficulties in learning, just as she herself had done.

For years, traditional phonics-based spelling approaches had been tried for Paula without success. During the first year at university, she was supported by a tutor who encouraged her to think about words that she would need in her degree studies and to experiment with ways to learn these. They began with the word 'psychology':

> Tutor: How many sounds can you hear in the word 'psychology'?
> Paula: Three.
> Tutor: What are they?
> Paula: Psy-chol-ogy.

Even though there are four syllables in this word, the tutor decided to concentrate on the sounds the student could distinguish herself. She wrote the word 'psychology' in lower case, drew three boxes and invited Paula to split these ten letters into the boxes to represent the sounds of the word:

> Tutor: . . . we should draw three boxes like this. . . Now you have to put some letters in each box. Which letters do you think for 'psy'? What goes next? What goes in the third box? Every letter must go in one of the boxes even if it is silent.

They discussed parts of the word Paula found difficult, with the tutor drawing attention to other words with similar letter clusters, both those in common usage and those that Paula had indicated she would need in her studies: 'y' as in 'sky', and 'my'; 'chol' with a silent 'c' as in 'cholera'; 'gy' as in 'energy' and 'geology'. The tutor talked her through the combinations of letters in each word-part, deliberately repeating the names of the letters several times as she did so. This took some time, until the whole word had been analysed and Paula could spell it. An hour later, however, she had forgotten the spelling, even when prompted to use the boxes. As she had employed a multi-sensory approach to teach the word, the tutor then decided to see if Paula could remember the spelling from the memory of the sounds of the combinations of letter names, rather than the visual combinations of letters. She asked Paula to 'switch off' her eyes and use her ears instead. Paula proved able to do this:

> Paula: 'Sy' has a 'y' like 'my' and 'try'. No, it has a silent letter as well, 'psy', then 'col'. No, another silent letter like 'cholera' . . . 'chol' 'o' – that's easy, it's the same sound as the letter. 'gy', like 'energy' and 'geology'. So 'psychology'. Is that right? Let me look now. Yes, I', pretty sure I'm right. Yes, that's it.

After three one-hour sessions, Paula was able to work out strategies for learning the words she needed. Later, she reported to the tutor that she was to visit a school and teach a lesson as part of her training. She was very nervous, and decided to write out all the words she thought she would need. She planned to tell the children that she experienced a particular problem with spelling and that they could find ways to solve their difficulties as she had done. After the lesson she reported to the tutor that this strategy had been successful. In the next few months she wrote her university assignments using a word-processing programme with a spell check facility, and requested permission to use a dictionary during her end-of-year examinations. She successfully completed the first year of her studies. The spelling technique used with Paula was subsequently tried with three other adult students, with similar positive outcomes.

Schools' spelling and marking policies

Many parents may not know how to help their child to learn new spellings. In any case, parents (and caregivers) should not be assumed or expected to know how to help their children with spelling acquisition, just as they should not be expected or assumed to know how to help their children read or write in ways that are seen as acceptable and effective by the school. Rather, they should be supported by specific guidelines to help their children, and in order to reduce their own anxiety levels (Bentley, 2002). Guidelines that include step-wise descriptions of some of the methods outlined above may well be very welcome to some parents or caregivers, as are the specific step-wise reading tutoring programmes such as Pause Prompt Praise.

Spelling policies

Marking and spelling policies adopted by teachers and schools can also stimulate a fair amount of controversy. Bentley (2002), for example, refers to the five-stage model of spelling acquisition and feels that students should be encouraged to make the transition from one stage of spelling development to another when they have mastered the previous stage. She is of the view that, for the most part, class or group spelling tests are a waste of time since learners will be at different stages in spelling acquisition. However, such spelling tests may be a required part of a school's approach to supporting pupils' literacy development, particularly in contexts where hierarchical lists of sound-symbol correspondences form part of a national literacy curriculum. Also, many teachers may feel that set spelling tests are very important to assess the development in spelling of a whole class or group. On the other hand, teachers' beliefs that spelling tests are a waste of time may reflect the arbitrary way in which many spellings are chosen for students to learn and how little they are tailored to the literacy needs of individual students.

In order to identify the stage of development a student has reached in his/ her spelling, it is very important to take the time to scrutinize samples of the students' writing very carefully. A student who is tired and/or in a hurry may make more errors than s/he does in normal circumstances. Students' spelling errors often span the developmental stages (Bentley, 2002). There is probably no one rule about how long a student might remain at one stage of spelling development. A crucial consideration is how to ensure that, overall, a student is becoming more skilled in spelling acquisition and, if s/he remains 'stuck' at one stage, to work out ways of supporting him/her to move on to the next.

Schools should also have very clear marking policies. On the one hand, it can be very demoralizing for some students repeatedly to receive back scripts covered with correctional markings. On the other hand, there has to be a rational, structured and pedagogically sound approach to ensuring that students learn how to recognize mistakes and take some responsibility for correcting them. Some teachers may feel it is appropriate to encourage students to proofread their own, or peers', work before handing it in, and/or, perhaps, to correct only words or sentence structure with which they feel students should already be familiar. Whatever strategy a school chooses – for example, words from a leveled list that they are expected to have mastered, in a word frequency approach such as that of Arvidson (1970) – it should be supported by reasoned pedagogical argument and be clear to students and parents.

Conclusion

English orthography is complex and irregular, and many students experience difficulty in learning to spell accurately. Good spelling is a vital component of communication through writing. School leavers who have not acquired spelling accuracy during their school years may well regret this later in life. Public audiences make harsh judgements on the basis of poor spelling.

Accurate spelling is not automatically transferred from learning formal spelling lists into students' writing unless the words that have been learnt are immediately relevant to what the student wishes or needs to express. Teachers need to develop their own understandings about spelling and learning to spell so that they can construct intervention strategies which meet the needs of individual students, and lead them towards correct spelling. A number of researchers proposed a developmental model of spelling acquisition, awareness of which can enable teachers to assist learners to improve their spelling competence in the context of their own writing. Appropriate support for the few students who experience very serious difficulties in spelling acquisition may be provided through multi-sensory teaching approaches which focus on different modalities: auditory, visual, kinaesthetic and tactile. Schools need clear spelling and marking policies which encourage writing and spelling accuracy, without demoralizing students with spelling difficulties by being limited to marking excessive corrections on students' written text.

7 Responsive approaches to assessment

Introduction

Assessment of literacy learning in schools has a particular impact on achievement (Murphy, 2002). It acts to create identities of students-as-literacy-learners that interact with those identities they already have and thus serve to reinforce or undermine the motivation to strive for future achievement in literacy development. Students' sense of themselves as having the potential to be effective in the community of literacy practices may be constructed and/or constrained by the forms of assessment that are used. Assessment should address the need to build students' identities and not destroy them.

In this chapter we examine inherent problems and difficulties associated with standardized forms of assessment that seek to compare students' performance against national or regional age norms, and with some 'diagnostic' tests which may be overly focused on detecting problems with surface or structural features of writing, reading or oral language. In recent years, in order to plan appropriate teaching approaches for students experiencing difficulties, there has been a recognition that barriers to students' literacy development arise from the interaction between the students and their learning environments. This emphasis implies a broader conception of what needs to be assessed beyond simply the characteristics of the individual learner and what has been achieved over a particular period of time. We acknowledge that literacy learning takes place in multiple localities (Street, 1993; Gee, 2000) and view the assessment of literacy difficulties as needing to take account of the real-life contexts in which those difficulties occur. We discuss the question of how to assess the learning environments in which learning occurs and to be responsive to the different knowledge, experience and cultural understandings of literacy within the diverse communities in which students are living. Assessment of the performance of individual students is also clearly important, and we discuss literacy assessment strategies and procedures that can indicate improvement and are sensitive enough to detect relatively small changes over relatively short time periods (for example, after one school term, or after a six-week teaching unit) for students who experience difficulties. We note the importance of providing some measure of text difficulty, as one key descriptor of a student's current reading achievement. We also focus on four important domains of measurement of literacy: comprehension, rate (fluency), accuracy, and quality. We present suggestions for assessing each of these dimensions. These include re-telling of stories, timed audio-taped samples of reading and oral language, and timed samples of student writing in responsive social contexts. Finally, the chapter notes some of the issues involved in literacy assessment of students whose language of instruction is different from their home language.

Problems and difficulties associated with standardized forms of assessment

Underlying particular forms of assessment that are used to identify students' literacy needs are assumptions that carry particular implications. Some of these assumptions contradict the concept of inclusion. For example, available resources have often dictated the kind of special educational provision that is made for individual students (Cline, 1992). To determine eligibility for support services, additional or alternative provision depends on norm-referenced assessment designed to enable a comparison of individual pupils' achievement with that of peers, and therefore identify some students who are sufficiently 'different' to qualify for exceptional support.

Standardized tests reflect views of intelligence as an innate capacity that is assumed to be randomly distributed throughout populations. Such views enable a statistical definition of 'need', in terms of the number of students who can access resources. This underlying assumption discounts a view of students as having the potential to achieve very highly, given the right learning opportunities. Norm-referenced tests of ability and attainment can 'determine selectively the way in which issues are discussed and solutions proposed' (Broadfoot, 1996). The influence of psychometric approaches to measuring human achievement therefore can lend support to deterministic views of ability and achievement. These views can limit teachers' expectations of what to expect of certain students, and restrict future developments in assessment practices.

In addition, for some students, for example those from economically poor family background, lowered expectations can lead to a reproduction in society of underprivileged groups (Tomlinson, 1988). Special educational arrangements may appear to be the result of rational and pragmatic assessment of pupils. This, however, is questionable (Habermas, 1974). Tomlinson (1988) considers that the function that some special educational provision serves in maintaining the power of the privileged and dominant groups in society is a powerful determining factor in explaining its existence:

> The ideas of critical theorists can suggest that the stupidity or dullness of some individuals or social groups is not necessarily self-evident or 'true'. Acquiring the label and being treated as 'less-able' is likely to be the result of complex social economic and political judgements and considerations.
>
> (Tomlinson, 1988, p. 45)

The performance that is measured by psychometric tests may reflect a history of inappropriate teaching and inappropriate curricula as much as capacities or characteristics of the individual learner. The same low test score may reflect quite different individual learning histories and learning opportunities. Some commentators believe that schools help to reproduce societal patterns of control and subordination linked to the economic context (Bourdieu and Passeron, 1973). There is a contradiction between the rhetoric of education to promote equality and the reality that the system of education functions to reproduce the children of underprivileged groups into powerless positions in society. 'Success' and 'failure' are social categories whose labels serve the vested interests of dominant, powerful groups in society. They are not objective 'givens'. The social, economic and political status quo requires some children to fail in the education system. This position explains individual student failure as much as the supposition of a deficit in the child.

There is a crisis in education in a post-industrial age where achievements assessed through reading and writing are the prerequisites to obtaining a job with a salary above subsistence level. The inability of illiterate citizens to find well paid employment is both explained and legitimised if they have been labelled in advance through special education:

> Special education reproduces and controls lower-status groups, and legitimates their life-long treatment, but is, in itself, an acceptable, legitimating, humane development.
>
> (Tomlinson, 1988, p. 49)

Low scores on standardised tests of reading and spelling can easily lay the blame for failure on the child, and/or the family and cultural background and also absolve schools from taking responsibility for that child's progress in academic learning:

> The way the black and working-class Johnnys with reading problems are dealt with will usually ensure that they are reproduced into the low-status sections of society.
>
> (Tomlinson, 1988, p. 55)

In the case of specific difficulties in literacy, such as 'dyslexia', some groups of parents have found a way of removing the stigma of failure from their children and of normalising them:

> The dyslexia label says to parents, 'Your child has a problem, but your child is normal' . . .
>
> (Booth and Goodey, 1996, p. 5)

To some extent the views of Tomlinson, Bourdieu and Passeron outlined here in relation to the marginalisation of particular groups of children in schools, and later in society as adults, reflect some of the concerns of the discussion of equity issues in previous chapters. On the one hand identification and labelling may bring additional resources, but on the other it may serve to perpetuate the existing social order, by locating the source of poor achievement within individuals and their families, rather than within pedagogical practices in classrooms and schools.

Issues associated with the use of non-standardized assessment tools

Directly connected to the issues above are the challenges teachers face in choosing appropriate non-standardized assessment tools for evaluating students' literacy achievement and addressing the needs of students' learning through ongoing in-class assessment practices. In the New Zealand context, Crooks (1988, cited in Clarke, Timperley, and Hattie, 2003) draws the following conclusions:

- Classroom evaluation affects students in many different ways, such as guiding their judgement of what is important to learn and reducing or enhancing their motivation and self-perception of competence.
- Classroom evaluation often emphasises recall or recognition of isolated pieces of information rather than how that information fits within a broader framework of meaningful interrelationships and understandings.
- Too much emphasis is placed on grading and too little on assisting students to learn, with the undesirable effects of reducing intrinsic motivation and creating evaluation anxiety.
- Feedback could be made more effective if it focused students' attention on progress in mastering particular tasks, was given soon after the task was completed, and was specific.

- Cooperative groups that are encouraged to monitor their individual and group progress enhance learning.
- Evaluation standards need to be high but attainable.
- Evaluation tasks should be selected to suit the goals that are being assessed.
- Evaluation enhances learning if it includes important skills, knowledge and attitudes.

(Clarke, Timperley and Hattie, 2003, p. 11)

Caygill and Eley (2001) further contend that, 'any assessment activity should be appropriate to the purposes of the assessment, to the curricula objectives, and to the students being assessed' (p. 2). This is particularly important if schools are to avoid disadvantaging some students by ignoring their prior literacy knowledge and experiences as learners. Harrison, Bailey and Dewar (1998) identify that students' previous experiences with assessment activities will influence and affect their interpretation of what they are asked to do as well as their ability to respond with what they have learned. Due consideration must also be given to the ways in which the tasks themselves can affect the reliability and validity of the judgements that will later be made about the learner (Pearson, Destefano and Garcia, 1998). In addition, Sligo, Fontaine and O'Neill (1999) contend that how the assessors are perceived by students to be engaged or interested in their task of assessing students, will in many cases influence the quality of the work that the students will subsequently submit.

Other challenges associated with assessment are concerned with teachers' knowledge and understanding about the place of assessment within their classroom programmes. Peddie (2000), in his evaluation of a professional development programme supporting assessment, reported that almost 40 per cent of teachers surveyed reported difficulty with the use of formative assessment, giving student feedback and aggregating and reporting data. Daniel and King (1998) further contend that although measurement and testing are expected to be integral to teachers' programmes, many teachers report their training in the use of specific assessment types and their knowledge of assessment purposes to be inadequate. Given this concern, the validity of assessment practices for measuring and reporting on the wide range of specific literacy skills required across the curriculum, may well be open to question (Hager and Gable, 1993). As Clay (1998) contends, this can result in teachers wrongly identifying and accepting particular behaviours and/or skills as indicative of concept learning.

Assessment for learning

In many countries there has been a shift in emphasis in recent years from views of assessment as a tool to ascertain achievement levels in individual learners, and across whole cohorts at particular points in time, to a focus on assessment as a tool for enhancing learning. The New Zealand Curriculum Framework (Ministry of Education 1993), for example, suggests that:

> Assessment of individual students' progress is essentially diagnostic. Such assessment is integral to the teaching and learning programme. Its purpose is to improve teaching and learning by diagnosing learning strengths and weaknesses, measuring students' progress against the defined achievement objectives, and reviewing the effectiveness of teaching programmes.
>
> (Ministry of Education, 1993, p. 24)

The Ministry of Education documents, 'Assessment, Policy to Practice' (1994), 'English in the New Zealand Curriculum' (1994) and 'Planning and Assessment in English' (1994) build on these principles. The 'Planning and Assessment in English' document identifies the following seven key assessment points:

- Teachers need to plan to collect assessment information as part of the teaching and learning programme.
- The achievement objectives selected for a unit of work provide the basis for appropriate criteria to assess against and report on.
- Specific outcomes for a unit of work relate to the achievement objectives and provide a focus for assessment.
- Teachers need to use a range of tasks and procedures to meet the different purposes of assessment.
- The type of assessment (diagnostic, formative, or summative) used on any one occasion needs to be suited to the purpose of the assessment.
- Students should be actively involved in the assessment process as appropriate to their stage of development.
- To report reliably on students' achievements, information needs to be collected over a period of time and in a variety of contexts.

(Ministry of Education, 1997, p. 56)

In both New Zealand and the UK there has been a move away from assessment methods that serve only summative or 'assessment of learning' purposes. In both countries, the shift in emphasis in the purpose of assessment has resulted in a focus on 'Assessment for Learning' (AfL) which means:

> . . . using evidence and dialogue to identify where pupils are in their learning, where they need to go and how best to get there.
> (http://www.standards.dfes.gov.uk/personalisedlearning/five/afl/, accessed 27 March 2005)

The Department for Education and Skills (DfES) in England defines AfL as follows:

> Assessment for learning is the ongoing day-to-day formative assessment that takes place to gather information on what a child or group of children understand or do not understand and how future teaching will be adapted to account for this. Effective ongoing day to day assessments would include effective questioning; observations of children during teaching and while they are working; holding discussions with children; analysing work and reporting to children; conducting tests and giving quick feedback and engaging children in the assessment process.
> (http://www.standards.dfes.gov.uk/primary/features/primary/ 1091819/1092063, accessed 27 March 2005)

Advice given on putting AfL into practice suggests that:

> Assessment for learning should:
> - be part of effective planning of teaching and learning;
> - focus on how pupils learn;
> - be recognised as central to classroom practice;
> - be regarded as a key professional skill for teachers;
> - be sensitive and constructive because any assessment has an emotional impact;
> - take account of the importance of learner motivation;
> - promote commitment to learning goals and a shared understanding of the criteria by which pupils will be assessed;
> - provide constructive guidance for learners about how to improve;
> - develop learners' capacity for self assessment and recognising their next steps and how to take them;
> - recognise the full range of achievement of all learners
> (http://www.standards.dfes.gov.uk/primary/features/primary/ 1091819/1092063)

Ongoing formative assessment

As we noted above in our discussion of 'Assessment for Learning' (AfL), assessment that informs students' learning is an ongoing, continuous, formative process that provides teachers with formal and informal opportunities to notice what is happening during learning activities, to recognize where the learning of individuals and groups of students is going, and how they as the teacher can help take that learning further. Teachers who are able to reflect on whether they have interacted effectively with all students, used the most appropriate teaching strategies and helped students to reflect on what it is they are doing themselves, are able to take students further along an independent learning pathway. By engaging students in learning conversations that include responsive feedback, teachers such as these are also able to help students to monitor their own learning:

> Learning happens as a result of what teachers and students think, do and talk about. Assessment for learning is based both on what teachers notice informally and on the information that they choose to collect and record about learning.
>
> (Ministry of Education, 2004, p. 1)

Effective teachers use assessment information to determine what it is that students already know and understand. They then adjust their teaching for individual students and groups of students accordingly.

> In practice, this means clear evidence about how to drive up individual attainment; clear feedback for and from pupils so there is clarity on what they need to improve and how best they can do so; and a clear link between student learning and lesson planning.
>
> (http://www.standards.dfes.gov.uk/personalisedlearning/five/afl/, accessed 27 March 2005)

Teachers who do this are sometimes called 'reflective practitioners' (Schön, 1983, 1987) because they notice what is different or unusual about patterns of progress in student learning, and think carefully and deeply about what assessment information is telling them about student understandings, and also more particularly about their own teaching. Based on these outcomes, these teachers then ask themselves questions about what they should or can do differently. They then use their professional knowledge, their knowledge of a range of pedagogical strategies, and evidence about their students' current knowledge and understandings to connect to and respond to the thinking of each student.

Quality feedback, directly linked to assessment information, provides the basis of learning conversations. Such conversations help students to:

- confirm the intended outcome of the learning;
- become motivated to continue or move on;
- accept responsibility for their own learning;
- assess their own learning;
- identify their next learning steps.

Feedback to students is most effective when it:

- focuses on the tasks and the associated learning, not the student;
- confirms for the student that he or she is on the right track;
- includes suggestions that help the student (that is that scaffold their learning);
- is frequent and given when there is opportunity for the student to take action;
- is in the context of a dialogue about the learning.

(Ministry of Education, 2004, p. 16)

When feedback connects directly to specific and challenging goals that relate to students' prior knowledge, experience and cultural understandings, students are better able to focus more productively on new goals and next learning steps. In this situation students are more likely to acknowledge their own skill levels and/or gaps and identify where they need and want to take their learning in the future. Thus students are in a better position to become active learners rather than passive recipients of knowledge.

Responsive task-focused feedback

In order to enable teachers to engage in conversations that link back to and promote students' learning outcomes, the Ministry of Education in New Zealand has developed a series of authentic examples of students' work that illustrate learning, achievement and quality in relation to the levels described in each of the national curriculum statements. These nationally moderated examples of students' work are known as the New Zealand Curriculum Exemplars (www.tki.org.nz/r/assessment/exemplars/index_e.php) and are available for both English medium and Māori medium teachers and students. Using a wide range of authentic examples of students' work, exemplars illustrate key features of learning, achievement, and quality at different stages of student development and can be used by students and teachers to identify next learning steps, and also to guide teachers in their interpretation of the curriculum levels.

Annotations on each of the students' work samples draw attention to the important features of the work and serve to illustrate learning, achievement and quality in relation to the levels described in the national curriculum documents. Further, the indicators of quality and achievement that form the basis of the annotations are set out in matrices that show learning progressions through the curriculum framework from level 1 to level 5. Schools and teachers can use the exemplars and matrices in a number of different ways, in order to promote the professional learning of teachers and further learning of students at an individual, class and school level.

Teachers can compare a student's work sample with the exemplars, in order to identify specific aspects that the student has achieved and those that they need to work on. Once identified, particular indicators from the relevant matrix can also be identified, and new learning goals can be prioritized. Teachers can also use the matrices and exemplars collaboratively with the student to review learning outcomes by again comparing the progress they have made in relation to the samples of work and matrix indicators. In so doing, teachers are able to exemplify the next learning steps while also raising expectations and collaboratively working towards measuring performance and raising achievement. Once students have had this process modelled by the teacher and are familiar with it, they are better placed to use the matrices and exemplars for self and peer review, independent of teacher support. In this way, students learn to evaluate their own work and development and thus shape their own next learning steps. Through collaborative assessments of this kind, teachers can also identify individual teaching and learning needs and respond accordingly.

Teachers can also use the matrices and exemplars to moderate the work of a whole class by comparing the work of the class in relation to particular indicators. In this way, teachers can consider and discuss student achievement from common understandings and use these understandings to develop next learning steps. By comparing class and/or school-wide work samples, teachers can refine their own teaching expectations, inform their own teaching practices and thus reach a more consistent understanding of learning expectations at a class and school level. This information, used to inform classroom planning, is more likely to support appropriate goals for class and school learning programmes. Teachers can also use this information to discuss the work of their students with parents and caregivers. By discussing and exemplifying a child's achievement and progress in relation to selected samples of work, parents and caregivers are able to be better informed about what work at a particular curriculum level looks like and how they too can better support the next learning steps. Likewise, school boards can use this information to focus in on aspects of learning that need to be developed, in order to identify strategic targets and then assess whether these targets are being met.

Teachers are able to access on-line exemplars as well as links to other relevant curriculum materials. Teachers are also able to access on-line case studies of how the exemplars are helping teachers and students to engage in rich collaborative discussions focused on improving learning. The national New Zealand exemplars and matrices have also been used in some New Zealand schools as the basis for developing their own school's exemplars in targeted learning areas. The resulting exemplars are used to further discuss and refine the teaching and learning programme.

Interactive formative assessment

An example of interactive formative assessment within the individual student's zone of proximal development is to be found in the work of Glynn and McNaughton (1975). These researchers reported on an approach to assessing both reader and tutor behaviour within the context of students' one-to-one oral interactions with a teacher or a tutor around a specific reading text. This approach allowed the researchers a means of assessing the characteristics of teacher and tutor interactions when working within the zone of proximal development with students experiencing reading difficulties. This assessment approach has been used to provide feedback and professional development to parent, peer and teacher tutors of reading over 30 years. Reflecting on this study after this time, Glynn and McNaughton (2002) suggest the following four operational principles that have guided their use of direct observation to assess reading performance:

1   Continuous observational assessment of reading performance in children's regular classroom contexts. This allowed for the assessment of quite small changes over time, and generated information sensitive enough to provide the teacher with detailed feedback on changes in individual children's reading. This type of information was not available from standardized tests of reading achievement.

2   Combinations of systematic observation and recording with appropriate theoretical understandings of how children learn to read. This required careful operational definitions of constructs such as reader self-corrections as responses to semantic and syntactic information within meaningful texts (Clay, 1972).

3   Multiple measures of reading performance. One-off summative assessments of word knowledge or of reading rates and reading accuracy, which yield a reading age score were found to be too gross and lacking in the detailed information needed to assist individual children improve their reading. Consistent with the sociocultural view that literacy learning occurs within interactive social contexts, it was important not just to observe and record errors, but also to obtain information on specific characteristics of readers' responses to those errors, such as whether readers were responding to semantic or syntactic features of the words and texts they were reading. Glynn and

McNaughton (2002) endorsed the use of a range of measures covering both accuracy (for example, percentage of words read incorrectly), rate (for example, the percentage of words read correctly in a three-minute sample), and the advancement through text levels of increasing difficulty within a given time (such as a school term). Data on text difficulty level gains plotted against time indicated that although the prime concern of gathering interactive reader and tutor data was to improve reading performance within individual students, it was also possible to compare changes in performance over time between children.

4   Measuring the interactions between readers and tutors, and not just readers' responses alone. Many reading behaviours occur in specific interactive contexts, which incorporate teacher prompts (as likely antecedents of reader behaviours) and differential tutor responses to errors, as well as tutor social reinforcement (as likely consequences of specific reader behaviours). This also recognizes that such teacher behaviours are likely to vary between different children and according to the difficulty and other characteristics of the text being read. In some ways, this approach anticipated the concept of ecological assessment (Ysseldyke and Christenson, 1987, 1993; Ysseldyke and Thurlow, 1994; Brown et al., 2000). Ecological assessment is a major dimension of inclusive education, which locates reading difficulties not just within the reader, but also within the interaction between children and the learning contexts available to them.

The purpose of assessment in an inclusive education paradigm involves finding out what modifications need to be made to tasks, settings, or teacher behaviour in order to more fully include children with special needs or learning difficulties. The fine-grained continuous measures employed in the earlier study with Pause Prompt Praise pointed in this direction (Glynn and McNaughton, 1975). This study suggested that the same teacher, using her intuitive judgement, was advancing some children through texts of increasing difficulty more readily than others, despite the similarity in reading performance of some of these children. Feedback on specific dimensions of tutoring behaviour, such as the use of Pause (delay) providing differential attention to errors and differential reinforcement of reader behaviours, it was thought, might facilitate changes in the effectiveness of teacher behaviour.

These four observation principles informed and guided the development of the continuous assessment procedures that underpin the Pause Prompt Praise reading tutoring programme reported in Chapter 4.

Figure 1 illustrates the four principles in use in the context of the Pause Prompt Praise programme. The behaviours to be observed and recorded are consistent with theoretical perspectives that depict independent reading as

READER		TUTOR RESPONSE								READER		
TYPE OF ERROR		PAUSE	PROMPT			PRAISE				ERROR CORRECTION		
(1) correct word from the text	(2) word read by mistake or word omitted	(3) wait up to 5 seconds unless self-corrects before then	(4) to read on or read again	(5) to think about the meaning of the word	(6) to think about the look or sound of the word	(7) if reader's word is nearly correct	(8) if reader self-corrects No tutor help	(9) if reader uses tutor prompt to correct error	(10) if reader tries hard or works well	(11) reader self corrects error without help from tutor	(12) reader corrects error after tutor prompts	(13) reader is told the word by tutor
1												
2												
3												
4												
5												
6												
7												

Figure 1 Recording Sheet for analysis of reader and tutor interaction with Pause Prompt Praise

learning to use all sources of information (both contextual and letter-sound) to 'make sense' from written text. They are also consistent with applied behaviour analysis perspectives that utilize the power of both antecedents and consequences in changing behaviour (Wheldall and Glynn, 1989). Further, multiple measures are taken of both reader and tutor behaviour, enabling analysis of the interaction between the two. For example, student's errors may provide differential antecedents for teacher responses, while certain teacher behaviours (for example, pausing) may act as a powerful antecedent for students to engage with the text. Multiple measures are also able to provide a more detailed framework for feedback on tutor implementation of the procedures.

Figure 1 also illustrates how the reader-tutor interaction in Pause Prompt Praise can be completed from a brief tape recording of a few minutes' tutoring of oral reading from a continuous piece of text. Reader and tutor behaviour can be observed and recorded as frequently and continuously as required.

In Figure 1, column 1 is for recording the text word that was read incorrectly, and column 2 is for recording the reader's actual response (either the incorrect word, or leave a blank if no attempt was made at the word).

Analysis of the responses in column two enables the tutor to assess whether the error:

- is close in meaning to the correct word,
- follows the appropriate syntax required by the sentence,
- matches the letter-sound information in the word,
- whether error is simply a 'non-attempt'.

When an error occurs, the tutor's first task is to pause. The pause prevents the tutor from interrupting too soon. This may allow readers to notice for themselves that what they have read may not quite make sense, and, possibly, to self-correct. Tutors should pause either for up to five seconds, during which a self-correction may occur, or, alternatively, until the reader has reached the end of the phrase or sentence containing the error. If an appropriate pause has occurred after each error, a tick is entered in column 3 (tutor behaviour). When a self-correction occurs, a tick is placed in column 11 (child correction). When the tutor provides specific praise for this (self-correction) a tick is placed in column 8 (tutor praise).

The pause also allows the tutor time to decide which of three kinds of error has occurred, whether it is a non-attempt, a substitution that does not make sense, or a substitution that does make sense. After the tutor has paused, and if the reader has not self-corrected, the tutor offers a prompt to help the reader with the word (see Prompt columns 4, 5 and 6 in Figure 1). Tutors are required to select one of three kinds of prompt, according to the type of error the reader has made. Moving from left to right, these three kinds of prompt correspond to the following three types of error.

1   **When the reader's error is a non-attempt** (which is not self-corrected after a tutor pause), the tutor prompts the reader either to *read on* or *read again* (Type 1 prompts). *Read on* prompts are used if the error is at the beginning or middle of a sentence or clause, and *read again* prompts are used if the error is near the end. Sometimes this kind of prompt is sufficient for the reader to 'pick up' the meaning of the word from the context of the sentence or story. When this happens, a tick is placed in column 4 (tutor prompts), and in column 12 because the reader has made a 'prompted correction'. If the tutor provides specific praise for this (prompted correction) a tick is placed in column 9 (tutor praise).

2   **When the reader's error is a word that does not make sense**, the tutor uses a 'meaning prompt' directing the reader's attention to what the word means (for example, a question referring to the picture, the context of the sentence, the page, the whole story, or to the reader's prior knowledge and experience. When this happens a tick is placed in column 5 (tutor prompts) and in column 12 because the reader has made a prompted correction. If the tutor provides specific praise for this (prompted correction) a tick is placed in column 9 (tutor praise).

3   **When the error is a word that *does* make sense** the tutor may then use a graphophonic 'letter or sound prompt' (Type 3 prompt), directing the reader's attention to what the word looks or sounds like. Note that this kind of prompt is offered only when the error suggests that the reader has already understood something of the meaning of the word. When this happens a tick is placed in column 6 (tutor prompts) and in column 12 because the reader has made a prompted correction. If the tutor provides specific praise for this (prompted correction) a tick is placed in column 9 (tutor praise).

When readers do not read the correct word after two tutor prompts, the tutor should tell the student the correct word. When this happens a tick should be placed in column 13. This is the 'bottom line', which tutors try to avoid. Although it has taken up considerable space to describe this assessment and recording of reader and tutor behaviour contingent on reader errors, it is in practice quite easy to do from listening to a brief audio tape of PPP tutoring. Only two or three examples are sufficient to conduct some powerful focused feedback for tutor training. Lengthy reader-tutor interactions can distract the child from attending to the text. Instead, tutors should focus on making their first two prompts as succinct as possible.

Authentic literacy assessment tools

In this section we illustrate literacy assessment tools in the context of Māori medium education in New Zealand because it is there that Māori educators are attempting to address issues of authentic evaluation of literacy learning that avoid the risk of formal standardized procedures identified above.

Oral language assessment tools

In New Zealand, Māori medium educators are facing the challenge of developing appropriate Māori language assessment tools, at all levels of education. Rather than translate existing English language assessment tools, two of the authors have involved themselves with the development of assessment tools that capitalize on the responsive context that can emerge between the learner and the assessor, and focus on the assessor helping the students to 'show what they can do' on a series of carefully constructed language learning tasks. In this context, the assessor attends closely and responds to the learners' engagement with the specific tasks, providing support and assistance with cues, or prompts, to keep the student engaged, but being careful not to supply the student with correct answers or solutions. Assessments in these situations have two particular characteristics. First, emphasis is on observation of both student and assessor behaviour. Second, student performance on the tasks is clearly scaffolded within the zone of proximal development, to access what the student can achieve, with the support of an interactive adult. While this assessment places the level of assessment in advance of what the students can do without support, the responsive, interactive and social nature of the assessment process provides richer information for effective feedback and 'feed forward', and for learning conversations that engage both student and teacher.

The following assessment tools were developed to monitor reading development.

Authentic assessment of reading

Information to assess the effectiveness of reading and writing programmes require data on students' learning outcomes as well as data on the processes or programming they have received.

Reading levels

In New Zealand, as in the United Kingdom, students' reading of English is monitored by assessing their performance on reading texts of increasing levels of difficulty. A range of different systems are in use. Colour-coded systems in the United Kingdom can be compared with the colour wheel levelling system (Ministry of Education, 1996) used in New Zealand junior classrooms. Once students have progressed through the colour wheel levelling system for emergent and early reading texts, stories taken from the New Zealand 'School Journal' are graded using the Elley Noun frequency count (Elley, 1975) and arranged according to suggested reading ages. Various readability systems are also available in both countries and used by some publishers to identify recommended reading ages of selected texts used in reading programmes.

Reading progress in Māori medium junior classrooms in New Zealand is monitored using the *Kete Kōrero* Framework (*Ngā Kete Kōrero* Framework Team, 1996a, 1996b) text levelling system, that uses a series of empirically determined 'bench mark' books to place other Māori language texts into levels of increasing difficulty.

Reading assessment procedures

Iti Rearea

This assessment is derived from the work of Glynn and McNaughton (1975) presented above. In a Māori language reading context, these procedures have become known as the '*Iti Rearea*' reading assessment procedure (Berryman, 2001, 2002). Three-minute taped oral reading samples in either English or Māori are used to assess students' reading accuracy and reading rate. Oral comprehension probes are also used to compare each student's reading rate with their ability to talk about what they have read. This information is used together with information on reading level. The '*Iti Rearea*' procedure involves four steps:

1   Preview of text. The assessor begins by introducing the story and relating it conversationally to the reader's experience. Students are then given three minutes of uninterrupted time to read the story for themselves.

2   Oral recall questions. Next, students are asked three prepared, oral questions about the section that they have read. If the student cannot answer any of the questions correctly, the assessor chooses another book at an easier level and begins again. If the student gives at least one correct answer s/he is asked to read the book aloud for a period of three minutes while their reading is taped. The assessor explains to the student that at the time signal s/he can read to the end of the sentence but then s/he must stop.

3   The three-minute, audio-taped sample of the student's oral reading from a text at their appropriate instructional level must be accurately

timed. At a later time, these audio-tapes are analysed by identifying the correct and incorrect reading that has occurred. This requires close attention to the text of the oral reading and a reading, analysis sheet on which the incorrect reading behaviours are recorded. The three-minute oral reading samples provide data on reading accuracy and reading rate (number of correct and incorrect words read per minute).

4   Oral cloze (comprehension) task. A section of the identical level text is then used with target words blanked out as a cloze exercise. The student is provided with a cloze card that provides them with the text and some illustrations. The assessor reads the story to the student who is asked to supply words that would fit appropriately in the gaps. Exact words (the exact word used in the text) and appropriate word substitutions (words that retained meaning within the text) are accepted. The individual scores on the oral recall section and scores on the oral cloze task are combined to give the measure of oral comprehension.

The reading assessments in both English and Māori continue until students reach the highest book level at which they can still read to criterion levels of accuracy and comprehension. Promotion to a higher level of text difficulty occurs when the student meets any two of the following three criteria:

1   reading accuracy level of 91 per cent or higher,
2   correct reading rate of 21 words or more per minute, or
3   combined oral comprehension score of 41 per cent or more.

Authentic assessment of writing

Collecting the writing samples

These writing assessment procedures are modelled on the English Standard 2 Survey's use of unassisted writing samples (Hamilton Education Board Resource Teachers of Reading, 1989) and can be used to assess students writing in English or in Māori. Large photographs with prompt words (provided in the language of instruction) may be used to help motivate students to write. Care should be taken to ensure that images shown in photographs are representative of the culture of the students. Photographs should serve only to suggest possible topics, leaving students free to write on any topic they like. The assessor may suggest further topics if asked for assistance by individual students.

Students require a sheet of lined paper and a pencil. They are instructed to head the paper with their name and the date and are given up to ten minutes to choose their topic and for any brief informal discussion. This time does not involve any form of written planning. Next, students are instructed to begin their ten minutes of writing, using pencil. The use of erasers is discouraged. At the end of ten minutes of independent writing, pencils are exchanged for pens. The assessor then asks students to try to improve their writing in any way they can, this time using the pen. A further five minutes is allowed for proof-reading. The exchange in writing instruments enables the assessor to differentiate between the writing sampled in the first ten minutes of writing with the writing and editing completed in the five minutes of proofreading. During the writing and proofreading times students are free to use resources from around the room to assist them with their writing, but asking others for words is discouraged. Where practical, the assessor notes any resources students used during their writing. After five minutes, the assessor gathers in students' stories for analysis.

Analysis of writing assessment data

Assessment of writing accuracy employs a definition of errors that was collaboratively arrived at by researchers, together with *kaumātua* (elders) and *whaea* (senior Māori women) (Glynn, Berryman, Atvars and Harawira, 1998). The definition included errors of punctuation, spelling, unrecognizable words, unclear messages, incorrect language structures and tenses. Errors in students' writing samples are marked with a highlighter, for the attention of the assessor only. Data on writing rate, accuracy, and quality (holistic ratings of 'audience impact' and 'overall language quality') together with additional information in the writing samples are collated for subsequent analysis. Data are gathered also on the increasing number of more difficult words that students use in their writing. Raters, who are unaware of students' names or the sequence in which the writing samples have been gathered, can be asked to provide holistic ratings of audience impact and language quality for every writing sample.

Assessing the classroom learning environment

As we noted in Chapter 2, Ysseldyke and Christenson (1987) argue that to improve literacy levels in classrooms, it is important to focus on classroom practice because it is at this level that changes can be made to facilitate learning effectively. Ysseldyke et al. identify a number of instructional factors in the classroom that influence student outcomes in all academic domains.

Based on their analysis of features in the learning environment that influence learning, Ysseldyke and Christenson (1987) designed 'The Instructional Environment Scale' (TIES) (Yssledyke and Christenson, 1987, 1993; Yssledyke and Thurlow, 1994). The purpose was to support the systematic collection of data to analyse contextual barriers to students' learning and identify starting points for designing interventions for individual students. Data are gathered through classroom observation and interview with both pupil and teacher on twelve components of teaching:

> Instructional presentation: Instruction is presented in a clear and effective manner; directions contain sufficient information for the student to understand what kinds of behaviours or skills are to be demonstrated; and the student's understanding is checked before independent practice.
>
> Classroom environment: The classroom is controlled efficiently and effectively; there is a positive, supportive classroom atmosphere; time is used productively.
>
> Teacher expectations: There are realistic yet high expectations for both the amount and accuracy of work to be completed, and these are communicated clearly to the student.
>
> Cognitive emphasis: Thinking skills needed to complete assignments are communicated explicitly to the student.
>
> Motivational strategies: The teacher has and uses effective strategies for heightening student interest and effort.
>
> Relevant practice: The student is given adequate opportunity for practice with appropriate materials. Classroom tasks are clearly important to achieving instructional goals.
>
> Academic engaged time: The student is actively engaged in responding to academic content; the teacher monitors the extent to which the student is actively engaged and redirects the student when the student is not engaged.
>
> Informed feedback: The student receives relatively immediate and specific information on his or her performance or behaviour; when the student makes mistakes, correction is provided.
>
> Adaptive instruction: The curriculum is modified to accommodate the student's specific instructional needs.
>
> Progress evaluation: There is direct, frequent measurement of the student's progress toward completion of instructional objectives; data on pupil performance and progress are used to plan future instruction.
>
> Instructional planning: The student's needs have been assessed accurately and instruction is matched appropriately to the results of the instructional diagnosis.
>
> Student understanding: The student demonstrates an accurate understanding of what is to be done in the classroom.
>
> (Ysseldyke and Christenson, 1987, p. 21)

The instructional environment scale provides the means for a thorough analysis of the quality of teaching and learning contexts in which students are placed.

Assessment focuses on any or all of the 12 components listed above, and will generate the kind of specific information needed for effective teacher professional development. The 12 components provide a blueprint for teachers to improve their pedagogical practice in ways that will clearly enhance student learning. However, these components of effective instructional environments are presented as being under the control of and modifiable by the class teacher.

This type of analysis provides an important assessment, which removes the 'blame' for poor student learning from students, and locates the responsibility for creating responsive learning environments with their teachers. However, this type of analysis appears to place little emphasis on the need for classroom pedagogy to build upon knowledge and experiences that students bring to the classroom. It is not yet so easy to see how attention to these 12 components will necessarily increase teacher responsiveness to students from different language and cultural backgrounds. Teacher and student interactions around shared tasks, learning conversations and co-construction of learning may well occur, but do not appear to be as explicitly targeted in TIES II, as they are in approaches such as responsive written feedback, Pause Prompt Praise, and some of the oral language assessment tools presented elsewhere in this chapter.

Conclusion

In this chapter, we have discussed how uninformed applications of standardized assessment of literacy can have a negative impact on achievement and can undermine the identities of students-as-literacy-learners which in turn can have a destructive influence on the identities they already have of themselves.

Assessment can therefore serve to either reinforce or undermine the motivation to strive for future literacy development and achievement. Students' sense of themselves as having the potential to be effective in the community of literacy practices may be constructed and/or constrained by the forms of assessment that are used with them. Assessment therefore must aim to build on students' experiences and identities and not marginalise or destroy them. Despite the importance of assessment in education today, many teachers highlight the lack of professional development in assessment design, implementation and analysis.

This chapter contends that assessment needs to be an ongoing, continuous and formative process. This provides teachers with formal and informal opportunities to notice what is happening during learning activities, to recognise where the learning of individuals and groups of students is going, as well as to understand how they as teachers can help take that learning further. This process begins by ensuring students receive appropriate literacy learning goals and are engaged in interactive learning conversations throughout their literacy activities. Learning conversations are based on evidence from assessments and observations carried out in authentic learning, contexts. Learning conversations include responsive feedback that connects to the student's own generated evidence of learning and feed forward to help the student identify their next most appropriate learning steps. Exemplars of other students' learning can also provide a responsive context in which learning conversations can occur. In so doing teachers can help students to become more independent literacy learners and also monitor their own literacy learning.

8 Collaborative community and school partnerships in literacy

Introduction

This chapter adopts the view that school-sanctioned literacy is only one of many different literacies in people's lives (Street and Street, 1995) and that a number of 'mediators' of literacy, siblings, parents, carers, relatives, community members (Gregory, 1998; Gregory et al., 2004) as well as school staff can support literacy development among students who experience difficulties. We describe the role that significant others, as 'experts', can play in 'scaffolding' learning, (Bruner, 1996) or in offering 'guided participation' (Rogoff, 1990) by creating responsive, social contexts for literacy learning.

In this chapter, we discuss studies which demonstrate how home and community literacy practices contribute to reading success at school. By presenting examples of successful home and school literacy partnerships, we also illustrate the potential of home-school partnerships to support students' literacy learning. Several of these examples are built around the use of programmes described in Chapter 3, as well as responsive written feedback procedures described in Chapter 4. These examples illustrate the importance of schools addressing the issues of cultural differences between home and school in how they collaborate with families and communities to construct their literacy learning tasks and contexts, how they recognise and affirm literacy values and practices that are evident in different cultural communities, and how they understand and respect the dynamics of partnerships between parents and teachers.

Perceptions of family support for children's literacy development

In some countries, for a considerable time now there has been a research focus on collaborative home and school literacy partnerships, and the significance of relationships between family processes and children's progress at school. Until recent years, it was a common surmise that the homes of poor working class and ethnic minority-culture families are less worthwhile environments for children to acquire literacy than those of culturally dominant, middle class families. For example, in a study in the UK, Hannon and McNally (1986) found a 27-point difference in mean reading test scores between middle class and working class 7-year-olds. As part of the National Child Development Study (Davie, Butler and Goldstein, 1972), tests of reading attainment were carried out at 7 years old on all the children born in one week in 1958, 30 per cent of whom showed relatively poor achievement in reading. This poor achievement correlated strongly with a number of home factors, including social class. The children of semi-skilled, manual working class fathers were more than twice as likely to be poor readers as those whose fathers held professional or technical posts.

Gregory (1996) notes that, for many years in the UK, bilingual homes were also viewed as less beneficial environments for children's literacy learning in English than English monolingual homes. In 1967, for example, at the time of the Plowden Report (HMSO, 1967) references to bilingualism were largely negative:

> The argument in the report runs as follows: 'Immigrant children' are 'deprived' and at a disadvantage in school owing to the poor educa-tion of their families. In addition, they will be 'handicapped' by their unfamiliarity with the new language and culture . . . The solution to children's needs during the 1960s was, therefore, seen to lie in *assimi-lation* of immigrants through tighter control of new arrivals, through *bussing* children to other schools when the proportion of immigrants reached 33 per cent and through providing a *'compensating environ-ment'* by *'enriched intellectual nourishment'*.
>
> (Gregory, 1996, p. 5)

The 'literacy-deficient' view of some pupils' families presents a number of difficulties for those attempting to conceptualise appropriate ways in which to support the improvement of children's literacy. Hannon (1999), amongst others, points out that this view misses opportunities for drawing on existing patterns of family literacy to inform children's learning. Moreover, the school is absolved from responsibility for addressing the literacy difficulties of pupils if their families are seen as 'literacy-deficient'.

These views on the ability of families with little history of literacy to sup-port their children's literacy development are pessimistic. However, a number of studies from across the world, for example research carried out in New Zealand for over 25 years ((McNaughton, Glynn, Robinson and Quinn 1981, 1987; Glynn and McNaughton, 1985; Glynn, 1995; Bishop et al., 2003;

Glynn, Berryman, Grace and Glynn, 2004) have challenged such deficit theorizing and the deficiency model of poor working-class and ethnic minority-culture families (Blackledge, 2000). These studies appear to offer a very strong reason for believing that many families from across the social and ethnic spectrum may have the potential to provide a very important additional resource in supporting the literacy acquisition of children who experience difficulties. In the UK, as Wragg et al. (1998, p. 269) note:

> The Plowden Report (1967) on primary education devoted a whole chapter to the role that could be played by parents. Young and McGeeney (1968) experimented in London schools by involving parents in attending school functions, hearing their children read, and various other forms of participation. They found some improvements in reading performance compared with control schools where there was no such participation.

Hewison and Tizard's (1980) study of the reading attainment of 7-year-old working-class children in Dagenham showed that half of the parents of working class children who were competent readers regularly heard them read although none of the parents had been encouraged by the school to do so. Subsequently, a number of research studies were set up to investigate the hypothesis that parental support at home for school-related literacy had a significant effect on improvement of children's reading. For example, in the Haringey Project (Tizard, Schofield and Hewison, 1982) every child chosen at random in the two top infant classes, in a study based in two multiracial inner-city schools in London, was heard reading from books sent home by the class teachers for two years. The results indicated a highly significant improvement among pupils who were heard reading at home in comparison with other pupils. There was no comparable improvement among those pupils who received the extra tuition in school.

Most children are already competent learners by the time they enter pre-school or school, and after they have done so they continue to participate in responsive, social learning contexts at home. At this point many children are becoming literate in two major socialisation settings, each of which functions to teach specific forms of expertise. However, the relationship between home and school settings can foster collaboration and interdependence or separation and disconnectedness, with corresponding positive or negative impacts on children's progress at school. There are important differences in views about the power relationship that should exist between schools and the families of students experiencing literacy difficulties and, therefore, of ownership of home-based literacy strategies and programmes. Wragg et al.'s (1998) summary of the manner in which parents were involved in the reading development of their children in the schools surveyed during the Leverhulme Primary

Improvement Project, for example, reflects an imbalance of power and assumptions of teachers as the primary, or sole, source of expert knowledge about individual children. In Wragg et al.'s (1998) study, most schools professed to involving families in children's literacy acquisition. However, as Wragg et al. noted, beneath the surface, commonly there was tension and confusion over the role that parents who had been invited into the classroom as volunteer helpers should perform:

> The generally positive reaction of schools to the involvement of parents is a strong foundation stone on which to build, but there should be no doubt about the gaps, misunderstandings and lack of knowledge that exist, even in schools as effective generally as the ones studied in this research. . . . Unwittingly perhaps, some schools may patronise their children's parents by glossing over their concerns, assuming that they are capable of very little beyond the most rudimentary, or, in the case of ethnic minorities, assuming too readily that they may not be equipped to help.
>
> (Wragg et al., 1998, pp. 269–70)

In the context of literacy learning in bi-lingual families, by the mid-1970s in the UK this negative portrayal of the family's contribution to children's educational progress had been replaced, in official rhetoric at least, by a positive recognition of the linguistic and cultural backgrounds of many pupils. Gregory (1996) notes the recommendation of the (1975) Bullock Report that no child should be expected to:

> live and act as though school and home represent two totally separate and different cultures which have to be kept firmly apart. The curriculum should reflect many elements of that part of his life which a child lives outside school. . . . Their bilingualism is . . . something to be nurtured and one of the agencies that should nurture it is the school'
>
> (HMSO, 1975, para 20.5–17)

Some local education authorities took part in a pilot project to provide teaching in the mother tongue within mainstream schools. However, such initiatives came to a halt in the 1980s as a result, according to Gregory (1996) of the image of high cost and lack of evidence of positive impact on the learning of English. In 1985, the Swann Committee reported that 'community languages' are best taught outside the state school system (Education for All, HMSO, 1985). Since 1988 and the introduction of the Education Reform Act it is expected that equal opportunities will be integral to the development and evaluation of schools' curricula, but whether offering the same curriculum to all children ensures equality of opportunity in practice is open to question.

More recently, insights gained from a study of the literacy practices of three bi-lingual Puerto Rican 5 year-olds (Volk and de Costa, 2004) 'contradict stereotypes of Latino families' and demonstrate that many of these may be 'people rich' and have 'substantial funds of knowledge relevant to literacy teaching and learning shared through mediating networks' (p. 37). Children's developing literacy was 'mediated by a network of people that included their teacher, parents, peers, siblings, extended family members, family friends, Sunday school teachers and pastors' (p. 26). Literacy events were observed as:

> . . . co-constructed by multiple participants and were syncretic. Julializ and Fidelia (two students in the study) along with their siblings and parents, drew on Spanish and English, their own experiences with school and religious texts, both oral and written texts encountered at home and in the community, on the US mainland and in Puerto Rico. Different literacies and languages were blended and reinvented as the children built on what they had learned in school and developed new skills to take back there. These reinvented literacy practices stand as a challenge to impoverished images of learning at home and conceptions of literacy as an individual task.
>
> (p. 37)

Most children spend their first few years living at home with parents, siblings and other immediate and extended family members. Here, they successfully acquire their first language and learn to use that language to enhance social and cultural relationships with adults and peers, and, often, to achieve important literacy learning. Many families play a major role in providing opportunities for literacy development, and in providing structured, responsive and supportive contexts for their children's learning. Along with other researchers (Farver, 1993; Gregory, 1998), Volk and de Costa, (2001) note that older siblings can attune their teaching to the current level of younger children's literacy development and thus act as mediators of literacy learning in ways that enhance the literacy learning of themselves and the younger siblings. Volk and de Costa (2001) conclude that the findings of this study:

> . . . point to the importance for teachers of looking beyond the replication of school experiences at home to the range of literacy interactions and people in children's lives and of recognising them as genuine resources for literacy learning. Interacting with network members, asking questions and listening to their perspectives on literacy, and observing them interact with children may provide

teachers with a new appreciation of network members' skill as teachers. In order for these interactions to occur, teachers must find new ways to be a part of children's families and to bring parents and other significant teachers into schools along with literacy practices from homes and communities.

As teachers learn what counts as literacy at home, it would be equally important for them to make explicit what counts as literacy in their own classrooms to themselves as well as to the children and to their families. Once that is clear, they can experiment with techniques and materials used at home in ways that complement their own approaches. They can also help network members understand the learning potential of activities such as making lists, reading the newspaper or the Bible, and reading, telling and reciting stories. By interweaving different approaches, teachers will make it possible for children to draw on what they learn in both settings when interacting with print. Then differences, rather than being seen as obstacles, can be understood as 'a springboard for learning' (Gregory, 1996: 6), a varied collection of resources on which children, network members, and teachers can draw in constructing a joint culture of literacy in the classroom.

(Volk and de Costa, 2001, p. 221)

Community-based literacy learning

In some communities, children may have acquired literacy in schools outside the regular state school system quite unbeknownst to teachers in mainstream schools. Duranti, Ochs and Ta'ase (2004), for example, draw attention to the function of religious schools in promoting children's literacy acquisition:

> For centuries, religion has promoted literacy. Jews, Muslims and Christians alike rely on written scriptures and instruct their congregations how to read passages within them. . . . Far more than public schools, religious schools serve as the cornerstone of literacy across nations.
>
> (Duranti, Ochs and Ta'ase, 2004, p. 159)

They note how, for example, in every pastor's school in Western Samoa, 'initial literacy instruction has been accomplished in exactly the same way, through what is called the *Pi Tautau*, published by the Congregational Christian Church. The *Pi Tautau* is:

> . . . a large poster displaying the Samoan alphabet, with Arabic and

Roman numerals along the bottom. Each letter is accompanied by a picture of an object beginning with that letter. As the literacy lesson begins, you sit cross-legged on the floor with the other children in front of the teacher, who is seated on a chair, holding the *Pi Tautau* on her lap. Over time you come to understand what is expected of you. Each lesson the teachers points to the picture on the top left hand corner and asks the class to collectively recite first the letters and their corresponding images, then the letters alone and finally the Arabic and Roman numerals from one to ten.

(Duranti, Ochs and Ta'ase, 2004, p. 160)

In many places outside Western Samoa, for example in California, Samoans have formed communities based around their local church, an important element of which is the religious school where children are introduced to the letters, words and numbers represented in the *Pi Tautau*:

The *Pi Tautau* is thus an instrument and a symbol of continuity and even ... a tangible and safe anchor for keeping the children of Samoan descent in southern California connected to the language of their parents and grandparents.

(Duranti, Ochs and Ta'ase, 2004, p. 165)

Duranti et al. suggest that 'educational research needs to reconfigure the relation between home and school and between home and community' to recognize that, for many communities:

... the boundaries of school go beyond the public school to include religious school and community extends beyond the neighbourhood to embrace the 'church village', a place where change and tradition can be safely negotiated.

(Duranti, Ochs and Ta'ase, 2004, p. 169)

Gregory (2004) draws from a number of research studies across the world into literacy practices in different communities of economically disadvantaged groups, including the work of Duranti, Ochs and Ta'ase above, as well as her own work in the UK in Spitalfields, East London, to outline 'principles and practical implications for future family literacy involvement' (Gregory, 2004, p. 268). Among these are:

- 'Recognise and acknowledge the variety of literacies and "funds of knowledge" in the lives of children and their families as practices through home and community activities' (Gregory, 2004, p. 269).

- 'Understand and support the value of different mediators of literacy
  ... in children's literacy development (Gregory, 2004, p. 270).

A number of studies have begun to demonstrate how children are often initiated into literacy through collaborative group activities where the traditional cultural knowledge of a community is passed down through a variety of mediators. Many Bangladeshi British children in Gregory's Spitalfields study were involved in out-of-school Qur'anic classes and/or Bengali classes of up to 30 children where the teaching was very formal and the children's role was to listen, repeat, practise and be tested. Children might also read English school books informally with older siblings where the 'tutor' might synthesise Qur'anic and school literacy practices to scaffold literacy learning. Some researchers, for example Volk and de Costa (2004) (see above), have pointed to 'the special role which may be played by older siblings in linguistic minority families where parents do not speak the language ... and to suggest that the ways in which children learn from older siblings in the home environment may have implications for school learning' (Gregory, 1998, p. 36). Play between young children and older siblings can initiate children into mainstream school literacy practices and the role of the teacher (Gregory, 2004; Williams, 2004). In the context of the Spitalfields study above, Gregory (1998) notes features of play-teaching where older siblings taught younger siblings the content of recent classroom literacy lessons delivered by their own teachers but use the teaching style of their community language classes outside the mainstream school:

- The older child provides a model, demonstrating what the younger sibling should do.
- The older child checks up on past learning and directly instructs the younger.
- The older sibling provides alternatives if the younger child is in difficulty.

Gregory comments that where older siblings mediate the literacy learning of younger siblings through culturally-relevant teaching practices, 'it is clear that teachers have found the 'perfect partners' (Gregory, 2004, p. 104). Gregory documents how younger siblings are taught to listen and repeat, as in Qur'anic and Bengali classes. A second strategy used by older siblings is 'tandem reading', typified by the younger child echoing the older sibling's words. 'Chained reading' was also observed, the older sibling beginning to read aloud, younger child taking over until s/he needed help, the older sibling supplying the difficult word, and so on. The older child's strategy could also move on to asking questions on the text. In summary, the more experienced sibling's strategies were often characterized by:

(1) sustaining a fast-flowing pace
(2) providing a firm 'scaffold' which is only very gradually removed (the older child at first expects repetition or echoing of one word only which gradually increases as the younger child gains in confidence);
(3) expecting a high level of accuracy after the initial stage which is reinforced by frequent (though not constant) correction of the younger child;
(4) allowing (perhaps expecting) the younger child to repeat a word correctly before continuing reading;
(5) a total lack of evaluative comment e.g. 'good girl/boy' etc;
(6) explicit 'modelling' but a complete lack of questioning during the reading of the text;
(7) text-based questions with right or wrong answers (display questions) following the reading.

The whole interaction is marked by a high number of exchanges with no breakdown in communication. Exchanges take place rhythmically with a musical synchrony reminiscent of movements between parent and very young infant . . .

(Gregory, 1998, p. 47)

Home/school literacy schemes are 'most successful when teachers are knowledgeable about the strengths of their communities and encourage a syncretism of practices' (*ibid*, p. 275). Gregory concludes that teachers have much to learn from some of these older siblings in building upon such finely tuned scaffolding in reading lessons.

The nature of home-school collaboration

A number of theoretical approaches can be employed to comment on the nature of home-school literacy partnerships. Whether one adopts concepts of family resource and cultural capital (Nash, 2001), or a *kaupapa* Māori framework (Smith, 1997) or a developmental systems model (Tangaere, 1997) or a sociohistorical perspective (McNaughton, 1995), or a behaviour analysis interactionist perspective (Wheldall and Glynn, 1989), there is general agreement among educational theorists that positive family–school relationships are vital to effective schooling. McNaughton and Glynn (1998), for example, argue that home and school exercise joint influences on children's literacy learning. However, facilitating a responsive approach to learning in one context or the other depends firstly on home and school knowing and understanding what literacy values and practices are operating in the other. Regular and reliable exchange of information between home and school about children's learning and behaviour is a minimum requirement if home and school are to collaborate effectively in enhancing children's literacy learning.

The long-standing concern of McNaughton and Glynn (1998) to understand and promote effective forms of collaboration is heightened in the present educational context, where there is an increasing need for more effective ways to promote educational equity in the face of increasing ethnic, language and socioeconomic diversity (Wilkinson, 1998). Particular challenges arise when parents and teachers come from different ethnic and cultural groups. In these cross-cultural contexts, best practice models of family, community and school relationships are sorely needed.

McNaughton and Glynn (1998) believe that it is important to develop some understanding of what we mean by collaboration. They view collaboration as ideally entailing shared expertise between educationalists and family caregivers. However, sharing expertise requires shared understandings about goals of teaching and learning, and about processes of teaching and learning. It also requires shared actions relating to goals and understandings. This sharing is not unidirectional, but reciprocal, so that agents in each setting are able to learn from and complement each other. McNaughton and Glynn (1998) believe that this form of sharing does not undermine the expertise of the teacher, but extends and enhances it. Berryman et al. (2002), working in a Māori context, believe that the general characteristics of effective collaboration are partnerships where:

- The *mana* (power and authority) and expertise of each partner were acknowledged.
- Collaboration with the partner is culturally appropriate and responsive.
- Partners learned from each other and changed their behaviour accordingly.

Many parents may welcome strong directives from teachers, at least in the initial stages of supporting the literacy acquisition of children who experience difficulties. In some countries there are examples of literacy initiatives involving parents which reflect what Dale (1996) has identified in a UK context as an 'expert model' of partnership arrangement between schools and families. Here the parent is seen as reliant on the professional with expertise in deciding what needs to be done. The teacher is assumed to have expertise with which to decide what needs to be done. Parental involvement is not of prime importance except to provide information. The teacher-directed model is reflected in initiatives such as Topping's (1996) 'Paired Reading' programme where families:

> . . . commit themselves to an initial trial period in which they agree to do at least five minutes Paired Reading on five days each week for

about eight weeks. Grandparents, siblings, friends and neighbours can be encouraged to help, but must all use the same technique – the target child is deliberately asked to quality control the tutoring they receive.

(Topping, 1996, p. 46)

Topping (1996, p. 48) is quite prescriptive about the choice of family for a pilot project in a school. 'A small group of fairly well motivated families is a good choice for a first effort' where children 'have easy and frequent access to a wide range of books'. He describes the 'rules' of his 'Paired Reading' method as 'engineering in' behaviour which is approved of by the expert and 'engineering out' behaviours seen as 'undesirable':

> Much verbal praise and non-verbal approval for specific reading behaviours is incorporated. Undesirable behaviours are engineered out of the system by engineering in incompatible positive behaviours.
>
> (ibid)

He warns against assuming that 'any old thing that two people do with a book' constitutes 'Paired Reading' and advises strong directive from teachers to parents about how the technique should operate. Teachers should:

> . . . check on the technique, offer advice, and coach as appropriate
>
> (Topping, 1996, p. 48)

Whilst some parents may welcome such clear directives from teachers, others may be very concerned about involving themselves in initiatives where the intention is to 'engineer in' behaviour seen as 'desirable' by those who may understand little of the child's background. This is not to critique the 'paired reading' technique itself, but to look closely at the underlying assumptions on which the implied school-family partnership of unequals is framed.

In the UK there are examples of individual parent-led initiatives which reflect another of Dale's (1996) models of partnership between home and school, the 'consumer' model, which has arisen out of a sense of concern that schools are not able to address the particular literacy needs of some individual children. Sometimes the resources available to the school are felt to be inadequate. Sometimes there is a difference of opinion between families and schools over the root cause of children's difficulties in literacy and, therefore, what might constitute an appropriate response to address the difficulty.

Heaton (1996), for example, notes that, for her, it is extremely important to feel that she has the ability and power to offer appropriate support and help to her own child and that teachers will listen to her when she wishes to discuss the barriers to literacy learning faced by her child. Heaton is one of a number of writers (Ostler, 1991; Heaton, 1996; Riddick, 1996) who have described particular techniques and practices that they, as parents of children described as 'dyslexic', have found useful both in obtaining the additional or alternative educational provision that they have felt necessary to meet their children's learning needs and also in supporting their children in their day-to-day living. From a questionnaire completed by parents and carers of students identified as dyslexic, Heaton (1996) offers advice to families on how to empower themselves to draw upon their knowledge about their own children in deciding what services are required for their child. This includes:

- being prepared to have to organize a management system for, and spend time on, all the paperwork involved in making the case for recognition and assessment of the student's difficulties in literacy acquisition;
- being proactive in finding out about difficulties in literacy, appropriate teaching methods and common terminology;
- maintaining close liaison with the school and every year ensuring that the student's teachers are aware of the difficulties s/he experiences;
- working out practical strategies for personal organization;
- teaching strategies for dealing with potential difficulties with the concepts of time, space and direction.

In some schools the consumer model of parent-school partnership might be experienced as uncomfortable for a number of reasons. Parents might be felt to usurp some of the power and control more usually owned by professionals inside educational institutions. Also, there is an inherent inequality in a market system which ensures that children whose parents are the most literate, persistent and articulate are advantaged (Audit Commission, 1992; Gross, 1996). There may therefore be a very real concern about the way in which, as Gewirtz et al. (1995) comment, in the UK, education is viewed as a commodity.

Proper consideration of the location of power and its significance is a very important component in conceiving ways in which families might support the literacy development of their children. Parent-educators have the potential to make a major impact on children's learning and, as a number of researchers have indicated, support the literacy acquisition of those who experience difficulties (Glynn et al., 1979; Ostler, 1991; Heaton, 1996; Riddick, 1996). The corollary of recognising this potential impact is a need to accord respect both to the role of parent-educators and to the families themselves by sharing information about children's progress and acknowledging that families also have expertise that should be harnessed to support children's learning:

A successful partnership needs a two way flow of information, knowledge and expertise. There are many ways of achieving partner-ship with parents but the following are common features of effective practice:

Practitioners show respect and understanding for the role of parents in their child's education

The past and future part played by parents in the education of their children is recognised and explicitly encouraged . . .

The knowledge and expertise of parents and other family adults are used to support the learning opportunities provided by the setting . . .

Relevant learning activities and play activities, such as sharing and reading books, are continued at home.

Similarly, experiences at home are used to develop learning in the setting, for example, visits and celebrations.

(QCA and DfEE, 1999 quoted in Mittler, 2000, pp. 155–6)

These indicators imply an equitable power relationship in the partnership between home and school. There is a very careful balance to be considered especially where the partnership arrangements that exist between families and schools and the degree of schools' responsiveness to family culture can serve to include, or alienate, young people. This may be important in cases where those whose experience of difficulties in acquiring literacy makes them particularly vulnerable to criticism or comment by others unaware of family circumstances or cultural background.

Collaboration is multidimensional and the different dimensions are inter-linked. For example, specific guidance for families on how to carry out reading activities at home may contribute to children's progress at school. But one constraint on the full effectiveness of this guidance is the degree to which families feel they have an influence over school processes and goals (Delgado-Gaitan, 1990). Collaboration implies interdependence between parents and teachers. This is shown when well written and enjoyable narrative texts in a home language are made available for families to read with their children, and thus may contribute to extended reading at home. But effectiveness of the pedagogies adopted by families is dependent on goals about school learning being shared between educators and families (Gallimore and Goldenberg, 1993).

As we have already commented in relation to the work of Gregory (1996), Volk and de Costa (2004) and Duranti et al. (2004), one important dimension of effective collaboration is the role of teachers' knowledge of students' par-ticipation in family and community literacy contexts. This raises questions about what sorts of knowledge teachers might need, as well as what sorts of knowledge should be developed through teacher professional development.

Before arriving at answers to these questions, we need first to consider issues surrounding the forms collaboration can take (McNaughton and Glynn, 1998).

Deliberately arranged collaboration, in the sense in which we have defined it, can take two complementary forms. One form involves incorporation of school-like activities into family activities. This may happen where families begin to use forms of literacy that share properties with school forms of literacy. Research examples we will discuss further below include procedures for supporting oral reading (Pause, Prompt and Praise, already introduced in Chapter 4), and patterns of reading storybooks to pre-school children.

A second form of deliberate collaboration involves incorporation of community activities into school activities. This occurs where schools take seriously the notion of teaching to children's strengths and starting from where children 'are at':

> Where children are at is to some degree where their families and communities are at
>
> (McNaughton and Glynn, 1998, p. 5)

Both forms of collaboration have long traditions in the education system in some countries. For example, in New Zealand sending books home in Year 1 for family members to hear beginning readers read has been a standard educational practice for nearly 40 years. Another example, also in New Zealand, can be found in some Native Schools in the nineteenth century where Māori language forms were incorporated into texts as a bridge to reading English (Simon and Smith, 1998). Similarly, the much celebrated 'Ready to Read' (Department of Education, 1985) texts for beginning reading instruction were constructed on the basis of incorporating familiar language and topics drawn from children's experiences of home and community.

Both forms of collaboration require teachers to have generic knowledge and also particular knowledge about their students' communities. Incorporating school-like activities into family practices requires a generic understanding of the forms that language and literacy practices could take within these communities. A generic understanding of cultural identity is also required because language and literacy practices both reflect and construct cultural identities, and because family language and literacy practices are everyday life events forming part of children's social, economic, political, cultural and historical contexts. We have already noted the crucial role of religious schools in literacy learning, and in maintaining traditional cultural practices in some communities. McNaughton and Glynn (1988) argue that in addition to this generic knowledge, if schools are to establish effective collaboration with home around literacy learning, teachers need specific knowledge about the literacy practices of particular families of students in their classes, for example the extent to which older siblings habitually mediate the literacy learning of younger children within the family (Gregory, 1996). The diversity in ways of using language within cultural groups may be as wide as, or wider than, the differences between such groups (McNaughton, 1996).

Parent involvement in reading

We have already discussed one example above of a school-directed approach to involving parents in children's reading development (Topping, 1996). There are a number of other examples around the world of researchers trialling home-school collaborative literacy initiatives which set out to share understandings of goals and processes of teaching and learning, and aim to share expertise between educationalists and family caregivers in a reciprocal way so that teachers, families and community members are able to learn from each other. 'Pause Prompt Praise' reading tutoring procedures, piloted in South Auckland in 1977 and described in Chapter 4, are an example of a project of this sort that is especially salient in conceptualising how to support the reading of young people who experience difficulties in literacy acquisition. A further study incorporating 'Pause Prompt Praise' together with strategies for enhancing children's writing was carried out with parents of students experiencing difficulties in literacy, and their teachers in nine Rotorua primary schools, (Glynn, Berryman and Glynn 2000a, 2000b).

Three examples of collaboration between parents and the home-school liaison teachers in the 'Rotorua home and school project' (Glynn, Berryman and Glynn, 2000a, 2000b) illustrate how teachers at school gained experience and understanding of their students' home contexts for literacy learning. At the beginning of this study teachers perceived parents of participating students as needing a great deal of support if they were to assist their children's progress at school, given the extremely adverse economic circumstances with which many were coping. Transiency was also identified as being extremely problematic for parents and students in these schools. However, the researchers in this study who did visit children's homes found otherwise. Researchers found that these parents cared deeply about their children's reading difficulties at school, and were highly motivated to do something to help them. It appeared that very few teachers had had contact with, or direct knowledge of, their children's families or homes other than what they glimpsed of parents in the school setting.

The first example is of a Korean student, D, whose entire family were learning English as a second language. The fact that English was D's second language was the major reason offered by teachers for her apparent underachievement in reading. D's situation reflects a common perception in schools that second language learners are merely 'poor readers of English', rather than competent readers and speakers of their home language with a developing competence in literacy and language in English also. This family was highly motivated for D to learn English as quickly as possible. Both D's father and older sister (a Year 10 high school student) shared the work of implementing the 'Pause Prompt Praise' procedures as well as the structured brainstorm and responsive written feedback strategies with D. From the liaison teacher's and the researcher's home visits, it was clear that not only were all the programme components being implemented successfully, but also that many other learning activities were going on as well, as can be seen from the researcher's notes:

> When I got to the house, D was looking out the window expecting me, and Mr P came straight to the door. They had the books ready. D showed me the place where she does her study, a room with over 50 Korean books and two large desks. D can read fluently in Korean and read one of the books to me. She reads Korean books daily and her father's help is simply to tell her the unfamiliar words. She could read in Korean before she came to New Zealand. She writes a diary or journal every day in Korean, and also in English when the school asks for it. She likes reading in Korean and English. When I asked her which was harder, she thought a long time, and then said 'English'.
>   . . . Mr P had a list of carefully written questions which he said he had re-written three times, to get correct. I answered all these questions and asked if I could have the sheet to help me with my work. He had several other questions also. Why, and what was the poem in front of the parents' handbook? Who were all the people inside the front cover? (These were members of the project team). How could he think up enough (English) words for the brainstorming (writing) session? He wanted to know how long he should pause before prompting. He wanted to know if he should be teaching her in his 'bad accent', and if this made a problem. He also asked about the diary/ journal entries. He wanted to know who was supposed to do the correcting . . .
>
>   (McNaughton and Glynn, 1998, pp. 8–9)

When researchers commented to D (and her home-school liaison teacher) about how well, and how meticulously, all the various components of the programme were being implemented at home, she replied:

> Well, if my father says all these things need to be done, then they all get done.
>
>   (NcNaughton and Glynn, 1998, p. 9)

The second example comes from the researcher's notes of a home visit to a Pasifika (Pacific Island) family, who had been living in New Zealand for a number of years:

> When I went to the house, Mrs V was not yet home, so I waited in the car for half an hour before trying again. This time she was home, but appeared very flustered. She took me into the bedroom and sat me on the only chair while she and her daughter, M, sat on the bed. There were many people in the house, Mr F's adult sister, at least one teenage boy, two smaller children, a baby and M.
>
> M was very keen, and unpacked the books and started reading aloud while we were still talking. An older girl came in with the baby, and said something when Mrs V asked for the aunty to mind the baby. The baby was scratchy so I suggested she feed the baby while we did the session. We had only just started when the two younger children came in also, and wanted to join in. Almost the entire session was conducted with three children, and the baby interacting in the room . . .
>
> Mrs V was very enthusiastic about the programme and said she was doing it every day, and could see great improvements in M's reading. She had brought along her own uncle to the training session and he was trying the same procedures with his son who is at N school. His son had been 'sitting in the corner on his own because the teacher said he couldn't read'.
>
> He (uncle) went to the teacher and said, 'You're not doing your job properly' . . . Mrs V had a question ready for me. The sheet for the writing brainstorming session had no lines on it, so M couldn't write very well. Shouldn't there be lines on it? . . . This mother is doing an excellent job under difficult circumstances.
>
> (McNaughton and Glynn, 1998, p. 10)

The third example in the Rotorua Home and School Project involves the parents from one of the nine schools, who were all Māori parents with affiliations to the same tribe, *Te Arawa*, and the home-school liaison teacher (who was a respected elder) with affiliation to a different tribe, *Ngāti Porou*, but who had *whānau* (extended family) connections with *Te Arawa*. *Whānau* links enabled these parents to establish a collaborative, and collective, working relationship with each other, as well as with the home-school liaison teacher. From the beginning of the intervention phase of this project, these parents made arrangements to support each other in their learning, to share resources, to pass tape recorders and reading texts from one house to another, and to monitor and discuss the progress of all their children.

They regularly spoke in terms of 'our programme', 'our school', 'our tapes', 'our students' and 'our data'. Two of these parents, probably because of their very tangible ownership of the programme, were quite comfortable with approaching teachers when they believed the teachers were not adequately fulfilling their side of the home and school partnership. In this situation, culturally preferred styles of learning and interacting over-rode the boundaries of conventional Western parent-teacher relationship. Parents' ability to take the initiative in approaching teachers appeared to add great strength to the collaborative partnership between home and school, and certainly contributed to the reading and writing gains made by the students in the home and school programme at this school. Some time after the research had finished, parents in this community collaborated once more with the researchers when they shared their skills and expertise to film two videos about communities working collaboratively with schools to support the literacy achievement of students by building culturally competent and effective home and school partnerships (Berryman, Glynn and Glynn 2001a, 2001b).

Taken together, these three examples illustrate how teachers can effectively share knowledge and understanding with the parents and communities of the children they teach. In the first two examples, one parent, Mr P, was a recent migrant who was struggling to learn English as a second language, while the other parent, Mrs V, was coping with severe financial hardship and responsibilities for a large extended family. The learning contexts of the Korean and the Pacific Island households differed markedly in terms of the amount of material resources available and in the learning and the interaction styles employed for enhancing their children's literacy. The two homes also differed in terms of the space available to work in and the number of people sharing that space. Nevertheless, both Mr P and Mrs V were highly motivated to see their child succeed in reading and writing at school, and both were achieving success in implementing the programme with their own children at home. D and M brought to school entirely different understandings of what reading and writing was all about. When a teacher sent home a reading text, as seen in these examples, Mr P and Mrs V approached the task in dramatically different ways.

In example three, the children's parents, classroom teachers and home-school liaison teacher shared Māori as a common culture and language, even though most parents and students were second language learners. This established bases for common understandings about what the reading and writing tasks were all about, why their children found reading and writing difficult, and about how teachers and parents were accountable to each other in terms of their *whānau* connections. The flow of information between home and school, and the control of that information flow was reciprocal. Parents and *whānau* members could both initiate action and respond to teacher-initiated actions to help their children. In the first two examples, the information flow was largely unidirectional, and controlled by teachers. In the third example, the information flow was largely controlled by parents, and mediated through the home and school liaison teacher. In all three examples, researchers found they needed to facilitate the flow of information, in an attempt to provide teachers with a better understanding of the home learning contexts and of their Māori community.

Understanding culturally specific relationships

We have seen that culturally specific support can facilitate children's learning in a variety of contexts and with a variety of methods. In order to appreciate the culturally specific nature of the relationships between people in the sections of this chapter that relate to community and school collaboration in a Māori context, it is useful to understand some of the basic structures within Māori society, how this society is organized and some of the key roles and responsibilities of people within it.

First, there is not simply one single Māori nation, but a large number of separate tribal groups, each with its own ancestral history, its own dialect and its own special association with the land where the people have lived for several centuries. The largest societal structure is the *waka*, or specific canoe on which key ancestors first journeyed to New Zealand from diverse origins in the Pacific, and from whom all members of a particular tribe descend. Sometimes there are several different tribes whose members descend from the same *waka*, but from separate important ancestors known to have travelled on that canoe. The *waka* is a high-order, unifying concept, linking people from several different tribes, together with specific areas of land and landscape features. The *waka* provides the first level of a Māori person's cultural identity.

The second largest societal unit is the *iwi*, or tribe, in which membership and cultural identity is defined in terms of descent from a specific ancestor. After successive generations, many Māori people today can still demonstrate descent from several different key ancestors, enabling them to claim identity or standing in more than one tribe, but more importantly to establish functional family relationships with a large number of people living across the country, and also internationally.

Attachments to *waka* and *iwi* are deeply important to defining one's identity as Māori and subsequently one's spiritual, intellectual, social and emotional well-being. These attachments also provide strong relationships and responsibilities to particular land features, to important ancestors and to the many people who share this common heritage. Māori identity is defined in terms of one's relationships to important ancestors from the past and also in terms of contemporary relationships with a very large number of people to whom one is related, and to whom one is *whānau* (extended family).

Relationships through marriage, rather than through kinship or blood links, are referred to as *whanaunga*. The construct of relationships itself is referred to as *whanaungatanga*, meaning 'interconnectedness'. This is also widely used metaphorically to refer to ecological relationships between plants, birds, animals, and between people and their environment. Finally, the important process of making, forging or maintaining relationships is known as *whakawhanaungatanga*.

These cultural practices occur routinely at all kinds of gatherings and events, and serve to remind people of their interconnectedness and their need to maintain these extended relationships for the survival and well-being of all the people. The survival of these values and practices since the impact of colonization is arguably one of the key elements in the survival of the language and culture for Māori.

For regular and routine social interactions people live and socialize at the level of *hapū*, or sub-tribal groups comprised of a smaller number of *whānau* or extended family units, who are in regular contact with each other. Within a *whānau* structure and organization, individuals have both rights and responsibilities. Rights include the right to seek support and assistance (physical, mental, emotional and spiritual), while responsibilities include the responsibility to provide or contribute such support or assistance to others. There is a powerful interdependent relationship among *whānau* members, which establishes a strong sense of inclusion and collective identity. Family members from the same generation may all share particular kinship roles. For example, any or all of the sisters of a given grandmother may exercise a grandmotherly role in the nurturing and education of any of her grandchildren, and any or all of the brothers of the grandmother may likewise share in the nurturing and educational roles with their 'collective' grandchildren. Similarly, any or all of a child's uncles and aunts may share in nurturing and educational roles. These specific *whānau* relationships still operate in contemporary Māori society, even though the extended *whānau* may be living in different towns and cities. Where their culture is alive and well, Māori children and their parents can access the support and guidance of multiple *kuia* (grandmothers) and *koro* (grandfathers), as well as the company and support of many, many *tuākana* (elder siblings and cousins).

Across all these levels of societal structures and organization, collective relationship roles and responsibilities are crucial for Māori people's identity and well-being. In more traditional Māori society, inclusion in all of the different levels is dependent upon both genealogical descent (kinship) and on active participation, and exercising rights and responsibilities. However, in contemporary Māori society, while genealogy and kinship is still essential for asserting one's sense of belonging to a *waka* and to an *iwi*, membership at *hapū* and *whānau* level depends more on active participation and contribution to the well-being of the group. Furthermore, metaphoric *whānau*, or *whānau*-like, structures are regularly formed to address particular problems or challenges, or to achieve specific tasks. These *whānau* will operate along the lines of traditional kinship *whānau*, although their membership may cross kinship boundaries, and may even include non-Māori. However, procedures and decision-making will follow Māori protocols incorporating both the spiritual blessing and guidance of elders and working towards a consensus position before actions are undertaken by individuals, and the commitment of all members to work both to maintain and enhance the well-being of the group, and to work towards the achievement of the group's goals and tasks.

In summary, within both traditional kinship *whānau* and contemporary metaphoric *whānau*, relationships amongst members are crucial. Positions within each type of *whānau* carry both rights and responsibilities. When, in some communities, like the small rural community described in the following research, teachers and community members belong to the same kinship *whānau*, community and school collaboration takes on a very special quality.

Understanding culturally specific practices

Within a number of studies in different cultural settings reported throughout this chapter, we refer to the concept of cultural safety. This can be a highly contested and often misunderstood concept. In the context of this book, we are defining cultural safety as meaning the construction of supportive teacher-student relationships and forms of interactions in classroom and school learning activities, and teaching strategies that make it safe for students to be 'themselves'. That is, to talk, read and write about experiences and events that are familiar to them and their home cultures (McNaughton, 2002; Bishop et al., 2003). Students should not be required to leave their language, values, beliefs and literacy experiences at the school gate (Bishop et al., 2003). Rather, literacy practices in classrooms and schools should build upon those qualities and experiences from the home and incorporate them into school-based literacy activities. This position does not require that classrooms and schools will reproduce the exact cultural practices, and values of the students from every culture represented in their populations.

Rather, it requires classrooms and schools to construct new metaphoric spaces in which students from the various cultural backgrounds, and their teachers, feel safe to interact and learn from each other. However, the plight of indigenous students attending schools which require them to leave their culture at the school gate in order to participate in education, is somewhat different. Unless indigenous languages, values, beliefs and practices are represented and legitimated within classrooms and schools, schools will continue to contribute to the destruction of those languages and cultures which differ from those of their own. This constitutes a strong argument for indigenous peoples to establish their own schools and curriculum. However, it also constitutes an important learning opportunity for mainstream schools wanting to respond more effectively to learning and achievement by indigenous students. Schools often respond more appropriately to recent immigrant and ESL students, while the needs of their indigenous students are ignored or belittled (Glynn, 1998).

Merging personal and professional boundaries and commitments

The extent and the power of literacy expertise that is located, but often 'locked away', in families and communities is illustrated in the narrative between the third author of this book (Mere) and the home and school liaison teacher (Hiro), at one of the schools in the Rotorua Project outlined above (Glynn, Berryman, Grace and Glynn, 2004). Students experiencing reading difficulties who participated in a literacy programme implemented at home and at school improved their reading and writing over and above the levels achieved by students participating only in the regular school programme. There were two key reasons for the success of this partnership. The first was parents' and *whānau* members' successful implementation of both the Pause Prompt Praise reading tutoring programme (or its Māori language version *Tatari, Tautoko Tauawhi*) together with the two components of the writing programme, structured brainstorm and responsive written feedback writing programme (or their Māori language versions *Whakaputa Putawhakaaro* and *Tuhi Atu Tuhi Mai*). The second reason was the professional educational and cultural expertise of the home-school liaison worker. Because of her language and cultural expertise and her *mana* (acknowledged authority and standing), Hiro was able to engage Māori parents and *whānau* actively in the home and school project. The co-constructed narrative between Hiro and Mere (the third author), which follows, provides a context for understanding the power that collaborative home and school literacy partnerships have in improving children's literacy at school.

Hiro not only understood, but also affirmed, the cultural background of her students and their families. She did this by employing interpersonal processes that were characteristically Māori. She continually drew on this knowledge and expertise to improve the learning outcomes for all *whānau* members.

> Hiro: . . . I was a sort of liaison officer. I would sort of keep in touch with the parents concerned and with their children and with you. But besides keeping touch with the parents, I also had to encourage them to come forward because a lot of our Māori parents are a bit shy and that was a problem with a lot of them. They were keen enough in their own way but they were just shy, took a while to come to the meetings, but when they did come they were fine. It's just patipati [encouragement], I call it. You know, give them a little awhi [support]

and rub on the back and just have a quiet little korero [talk] to them and most of the time they open up.

(Glynn and Berryman, 2003, p. 42)

Awakening collective identity and collective responsibility

The children and *whānau* Hiro worked with became part of her life, and she part of theirs. Parents no longer identified themselves only as individuals. Values of individual achievement, and competition between individuals that are dominant in the majority culture, were gradually replaced by values of collective achievement and collective responsibility for the well-being of all students and *whānau* members. Through their participation in the project, and with Hiro's support and encouragement, *whānau* were affirming their cultural identity and validating the cultural understandings that came from experiencing school literacy from within a Māori worldview.

Mere: So, was this just advice about the reading and writing?

Hiro: No, whatever they asked.

Mere: Why do you think they came to you?

Hiro: As I said I think they trusted me. You build up that rapport with them by what you do and how you do it. You don't just necessarily give directions. I'm just used to doing things hands on, showing by example. I'm not a lecture type person. So perhaps they saw what I was doing and that I was happy with what I was doing, and that made them happy too. We'd have a cup of tea or coffee. Down here or in the staff room they were at home. They didn't feel uncomfortable. They felt safe.

Well they sort of formed their own whānau and helped each other too. That didn't matter that they weren't brother and sister and that word whānaungatanga [interconnectedness based on personal relationship] came out very strongly with that group of parents, with their 'network' going. We also had to share cassette recorders, and so one of them would finish with it, and go round the corner and pass it on the next one down the street. And so they did the rounds and the school supplied the recorders. I didn't have to go and pick them up from each one. They would just pass them on to the next one . . . And they helped each other in that way. Well even with the responsive writing. That's another way that whānaungatanga [family-style relationships] came out . . . they got sick of waiting for the teacher and they took control. I mean I started [by just] listening, but the busier I became, they decided that they would take control and they did.

Mere: What is whānaungatanga for you?

Hiro: It's being part of a family. Not necessarily blood ties. Having that family feeling working together is part of a whānau. And might all be from totally different areas but when you get together you all work towards the whānau goal, helping each other. Doesn't necessarily have to be brother, sister, mother, father.

Mere: That strong whānau network that had developed, I haven't seen it in any of the other places. How do you think you got it?

Hiro: That's the way our school is. Well we've got about 90 per cent [Māori students and whānau]. And that's the way our school is run. It's run like a big whānau whether you are in mainstream [English medium] or immersion [Māori medium]. Everything is whānau.

(Glynn and Berryman, 2003, pp. 47–9)

Hiro had taken a personal interest in, and developed a close understanding of, each of the families with whom she worked. Not only did she share in their work and successes, but she also shared in their pain and their grief. There were few boundaries drawn between her teaching and caring roles:

Hiro: Well there was one grandfather, who was having problems with his ex, and that child got hi-jacked by the ex and that grandfather had worked so hard. Yep and that was sad when he came to tell me that his grandson had been taken away by his grandmother, his ex. And then there was one, a parent that had all the time in the world, but he was too busy playing spacey games to listen to his own child read. And there was one mother who felt that she was not that good at Māori. But she persevered, borrowed dictionaries and everything. This made them work.

Then there was another one. Mum wasn't in the home but dad was working with the child. That was the difficult one cause he [the child] was taught in bi-lingual, taught to read in English first, and then he came to immersion. So that was a big step for him, he needed a fair bit of help for a start. And the father just needed help in sort of calming down, not losing it. But dad turned out really good. He went on to train as a teacher.

(Glynn and Berryman, 2003, pp. 46–7)

Initiating collective action and problem solving

In establishing this home and school partnership, it was essential that these parents and *whānau* members exercised some shared control over the context and direction of their learning. Balance of power, shared control and reciprocity between learning and teaching roles, are seen as elements of responsive, social contexts that promote independent learning (Glynn, 1985, 1995).

It was clear that Hiro and the school were embodying these concepts in their pedagogical practice. They believed *whānau* not only could but also should become involved in the literacy education of their children at school. With Hiro's help, it was not long before these parents who had up until then been the learners, began to take a share in the teacher role. While this could have become a potential source of conflict between home and school, because of Hiro's professional experience and *mana* (acknowledged authority and standing), the *mana* of the parents as well as the teacher were maintained. There was mutual respect and appreciation. Both groups were able to work alongside each other, learn from each other, and in many cases change their behaviour as a result. The central collective focus was as much on promoting the well-being of the whole group (teachers and parents) as it was on improving literacy outcomes for students. Participating in a *whānau* structure carries important responsibilities as well as benefits.

> Hiro: I like seeing people who are not in the education sector, parents and other *whānau* members, latching on to things in education and seeing the benefits.
>
> Mere: Do you think those parents latched on?
>
> Hiro: I think so. The majority of them I would say. The hardest part was getting them into that routine of working with the teacher. Mind you, it was hard getting the teacher into the routine too!
>
>   When it came to the responsive writing and brainstorming, well it ended up the parents decided they'd do it at home. They took it away from the teacher because they got sick of waiting [for the teacher to initiate partnership] and I can understand that, being a parent and a grandparent myself. But I can also understand the teacher who was only new to our school so he was still getting to know his children and still settling in. Some [teachers] don't take long you know, some only take five minutes but some take longer and I think that may have been where the difficulty was.
>
> Mere: Did you feel like you were piggy in the middle?
>
> Hiro: No, because the teacher was fine about it and so were they. They were quite happy. As long as there was someone there to do it, it didn't have to be the teacher. And it just kept going. I just felt that the teacher would need to sort of get himself faster into a routine. Yes, some take a bit longer than others.
>
>   (Glynn and Berryman, 2003, pp. 49–50)

This example of collaborative problem solving provided an opportunity for the cooperative and active learning roles of the teacher and *whānau* to be interchanged, while keeping intact the *mana* of teacher and parents.

Strengthen the whānau, strengthen student achievement

A key to parents' support of the project was Hiro's commitment as a *whānau* member to meeting their needs for cultural safety and comfort, rather than simply ensuring their compliance with the project requirements. Given the many competing demands made on parents' time and energy, she ensured that resources were always ready for them, that there was always time and space to meet where they felt comfortable and safe (and where there was always something to eat and drink). When asked why she thought none of her parents had dropped out, Hiro replied:

> Hiro: Perhaps because we had our regular meetings I fitted the meeting in after lunch before three o'clock so that they could stay and pick up their children and they didn't mind doing that because it wasn't inconveniencing them and sometimes it would be just one or two. Might be the whole lot. But if some were having problems then I would have a meeting with just one person at a time. I didn't [always] have them all together at once.
>
> Mere: Right. So, you actually had the group meeting, and I attended some of those, but you also had some individual meetings.
>
> Hiro: Yes, cause I felt well if they were shy about some of the things they were doing and weren't too confident, well on a one to one they would open up and they wouldn't be embarrassed in front of other people.
>
> (Glynn and Berryman, 2003, p. 46)

Hiro saw it as crucial that both children and *whānau* on the project should learn not only the specific tutoring skills, but also important independent living skills. She referred to one mother in particular who, because of her experience in the project, began a concerted effort to learn the Māori language, and went on to become a valued assistant in the school. This mother grew not only in self-confidence but also in self-efficacy:

> Mere: The mother you are talking about was actually one of the mums that I thought was shy. She's certainly not shy now!
>
> Hiro: Oh heck no. She runs that office [the school office] up there when the office ladies are away.
>
> Mere: She really became . . .

> Hiro: ... confident, her self-esteem is up there [indicating with hand]. That's what I like to see, confident in her own ability ... It's all been hidden in there and it's just coming out.
>
> (Glynn and Berryman, 2003, pp. 50–1)

The project provided an authentic context for learning for the *whānau*, and for Hiro herself. *Whānau* members succeeded in helping their children improve their reading and writing at school. Meanwhile, Hiro herself was fully engaged with the researchers in developing new assessment and intervention strategies for improving literacy throughout the *whānau*. While Hiro made the most of the professional development opportunities arising within the project, she did so in order to better equip herself to help other *whānau* members:

> Hiro: Well I had heard a little bit about it [the Rotorua Home and School Project]. I was getting excited too and that's why I pushed John [the school principal] to ask if we could go first in the first group because it sounded exciting. Anything to help our children and our parents help their children ... There wasn't much [professional development available] in assessment for our children in Māori medium. I've always felt we're still playing catch up. I'd actually like to take the senior staff on that whakaputa whakaaro, [structured brainstorming], tuhi atu tuhi mai, [responsive writing] one day at a hui – just take them through that. Because that's excellent for them.
>
> (Glynn and Berryman, 2003, p. 52)

Research on transition from primary to secondary school

Berryman and Glynn (2003) report another study carried out by a small rural Māori immersion primary school. Although students from this school typically completed Year 8 as highly competent speakers, readers and writers of Māori, having been in immersion education for at least seven years, they faced major problems on transition to mainstream secondary school where all teaching and assessment was conducted in English.

This is a problem encountered regularly by many first language speakers across the world who are required, on transition to schooling in a new country, to continue their education now delivered through the medium of another language. Their literacy skills and literacy experiences, and their high level of participation and competence in literacy practices in their first language are neither recognized nor incorporated into classroom pedagogical practice in their new school. Rather, these achievements are all too often regarded as problematic and as barriers to learning the new language.

This was certainly the case for these students literate in Māori on entering their local high school, where all teaching occurred in English. As a result of being assessed (in English) by the school's evaluation strategies within their first few days, they were identified among the lowest achievers with low expectations for academic success, and offered little or no access to effective second language teaching and learning support. This was a major blow to these students' self-esteem, and their view of themselves as competent and high-achieving learners. It was also a blow to the high expectations held for them by their primary Māori immersion school teachers, their families and community. Both school and community resolved that this situation should not occur again with successive cohorts of Year 8 students having to face similar disappointment and loss of self-esteem.

This school and community, in collaboration, decided to develop a plan to introduce reading in English to their Māori immersion students during the final ten-week term of their primary schooling, to equip them better for transition to secondary school. While these students had never been formally taught to read or write in English, they were fluent readers and writers of Māori. The plan included enlisting the assistance of the third author of this book, who has tribal connections and thus obligations to students, the teachers and families of this community. She also has expertise and experience in developing effective support strategies for Māori students in both Māori and English immersion settings. The plan also incorporated the strong preferences of the school and community for the English reading programme not to compromise the high level of Māori literacy their students were achieving, and to introduce the programme to their Year 6 and Year 7 students, as well as their Year 8 students. The programme provided individual English reading and writing tutoring support by adult family and community members for each of the 21 students, and was implemented both at home and at school. Tutors were trained in three specific literacy strategies. The first strategy, Pause Prompt Praise (discussed in Chapter 4), was introduced for individual responsive tutoring of oral reading in English, and the second and third strategies, structured brainstorming and responsive written feedback (discussed in Chapter 5), were introduced to improve the rate and quality of students' writing in English.

Berryman and Glynn (2003) summarize the literacy outcomes of this programme as:

1   Family and community tutors implemented the reading and writing strategies reliably and comprehensively, so that students received the programme components fully and in their correct format.
2   Students within each of the three Year groups achieved substantial positive English reading and writing gains, on a range of different measures including rate, accuracy and comprehension (reading) and rate, accuracy and quality (writing).

3   Overall, students in each of the year groups demonstrated their greatest reading and writing gains at the assessment points directly following their separate 10-week participation in the programme.

4   Students in the Year 7 and Year 8 groups maintained or improved their reading and writing gains at follow-up assessment points, 10 and 20 weeks after they participated in the programme, and were by then independent of their original tutor support. These follow-up points for the Year 8 students occurred after they had been attending secondary school for the first 10-week term. There was no follow-up for Year 6 students who had just completed their time in the programme at the end of the study.

5   Literacy skills in Māori were not compromised by adding literacy skills in English.

The community and teachers in this small rural primary school were able to take collective responsibility for addressing and solving a serious second language transition problem which was being encountered by their graduating students on entering secondary school. In the process, both community and school learned to respect and value the funds of literacy knowledge and experience held by the other, and how the depth of expertise available in both settings could be combined in a way that greatly benefited students' school literacy achievement.

Conclusion

Potentially, family members and local communities are important resources in supporting the literacy learning of all children, and are a valuable additional resource for those who experience difficulties. The attitude of any educational institution and educational professionals to the role of families and community members, as prime educators of children, is of great significance. The kind of home/community-school partnership arrangements that exist, and the way in which schools respond to family culture and background in literacy initiatives, can serve to include or alienate communities, families and their children. Embedded within particular approaches and strategies are a variety of preconceptions about the ability and right of families and/or carers from a diversity of backgrounds and cultures to support the literacy development of their children. It is fundamentally important for schools to recognize these preconceptions and assumptions in order to negotiate effective, appropriate home-school literacy programmes which can harness all available resources to address difficulties in literacy development effectively and help to maintain the 'broad-based' instruction (Wragg et al., 1998) required to support all students' literacy development.

McNaughton and Glynn (1998) have identified the importance of shared knowledge and understandings between home and school for the success of students' literacy learning at school. There are clear implications for teacher professional development in this. McNaughton and Glynn note that this will require not only courses that celebrate cultural diversity, but incorporate practical knowledge and experience of the literacy practices that are associated with that diversity. An important challenge for literacy education in many countries is responding to diversity in equitable ways (Wilkinson, 1998). The time has come to look critically at the range of opportunities for teachers to extend their knowledge and experience, especially in working alongside the families and communities of the students they teach.

9   Summary and conclusions

Introduction

This book has taken a sociocultural approach to understanding literacy, and to understanding how teachers and schools might be more responsive to students experiencing difficulties with literacy. Three major themes have emerged from exploring developmental and pedagogical theory and practice focused on these understandings. The first theme concerns the importance of a sense of personal agency and responsibility within students experiencing difficulties on the one hand, coupled with the importance of their interaction and guided participation (Rogoff, 1990, 2003) in a range of literacy activities alongside more skilled adult or peer mediators' on the other. The second theme concerns the concept of literacy as social practice, through which students engage with different communities of practice (Lave and Wenger, 1991, 1999; Wenger, 1998) at home, at school and in their communities. The third theme concerns the pedagogical challenges arising from taking a sociocultural approach to literacy.

Personal agency and guided participation in literacy learning

The human development perspective adopted in this book has been one in which cognitive development and social development are seen as mutually facilitative and inseparable. The paradox that individual cognitive development and literacy are acquired through interaction around shared activities in responsive social contexts recurs within every chapter. All students, but especially those experiencing difficulties, are construed as active agents who become literate by engaging with their world through their language interactions within social and cultural contexts. From this perspective, it is literacy achievement that drives cognitive development, rather than the reverse. A key to understanding the power of these social interactions around shared literacy activities is the Vygotskian concept of working in the zone of proximal development (Vygotsky, 1978, 1981a, 1981b). The role of the more-skilled adult or peer mediators working in this zone is to support students to participate in activities in which they are as yet unable to participate on their own. However, this book has taken the position that these mediators do not simply construct scaffolded support for students (Wood, Bruner and Ross, 1976) and then remove it when they judge that students can engage in the activities on their own. Rather, they engage in a process of guided participation in contexts where there is reciprocity and mutual influence. By engaging in guided participation with students experiencing difficulties with literacy, adult or peer mediators gain in knowledge and, expertise, and establish or deepen their relationship with students as much as students do with them.

Literacy as participation in social practice

Within this book also, literacy achievement is understood as participation in social practice. Students learn to speak and read and write in contexts that are responsive and social. Within these contexts students become literate not only through observing mediators model effective oral and written language structure and usage, but also through seeking some measure of control over the language interactions and by participating in learning conversations. Particularly powerful learning conversations for students experiencing literacy difficulties are those in which both parties share in determining the topics, the timing and directions of the discourse. Both parties benefit from participating in these conversations and interactions. They gain information about the topics and activities involved from the perspective of the other person (the less-skilled or the more-skilled) and they establish and deepen personal relationships. Through learning how to initiate and maintain a conversation around shared experiences, students experiencing difficulties are able to participate in communities of literacy practice. Within these communities of practice they begin to acquire shared language and cultural experiences and to expand their understanding and use of different kinds of text and literacy tools. These, in turn, will enable them to participate in wider and more varied communities of practice, each with their own characteristic literacy practices, at home, at school and in the community.

Pedagogical challenges arising from a sociocultural approach to literacy

Homes and communities each have their own distinctive funds of knowledge and experience, each leading to its own literacy activities and communities of practice. Before entering pre-school or school, students are already participating in communities of literacy practice, and may be proficient in the stories, songs, music and in engaging in conversations with both adults and peers about cultural events that take place in their homes and communities.

However, major pedagogical challenges arise when the literacy activities and practices of the school differ substantially from those in students' homes and communities, and where teachers have little or no understanding or appreciation of those home and community literacy activities. This issue has been fully explored by McNaughton (2002). When this happens, the literacy knowledge and practices students bring with them to school are neither validated nor affirmed by the school's own literacy practices. Other students may experience extraordinary difficulties in mastering the conventions of school literacy whose pedagogical strategies may bear little relationship to their everyday lives. In either case, students experiencing difficulties may be construed by some teachers as illiterate, or at least as having severe deficits in the specific literacy skills and knowledge needed to participate in the literacy practices of the classroom. Having positioned students in this way, teachers and schools may then immerse them in remedial programmes and contexts constructed to assist them acquire the knowledge and skills seen as prerequisite to participation in classroom literacy activities.

However, this is problematic because the tasks and activities generated within these remedial programmes may become so focused on technical tasks and become so fragmented and decontextualized that the social and interactive and meaning-making qualities of literacy activities may be degraded or destroyed. Hence, far from preparing or equipping students experiencing difficulties to participate more fully in classroom literacy activities, such programmes may result in excluding students from participating in the communities of literacy practice within the classroom. Solutions to this dilemma are suggested as more likely to emerge from pedagogies that encourage communities and schools to collaborate in creating new spaces in which students' home and community literacy activities, as well as school literacy activities, can be acknowledged and respected. One strategic approach to achieving this is for schools to widen the range of text materials they access in their literacy programmes to include oral texts, written texts and multi-media texts, with which students from more diverse cultural backgrounds can already engage with successfully. Another strategic approach is for teachers to share with family and community members some of the 'school ways' of engaging with classroom texts, such as collaborative negotiation and co-construction of meaning. Combining these two strategic approaches may lead to teachers coming to a deeper understanding of their social and interactive role in students' literacy achievement.

Perhaps classroom and school literacy goals for students experiencing difficulties with literacy might be extended to include widening the range of different texts that students can engage with, and increasing the range of communities of literacy practice in which their students can successfully participate.

References

Adams, D. (1995) *A Hitch Hiker's Guide to the Galaxy*. New York: Ballantine/Random House.

Adams, M.J. (1994) *Beginning to Read: Thinking and Learning about Print*. Cambridge, Mass: MIT Press.

Agar, M. (1994) *Language Shock: Understanding the Culture of Conversation*. New York: Quill, William Morrow.

Allan, J. (1995) How are we doing? Teachers' views on the effectiveness of co-operative teaching, *Support for Learning*, 10(3): 127–32.

Alton-Lee, A. (2003) *Quality Teaching for Diverse Students in Schooling: Best Evidence Synthesis*. Medium Term Strategy Policy Division, Ministry of Education, Wellington.

Ames, G. and Archer, J. (1988) Achievement goals in the classroom: students' learning strategies and motivation processes, *Journal of Educational Psychology*, 80: 260–7.

Andrews, R., Torgerson, C., Beverton, S., Locke, T., Low, G., Robinson, A. and Zhu, D. (2004) The effect of grammar teaching (syntax) in English on 5- to 16-year-olds' accuracy and quality in written composition, in *Research Evidence in Education Library*. London: EPPI-centre, Social Science Research Unit, Institute of Education.

Apel, K. and Masterton, J. (1998) Assessment and treatment of narrative skills: what's the story?, in *RTN Learning Book*, Rockville, MD: American Speech-Language-Hearing Association.

Arvidson, G.C. (1970) *N. Z. C. E. R. alphabetical spelling list, Book 2*, 2nd edn. New Zealand Council for Educational Research, Wellington.

Au, K.H. (1994) Portfolio assessment: experiences at the Kamehameha Elementary Education Program, in S.W. Valencia, E.H. Hiebert and P.P. Afflerbach (eds) *Authentic Reading Assessment: Practices and Possibilities*, pp. 103–26, Newark, DE: International Reading Association.

Au, K.H.(2002) Multicultural factors and the effective instruction of students of diverse backgrounds, in A. Farstrup and S.J. Samuels (eds) *What Research Says about Reading Instruction*, pp. 392–413, Newark, DE: International Reading Association.

Au, K.H. and Carroll, J.H. (1997) Improving literacy through a constructivist approach: the KEEP Demonstration Classroom Project, *The Elementary School Journal*, 97(3): 203–21.

Audit Commission (1992) *Getting in on the Act: Provision for Pupils with Special Educational Needs*. London: HMSO.

Bandura, A. (1982) Self-efficacy mechanism in human agency, *American Psychologist*, 37: 122–47.

Bandura, A. and Schunk, D.H. (1981) Cultivating competence, self-efficacy and intrinsic interest through proximal self-motivation, *Journal of Personality and Social Psychology*, 41: 586–98.

Barnard, R. (2003) Introduction, in R. Barnard and T. Glynn (eds) *Cultural Issues in Children's Language and Literacy: Case Studies from Aotearoa/New Zealand*. Clevedon: Multilingual Matters.

Barton, D. (1995) *Literacy. An Introduction to the Ecology of Written Language*. Oxford: Blackwell.

Barton, D. and Hamilton, M. (1998) *Local Literacies. Reading and Writing in One Community*. London: Routledge.

Bentley, D. (2002) Teaching spelling: some questions answered, in J. Wearmouth, J. Soler and G. Reid (eds) *Addressing Difficulties in Literacy Development: Responses at Family, School, Pupil and Teacher Levels*. London: Routledge Falmer, pp. 340–53.

Benton, R. (1993) *The Māori Language Needs of Te Kōhanga Reo*. Report prepared for the Chief Executive, Ministry of Maori Development. Wellington: New Zealand Council for Educational Research.

Berryman, M. (2000a) Helping kids in need: changing perspectives on positive training relationships between parents and educators for the new millennium. *Kairaranga*, Issue 1, Volume 1.

Berryman, M. (2000b) Whānau-of-interest: a kaupapa Māori response for improving Māori achievement. Paper prepared for presentation at the NZARE conference, University of Waikato, December.

Berryman, M. (2001) Toitū Te Whānau, Toitū Te Iwi: a community approach to English transition, unpublished Masters of Education Thesis, University of Waikato, New Zealand.

Berryman, M. (2002) A model of school-wide assessment: practices from a kura kaupapa Māori. Paper prepared for a keynote presentation at the National Assessment Regional Seminar, Waikato.

Berryman, M. and Glynn, T. (2003) *Transition from Māori to English: A Community Approach*. Wellington: New Zealand Council for Education Research.

Berryman, M., Glynn, T., and Glynn, V. (2001a) Pause Prompt Praise: building effective home and school partnerships (video). William and Associates for Specialist Education Services.

Berryman, M., Glynn, T. and Glynn, V. (2001b) Me hoki whakamuri, kia haere whakamua: building culturally competent home and school partnerships (video). William and Associates for Specialist Education Services.

Berryman, M., Glynn, T., Walker, R. et al. (2002) *SES Sites of Effective Special Education Practice for Māori 2001*. Draft report to the SES Board and Executive Team, Specialist Education Services.

Berryman, M., Langdon, Y., Boasa-Dean, T., Reweti, M., and Rau, C. (2002) Te pānui whā miniti: evaluating this reading tutoring programme in a Māori language context. Report to the Ministry of Education.

Berryman, M., Reweti, M., O'Brien, K., Langdon, Y., and Glynn, T. (2001) *Kia Puāwai Ai te Reo: Strategies and Activities to Help Students Write in Māori and in English*. Specialist Education Services.

Best, R. (1991) Support teaching in a comprehensive school, *Support for Learning*, 6(1): 27–31.

Bishop, R. and Glynn, T. (1999) *Culture Counts: Changing Power Relations in Education*. Palmerston North, NZ: Dunmore Press.

Bishop, R., Berryman, M., and Richardson, C. (2001) Te Toi Huarewa: effective teaching and learning strategies, and effective teaching materials for improving the reading and writing in te reo Māori of students aged five to nine in Māori medium education. Final Report to the Ministry of Education.

Bishop, R., Berryman, M., and Richardson, C. (2002) Te Toi Huarewa: effective teaching and learning in total immersion Māori language educational settings, *Canadian Journal of Native Education*, 26(1).

Bishop, R., Berryman, M., Richardson, C., and Tiakiwai, S. (2003) Te Kotahitanga: the experiences of year 9 and 10 Māori students in mainstream classrooms. Final report to the Research Division, Ministry of Education, Wellington.

Blackledge, A. (2000) *Literacy, Power and Social Justice*. Stoke on Trent, Staffs: Trentham.

Booth, T. and Goodey, C. (1996) Playing for the sympathy vote, *Guardian*, 21 May, p. 5.

Borkowski, J.G., Weyhing, R.S. and Carr, M. (1988) Effects of attributional retraining on strategy-based reading comprehension in learning-disabled students, *Journal of Educational Psychology*, 80: 46–53.

Bourdieu, P. and Passeron, J.C. (1973) *Reproduction in Education, Society and Culture*. London: Sage.

Bradley, L. (1981) The organisation of motor patterns for spelling: an effective remedial strategy for backward readers, *Developmental Medicine and Child Neurology*, 23: 83–91.

Broadfoot, P. (1996) *Education, Assessment and Society*. Buckingham: Open University Press.

Bronfenbrenner, U. (1979) *The Ecology of Human Development: Experiments by Nature and Design*. Cambridge, Massachusetts: Harvard University Press.

Brown, B. and Thomson, L. (2000) Cooperative learning in New Zealand schools. Palmerston North: Dunmore Press.

Brown, D., Moore, D., Thomson, C. et al. (2000) Resource teachers learning and behaviour: an ecological approach to special education, *Australasian Journal of Special Education*, 24(1): 5–20.

Bruner, J. (1990) *Acts of Meaning*. Cambridge, Mass: Harvard University Press.

Bruner, J. (1996) *The Culture of Education*. Cambridge, Massachusetts: Harvard University Press.

Calkins, L.M. (1991) *Living between the Lines*. Portsmouth, NH: Heinemann.

Cambourne, B. (1988) *The Whole Story: Natural Learning and the Acquisition of Literacy in the Classroom*. Auckland, NZ: Scholastic.

Cavanagh, T. (2003) Schooling for peace: caring for our children in school, *Experiments in Education*, 31: 139–49.

Caygill, R. and Eley, L. (2001) Evidence about the effects of assessment task format on student achievement. Paper presented at the British Educational Research Association, University of Leeds.

Cazden, C. (1988) *Classroom Discourse: The Language of Teaching and Learning*. Portsmouth, NH: Heinemann.

Clarke, S., Timperley, H., and Hattie, J. (2003) *Unlocking Formative Assessment: Practical Strategies for Enhancing Students' Learning in the Primary and Intermediate Classroom*. Auckland: Hodder Moa Beckett.

Clay, M. (1972) *Reading the Patterning of Complex Behaviour*. Auckland: Heinemann Educational Books.

Clay, M. (1975) *What Did I Write?* Auckland: Heinemann.

Clay, M. (1991) *Becoming Literate: The Construction of Inner Control*. Auckland: Heinemann.

Clay, M. (1993) *Reading Recovery: A Guidebook for Teachers in Training*. Auckland: Heinemann.

Cline, T. (ed.) (1992) *The Assessment of Special Educational Needs*. London: Routledge.

Committee of Inquiry into the Education of Children from Ethnic Minority Groups (personal author: Lord Swann) (1985) *Education for All*. London: HMSO.

Crandall, V.G., Katkovsky, W. and Crandall, V.J. (1965) Children's beliefs in their own control of reinforcements in intellectual-academic achievement situations, *Child Development*, 36: 91–109.

Croft, C. and Mapa, L. (1998) *Spell-Write*. Wellington: NZCER.

Crooks, T.J. (1988) The impact of classroom evaluation practices on students, *Review of Educational Research*, 58(4): 438–81.

Crystal, D. (ed.) (1995) *The Cambridge Encyclopedia of the English Language*. Cambridge: Cambridge University Press.

Dale, N. (1996) *Working with Families of Children with Special Needs: Partnership and Practice*. London: Routledge.

Daniel, L.G. and King, D.A. (1998) Knowledge and use of testing and measurement literacy of elementary and secondary teachers, *The Journal of Educational Research*, 91(6): 331–45.

Davie, C.E., Butler, N. and Goldstein, H. (1972) *From Birth to Seven: A Report of the National Child Development Study*. London: Longman/National Children's Bureau.

Davies, S. (2004) Barriers to belonging: students' perceptions of factors which affect participation in schools, in J. Wearmouth, T. Glynn, R.C. Richmond and M. Berryman (eds) *Inclusion and Behaviour Management in Schools: Issues and Challenges*. London: Fulton, pp. 322–41.

Delgado-Gaitan, C. (1990) *Literacy for Empowerment*. London: Falmer.

Department for Education and Employment (1998) *The National Literacy Strategy: Framework for Teaching*. London: DfEE.

Department for Education and Employment/Qualifications and Curriculum Authority (1997) *The Implementation of the National Literacy Strategy*. London: DfEE/QCA.

Department for Education and Skills (2001) *Special Educational Needs Code of Practice*. London: DfES.

Department for Education, Northern Ireland (1998) *Code of Practice for the Identification and Assessment of Special Educational Needs*. Bangor, NI: DENI.

Department of Education (1985) *Reading in Junior Classes with Guidelines to the Revised 'Ready to Read' Series*. Wellington: Department of Education.

Department of Education and Science (1967) *Children and their Primary Schools* (The Plowden Report). London: HMSO.

Department of Education and Science (1975) *A Language for Life: Report of the Committee of Enquiry Appointed by the Secretary of State for Education and Science under the Chairmanship of Sir Alan Bullock* (The Bullock Report): London: HMSO.

Dewes, T. (1977) The case for oral arts, in M. King (ed.) *Te aō hurihuri the World Moves On*, pp. 46–63. New Zealand: Methuen Publications Ltd.

Dewey, J. (1933) *How We Think*. Boston: Health (original work published 1909).

Dineen, J.P., Clark, H.B. and Risley, T.R. (1977) Peer tutoring among elementary students: educational benefits to the tutor, *Journal of Applied Behavior Analysis*, 10: 231–8.

Dombey, H. (1988) Partners in the telling, in M. Meek and C. Mills (eds) *Language and Literacy in the Primary School*. London: Falmer Press.

Donaldson, M. (1978) *Children's Minds*. London: Croom Helm Ltd.

Duranti, A., Ochs, E. and Ta'ase, E.K. (2004) Change and tradition in literacy instruction in a Samoan American community, pp. 159–70, in E. Gregory, S. Long and D. Volk (eds) *Many Pathways to Literacy: Young Children Learning with Siblings, Grandparents, Peers and Communities*. London: RoutledgeFalmer.

Dweck, C.S. (1975) The role of expectations and attributions in the alleviation of learned helplessness, *Journal of Personality and Social Psychology*, 31: 674–85.

Dweck, C.S. and Licht, B.G. (1980) Learned helplessness and intellectual achievement, in J. Garber and M.E.P. Seligman (eds) *Human Helplessness: Theory and Applications*. New York: Academic Press.

Dyson, A.H. (1997) *Writing Superheroes: Contemporary Childhood, Popular Culture and Classroom Literacy*. New York: Teachers College Press.

Dyson, A.H. (2003) 'Welcome to the Jam': popular culture, school literacy, and the making of childhoods, *Harvard Educational Review*, 73(3): 328–61.

Education Review Office (1995) *Kura Kaupapa Maori*. Wellington, NZ: Education Review Office.

Elley, W.B. (1975) *Assessing the Difficulty of Reading Materials: The Noun Frequency Method*. Wellington, NZ: NZCER.

Englert, C. and Raphael, T. (1988) Constructing well-formed prose: process, structure and metacognition in the instruction of expository writing, *Exceptional Children*, (54): 513–20.

Farrell, P. (1999) The management, role and training of learning support assistants, Research Report RR 161, London: DfEE.

Farver, J.A.M. (1993) Cultural differences in scaffolding pretend play: a comparison of American and Mexican-American mother-child and sibling-child pairs, in K. MacDonald (ed.) *Parent-Child Play: Descriptions and Implications*. Albany, NY: SUNY Press.

Fisher, R., Lewis, M. and Davis, B. (2000) Progress and performance in National Literacy Strategy classrooms, *Journal of Research in Reading*, 23(3): 1–15.

Flesch, R. (1994) *The Art of Readable Writing and How to Test Readability*. New York: Wiley.

Florian, L. and Rouse, M. (2001) Inclusive practice in English secondary schools, *Cambridge Journal of Education*, 31(3): 399–411.

Flower, L. and Hayes, J. (1980) The dynamics of composing: making plans and joggling constraints, in L. Gregg and E. Steinberg (eds) *Cognitive Processes in Writing*, pp. 31–50. Hillsdale, NJ: Erlbaum.

Fuchs, D., Fuchs, L.S., Mathes, P.G. and Lipsey, M.W. (2000) Reading differences between low-achieving students with and without learning disabilities: a meta-analysis, in R. Gersten, E.P. Schiller and S. Vaughn (eds) *Contemporary Special Education Research*, pp. 81–104. Mahwah, NJ: Erlbaum.

Gallimore, R. and Goldenberg, L. (1993) Activity settings of early literacy: home and school factors in children's early literacy, in E. Forman, N. Minick and C. Stome (eds) *Contexts for Learning: Sociocultural Dynamics in Children's Development*. New York: Oxford University Press.

Gee, J. (1990) *Social Linguistics and Literacies: Ideology in Discourses*. Basingstoke: Falmer Press.

Gee, J. (2000) New people in new worlds: networks, the new capitalism and schools, in B. Cope and M. Kalantzis (eds) *Multiliteracies: Literacy Learning and the Design of Social Futures*. London: Routledge.

Gentry, R. (1987) *Spel is a Four Letter Word*. Auckland, NZ: Scholastic.

Gewirtz, S., Ball, S.J. and Bowe, R. (1995) *Markets, Choice and Equity in Education*. Buckingham: Open University Press.

Glynn, E.L. and McNaughton, S.S. (1975) Trust your own observations: criterion referenced assessment of reading progress, *The Slow Learning Child*, 22(2): 91–108.

Glynn, T. (1985a) Contexts for independent learning, *Education Psychology*, 5(1): 5–15.

Glynn, T. (1985b) Contexts for learning: implications for mildly and moderately handicapped children, *Australia and New Zealand Journal of Developmental Disabilities*, 11(4): 257–63.

Glynn, T. (1987a) Contexts for independent learning for children with special needs, *Behavioural Approaches with Children*, 11(1): 5–19.

Glynn, T. (1987b) More power to the parents: behavioural approaches to remedial tutoring at home, in W.K. (ed.) *The Behaviourist in the Classroom*. London: Allen and Unwin.

Glynn, T. (1995) Pause Prompt Praise: reading tutoring procedures for home and school partnership, in S. Wolfendale and K. Topping (eds) *Parental Involvement in Literacy: Effective Partnerships in Education*, pp. 33–44. London: Cassell.

Glynn, T. (2003) Responding to language diversity: a way forward for New Zealand Education, in R. Barnard and T. Glynn (eds) *Cultural Issues in Children's Language and Literacy: Case Studies from Aotearoa/New Zealand*, pp. 273–81. Clevedon: Multilingual Matters.

Glynn, T. and Glynn, V. (1980) Centralisation of spelling gains into written expression with parent-teacher remedial programme, unpublished manuscript, Department of Education, University of Auckland, New Zealand.

Glynn, T. and Glynn, V. (1986) Shared reading by Cambodian mothers and children learning English as a second language: reciprocal gains, *The Exceptional Child*, 33(3): 159–72.

Glynn, T. and McNaughton, S. (1985) The Mangere home and school remedial reading procedures: continuing research on their effectiveness, *New Zealand Journal of Psychology*, 15(2): 66–77.

Glynn, T. and McNaughton, S. (2002) Trust your own observations: assessment of reader and tutor behaviour in learning to read in English and Māori, *International Journal of Disability, Development and Education*, 49 (2): 163–73.

Glynn, T., Berryman, M. and Glynn, V. (2000a) The Rotorua home and school literacy project: final report to the Rotorua Energy Charitable Trust and the Research and Statistics Division, Ministry of Education, Wellington.

Glynn, T., Berryman, M. and Glynn, V. (2000b) Reading and writing gains for Māori students in mainstream schools: effective partnerships in the Rotorua home and school literacy project. Paper presented at the World Congress on Reading, Auckland, New Zealand.

Glynn, T., Berryman, M. and Harawira, W. (1996) Kia puāwai ai te reo (Video). Audio Visual Production Section, Higher Education Development Centre, University of Otago.

Glynn, T., Berryman, M. and Weiss, S. (2003) Responding to the message: responsive written feedback in a Maori to English transition context. Paper presented at the International Conference on Language, Education and Diversity, University of Waikato.

Glynn, T., Berryman, M., Atvars, K. and Harawira, W. (1998) Assessing student learning and behaviour change within a kaupapa Māori setting. Paper presented at the NZARE conference, Dunedin.

Glynn, T., Berryman, M., Bidois, P., Furlong, M., Thatcher, J., Walker, R. and Atvars, K. (1996) Bilingual reading gains for tutors and tutees in a Māori language immersion programme, in B. Webber (ed.) *He Paepae Kōrero: Research Issues in Māori Education*, pp. 35–58. Wellington: New Zealand Council for Educational Research.

Glynn, T., Berryman, M., Grace, H. and Glynn, V. (2004) Activating whānau (extended family) processes within a community and school literacy partnership, He Puna Kōrero, *Journal of Māori and Pacific Development*, 5(2): 14–30.

Glynn, T., Berryman, M., O'Brien, K. and Bishop, R. (2000) Responsive written feedback on students' writing in a Māori language revitalisation context, in R. Harlow and R. Barnard (eds) *Proceedings of the Conference, 'Bilingualism at the Ends of the Earth'*. Hamilton: University of Waikato, Department of General and Applied Linguistics.

Glynn, T., Bethune, N., Crooks, T., Ballard, K. and Smith, J. (1992) Reading recovery in context: implementation and outcome, *Educational Psychology*, 12(3/4): 249–61.

Glynn, T., McNaughton, S., Robinson, V. and Quinn, M. (1979) *Remedial Reading at Home: Helping You to Help Your Child*. Wellington: New Zealand Council for Educational Research.

Glynn, V. (1992) Peer tutoring bilingual children in a cooperative learning classroom, *Many Voices: A Journal of New Settlers and Multicultural Education Issues*, May: 14–17.

Goldenberg, C. (1991) *Instructional Conversations and Their Classroom Application*, Educational Practice Report 2. Santa Cruz, CA: The National Center for Research on Cultural Diversity and Second Language Learning.

Goodman, K. (1967) Reading: a psycholinguistic guessing game, *Journal of the Reading Specialist*, 6(4): 126–35.

Goodman, K. (1986) *What's Whole in Whole-Language?* Portsmouth, NH: Heinemann.

Goodman, K. (1996) *On Reading*. Portsmouth, NH: Heinemann.

Graham, S. and Harris, K. R. (1993) Teaching writing strategies to students with learning disabilities: issues and recommendations, in L.J. Meltzer (ed.) (1993) *Strategy Assessment and Instruction for Students with Learning Disabilities*. Austin, Texas: Pro-Ed.

Graham, S., MacArthur, C., Schwartz, S. and Voth, T. (1989) Improving LD students' compositions using a strategy involving product and process goal-setting. Paper presented at Annual Meeting of the American Educational Research Association, San Francisco.

Graves, A., Montague, M. and Wong, Y. (1989) The effects of procedural facilitation on story composition of learning disabled students. Paper presented at Annual Meeting of the American Educational Research Association, San Francisco.

Graves, D. (1983) *Writing: Teachers and Children at Work*. Exeter, NH: Heinemann.

Graves, D. and Hansen, J. (1983) The author's chair, *Language Arts*, 60(2): 176–83.

Greenhalgh, K.S. and Strong, C.J. (2001) Literate language narratives of children with typical language and children with language impairment, *Language, Speech and Hearing Services in Schools*, 32: 114–25.

Greeno, J.G. (1998) The situativity of knowing, learning and research, *American Psychologist*, 53(1): 5–17.

Gregory, E. (1996) *Making Sense of a New World*. London: Paul Chapman.

Gregory, E. (ed.) (1997) *One Child, Many Worlds: Early Learning in Multicultural Communities*. London: David Fulton.

Gregory, E. (1998) Siblings as mediators of literacy in linguistic minority communities, *Language and Education*, 12(1): 33–54.

Gregory, E. (2004a) Bridges to literacy, in M. Nind, K. Sheehy and K. Simmons (eds) *Inclusive Education: Learners and Learning Contexts*, pp. 263–80. London: David Fulton.

Gregory, E. (2004b) Invisible teachers of literacy: collusion between siblings and teachers in creating classroom cultures, *Literacy*, July: 97–105.

Gregory, E., Long, S. and Volk, D. (2004) A sociocultural approach to learning, in E. Gregory, S. Long and D. Volk (eds) *Many Pathways to Literacy: Young Children Learning with Siblings, Grandparents, Peers and Communities*, pp. 6–20. New York and London: Routledge Falmer.

Gregory, E., Williams, A., Baker, D. and Street, B. (2004) Introducing literacy to 4 year olds: creating classroom cultures in three schools, *Journal of Early Literacy Learning*, 4(1): 85–107.

Gross, J. (1996) The weight of the evidence, *Support for Learning*, 11(1): 3–8.

Habermas, J. (1974) *Theory and Practice*, translated from the German by John Viertel. London: Heinemann.

Hager, J. and Gable, R. (1993) Content reading assessment: a rethinking of methodology, *The Clearing House*, 66(5): 269–73.

Hall, R. (1983) *Multiple Choice*. A play first produced at New Mexico State University, New Mexico.

Hamilton Education Board Resource Teachers of Reading (1989) Standard 2 Survey: Reading/Language. Hamilton Education Board.

Hannon, P. (1999) Rhetoric and research in family literacy, *British Educational Research Journal*, 26(1): 121–38.

Hannon, P. and McNally, J. (1986) Children's Understanding and Cultural Factors in Reading Test Performance, *Educational Review* 38 (3): 269–80.

Harris, K.R. and Graham, S. (1985) Improved learning-disabled composition skills: self-control strategy training, *Learning Disability Quarterly*, (8): 27–36.

Harrison, C., Bailey, M. and Dewar, A. (1998) Responsive reading assessment: is postmodern assessment of reading possible?, in C. Harrison and T. Salinger (eds) *Assessing Reading 1: International Perspectives on Reading Assessment*. London: Routledge.

Hattie, J. (1999) Influences on student learning. Inaugural address, University of Auckland at www.arts.auckland.ac.nz/edu/staff/jhattie/Inaugral.html

Heath, S.B. (1983) *Ways with Words: Language, Life and Work in Communities and Classrooms*. Cambridge: Cambridge University Press.

Heaton, P. (1996) *Parents in Need*. London: Whurr.

Hersen, M. and Barlow, C. (1977) Single case experimental designs: strategies for studying behaviour change. New York: Pergamon Press.

Hewison, J. and Tizard, J. (1980) Parental involvement and reading attainment, *British Journal of Educational Psychology*, 58: 184–90.

Hohepa, M., Smith, G., Smith L. and McNaughton, S. (1992) Te Kōhanga Reo. Hei tikanga ako i te reo Māori: Te Kōhanga Reo as a context for language learning, *Educational Psychology*, 12 (3/4): 333–46.

Hollings, M., Jefferies, R. and McArdell, P. (1992) *Assessment in Kura Kaupapa Maori and Maori Language Immersion Programmes*. Wairarapa: Wairarapa Community Polytechnic.

Houghton, S. and Bain, A. (1993) Peer tutoring with ESL and below-average readers, *Journal of Behavioral Education*, 3(2): 125–42.

Houghton, S. and Glynn, T. (1993) Peer tutoring of below average secondary school readers with Pause Prompt and Praise: successive introduction of tutoring components, *Behaviour Change*, 10(2): 75–85.

Jerram, H., Glynn, T. and Tuck, B. (1988) Responding to the message: providing a social context for children learning to write, *Educational Psychology*, 8(1/2): 31–40.

Johnson, D.W. and Johnson, R.T. (1992) Encouraging thinking through constructive controversy, in N. Davidson and T. Worsham (eds) *Enhancing Thinking Through Cooperative Learning*. New York: Teachers College Press.

Johnson, M. (2002) Multi-sensory teaching of reading in mainstream settings, in J. Wearmouth, J. Soler and G. Reid (eds) *Addressing Difficulties in Literacy Development: Responses at Family, School, Pupil and Teacher Levels*. London: Routledge Falmer.

Jones, I. (2003) Collaborative writing and children's use of literate language: a sequential analysis of social interaction, *Journal of Early Childhood Literacy*, 3(2): 165–78.

Kamehameha Schools (1993) *Native Hawaiian Educational Assessment 1993*. Honolulu: Kamehameha Schools Bernice Pauahi Bishop Estate, Office of Program Evaluation and Planning.

Karetu, S. (1977) Language and protocol on the marae, in M. King (ed) *Te ao hurihuri the World Moves On*, pp. 31–45. New Zealand: Methuen Publications.

Kawagley, A.O. (1995) *A Yupiaq Worldview: A Pathway to Ecology and Spirit*. Prospect Heights, IL: Waveland Press.

Klinger, J.K., Vaughn, S., Arguelles, M.E., Hughes, M.T. and Leftwich, S.A. (2004) Collaborative strategic reading, *Remedial and Special Education*, 25(5): 291–302.

Krampen, G. (1987) Differential effects of teacher comments, *Journal of Educational Psychology*, 79: 137–46.

Lave, J. (1993) The practice of learning, in S. Chaiklin and L. Lave (eds) *Understand-*

ing Practice: Perspectives on Activity and Context, pp. 3–32. Cambridge: Cambridge University Press.

Lave, J. and Wenger, E. (1991) *Situated Learning: Legitimate Peripheral Participation.* Cambridge: Cambridge University Press.

Lave, J. and Wenger, F. (1999) Learning and pedagogy in communities of practice, in J. Leach and B. Moon (eds) *Learners and Pedagogy.* London: Paul Chapman.

Lederer, J. (2000) Reciprocal teaching in inclusive elementary schools, *Journal of Learning Disabilities*, 33(1): 91–106.

Lewis, A. (1995) *Special Needs Provision in Mainstream Primary Schools.* Stoke: Trentham.

Limbrick, L., McNaughton, S. and Glynn, T. (1985) Reading gains for underachieving tutors and tutees in a cross age peer tutoring programme, *Journal of Child Psychology and Psychiatry*, 26(6): 939–53.

Lovey, J. (1995) *Supporting Special Educational Needs in Secondary School Classrooms.* London: Fulton.

Lunzer, E. and Gardner, K. (1986) *The Effective Use of Reading.* London: Heinemann.

Lüthi, Max (1970) Once Upon a Time: On the Nature of Fairy Tales. Bloomington: University of Indiana Press.

MacArthur, C. and Graham, S. (1987) Learning disabled students' composing under three methods of text production: handwriting, word processing, and dictation, *Journal of Special Education*, 21: 22–42.

Mair, M. (1988) Psychology as storytelling, *International Journal of Personal Construct Psychology*, 1: 125–32.

Mastropieri, M.A., Scruggs, T.E., Bakken, J.P. and Whedon, C. (1996) A synthesis of research in learning disabilities, in T.E. Scruggs and M.A. Mastropieri (eds) *Advances in Learning and Behavioural Disabilities.* Greenwich, CT: JAI Press.

McNaughton, S. (1995) *Patterns of Emergent Literacy: Processes of Development and Transition.* Melbourne: Oxford University Press.

McNaughton, S. (1996) Ways of parenting and cultural identity, *Culture and Psychology*, 2(2): 173–201.

McNaughton, S. (2002) *Meeting of Minds.* Wellington: Learning Media.

McNaughton, S. and Glynn, T. (1998) Effective collaboration: what teachers need to know about communities. Paper presented at the Annual Conference of the New Zealand Council for Teacher Education, University of Waikato, Hamilton, October.

McNaughton, S., Glynn, T. and Robinson, V. (1987) *Pause, Prompt and Praise: Effective Tutoring of Remedial Reading.* Birmingham: Positive Products.

McNaughton, S., Glynn, T., Robinson, V. and Quinn, M. (1981) *Parents as Remedial Reading Tutors: Issues for Home and School.* Wellington: New Zealand Council for Educational Research.

Medcalf, J.E. and Glynn, T. (1987) Assisting teachers to implement peer-tutored remedial reading using Pause Prompt and Praise procedures, *Queensland Journal of Guidance and Counselling*, 1(1): 11–23.

Medcalf, J., Glynn, T. and Moore, D. (2004) Peer tutoring in writing: a school systems approach, *Educational Psychology in Practice*, 20(2): 156–78.

Mehan, H. (1996) The politics of representation, in S. Chaiklin and J. Lave (eds) *Understanding Practice: Perspectives on Activity and Context*. Cambridge: Cambridge University Press.

Meltzer, L.S. (ed.) (1993) *Strategy Assessment and Instruction for Students with Learning Disabilities*. Austin, TX: Pro-Ed.

Ministry of Education (1993) *The New Zealand Curriculum Framework*. Wellington, NZ: Learning Media.

Ministry of Education (1994a) *Assessment: Policy to Practice*. Wellington, NZ: Learning Media.

Ministry of Education (1994b) *English in the New Zealand Curriculum*. Wellington, NZ: Learning Media.

Ministry of Education (1996a) *Exploring Language: A Handbook for Teachers*. Wellington, NZ: Learning Media.

Ministry of Education (1996b) *The Learner as a Reader*. Wellington, NZ: Learning Media.

Ministry of Education (1997) *Planning and Assessment in English*. Wellington, NZ: Learning Media.

Ministry of Education (1999) *Literacy Experts Group Report to the Secretary of Education*. Wellington: Ministry of Education.

Ministry of Education (2002) *Best Evidence Synthesis*. Wellington, NZ: Learning Media.

Ministry of Education (2004) Curriculum update, *He Korero Matauranga*, Issue 54, April.

Mittler, P. (2000) *Working Towards Inclusive Education: Social Contexts*. London: Fulton.

Moll, L.C. (1992) Literacy research in community and classrooms: a sociocultural approach, in R. Beach, J.L. Green, M.L. Kamil and T. Shanahan (eds) *Multidisciplinary Perspectives on Literacy Research*. Urbana, IL: National Council of Teachers of English.

Montgomery, J.K. and Kahn, N.L. (2003) You are going to be an author: adolescent narratives as intervention, *Communication Disorders Quarterly*, 24(3): 143–52.

Murphy, S. (2002) Literacy assessment and the politics of identity, in J. Soler, J. Wearmouth and G. Reid (eds) *Contextualising Difficulties in Literacy Development: Exploring Politics, Culture, Ethnicity and Ethics*, pp. 87–101. London: Routledge.

New Zealand Maori Education Commission (1998) *Report to the Minister of Māori Affairs*, Wellington.

Ngā Kete Kōrero Framework Team (1996) *Ngā Kete Kōrero Policy Project*. A report to Te Puni Kōkiri, Wellington: Te Puni Kōkiri.

Nind, M. and Wearmouth, J. (2004) *A Systematic Review of Pedagogical Approaches That Can Effectively Include Children with Special Educational Needs in Main-*

stream Classrooms. London: EPPI Centre, London University Institute of Education.

Norwich, B. (1994) Differentiation from the perspective of resolving tensions between basic social values and assumptions about individual differences, *Curriculum Studies*, 2(3): 289–308.

Open University (2002) Video programme 4, E801: *Difficulties in Literacy Development*. Milton Keynes: Open University.

Ostler, C. (1991) *Dyslexia: A Parents' Survival Guide*. Godalming: Ammonite Books.

Palincsar, A.S. (1986) The role of dialogue in providing scaffolded instruction, *Educational Psychologist* (21): 73–98.

Palincsar, A.S. (1998) Social constructivist perspectives on teaching and learning, *Annual Review of Psychology* (49): 345–75.

Palincsar, A.S. and Brown, A.L. (1984) Reciprocal teaching of comprehension: fostering- and comprehension-monitoring activities, *Cognition and Instruction*, 1(2): 117–75.

Palincsar, A.S., Brown, A.L. and Campione, J.C. (1993) First grade dialogues for knowledge acquisition and use, in E.A. Foreman, N. Minick and C.A. Stone (eds) *Contexts for Learning*. New York: Oxford University Press.

Pearson, P., Destefano, L. and Garcia, G. (1998) Ten dilemmas of assessment of performance assessment, in C. Harrison and T. Salinger (eds) *Assessing Reading 1: International Perspectives on Reading Assessment*. London: Routledge.

Peddie, R. (2000) *Evaluation of the Assessment for Better Learning Professional Development Programmes: Final Report*. Auckland: Auckland Uniservices for the Ministry of Education.

Pellegrini, A.D., Galda, L., Bartini, M. and Charak, D. (1998) Oral language and literacy in context: the role of social relationships, *Merrill-Palmer Quarterly*, 44(1): 38–54.

Pere, R. (1982) Ako: concepts and learning in the Maori tradition, Working Paper no. 17, Department of Sociology, University of Waikato.

Perera, K. (1979) The language demands of school learning, in course PE232 *Language Development*, Milton Keynes: Open University.

Peters, M. (1967) *Spelling: Caught or Taught?* London: RKP.

Phillips, G., McNaughton, S. and MacDonald, S. (2001) Picking up the pace: effective literacy interventions for accelerated progress over the transition into decile one schools. Final report to the Ministry of Education on the professional development associated with the Early Childhood Primary Links via Literacy (ECPL) Project. Auckland: The Child Literacy Foundation and the Woolf Fisher Research Centre.

Phillips, S. (1999) *Management Skills for SEN Co-ordinators in the Primary School*. London: Falmer.

Pickens, J., Glynn, T. and Whitehead, D. (2004) Students reading together: a modified reciprocal teaching approach to improve comprehension, peer interaction and strategy use, *SET Research Information for Teachers*, (3): 14–18.

Qualifications and Curriculum Authority/Department for Education and Employment (1999) *Early Learning Goals*. London: QCA/DfEE.

Rattray, D. (1999) Respect versus discipline: a native perspective. Paper presented at the 1996 World Indigenous People's Conference on Education. Center for Cross-Cultural Studies, University of Alaska, Fairbanks.

Reason, R. (2002) From assessment to intervention: the educational psychology perspective, in G. Reid and J. Wearmouth (eds) *Dyslexia and Literacy: Research and Practice*. Chichester: Wiley.

Reason, R. and Boote, R. (1994) *Helping Children with Reading and Spelling*. London: Routledge.

Rees, D. and the Education Department of Western Australia (2001) *Spelling Developmental Continuum*. Melbourne, Australia: Rigby Heinemann.

Riddick, B. (1996) *Living with Dyslexia*. London and New York: Routledge.

Riley, J. (2001) The National Literacy Strategy: success with literacy for all?, *Curriculum Journal*, 12(1): 29–58.

Rogoff, B. (1990) *Apprenticeship in Thinking*. New York: Oxford University Press.

Rogoff, B. (2003) *The Cultural Nature of Human Development*. Oxford: Oxford University Press.

Rogoff, B., Paradise, R., Mejia Arauz, R., Correa-Chávez, M. and Angelillo, C. (2003) Firsthand learning through intent participation, *Annual Review of Psychology*, 54: 1–15.

Royal Tangaere, A. (1997a) *Learning Māori Together: Kōhanga Reo and Home*. Wellington: New Zealand Council for Educational Research.

Royal Tangaere, A. (1997b) Te kōhanga reo: more than a language nest, Early Childhood Folio 3. A Collection of Recent Research. Wellington: New Zealand Council for Educational Research.

Salmon, P. (1998) *Life at School*. London: Constable.

Sanders, M. and Glynn, E.L. (1977) Functional analysis of a programme for training high and low preference peers to modify disruptive classroom behaviour, *Journal of Applied Behavior Analysis*, 10(3): 503.

Sapir, E. (1970) *Language: An Introduction to the Study of Speech*. London: Hart-Davies.

Sarbin, T. (1986) *Narrative Psychology: The Storied Nature of Human Conduct*. New York: Praeger.

Scardamalia, M. and Bereiter, C. (1986) The development of evaluative, diagnostic and remedial capabilities in children's composing, in M. Martlew (ed.) *The Psychology of Written Language: Developmental and Educational Perspectives*, pp. 67–95. London: Wiley.

Schön, D. (1983) *The Reflective Practitioner*. New York: Basic.

Schön, D. (1987) *Educating the Reflective Practitioner*. London: Jossey-Bass.

Schunk, D.H. (1989) Self efficacy and cognitive achievement: implications for students with learning problems, *Journal of Learning Disabilities*, 22: 14–22.

Scribner, S. and Cole, M. (1981) *The Psychology of Literacy*. Cambridge, MA: Harvard University Press.

Scriven, J. and Glynn, T. (1983) Performance feedback on written tasks for low achieving secondary students, *New Zealand Journal of Educational Studies*, 18(2): 134–45.

Simon, J. and Smith, L.T. (eds) (1998) *A Civilising Mission ? Perceptions and Representations of New Zealand Native Schools System*. Auckland: Auckland University Press.

Sligo, F., Fontaine, S. and O'Neill, D. (1999) Valuing structure over style, *New Zealand Educational Review*, 14 (May): 7.

Smith, G.H. (1995) Whakaoho whānau: new formations of whānau as an innovative intervention into Māori cultural and educational crises, *Koanga*, 1(1).

Smith, G.H. (1997) Kaupapa Māori as transformative praxis. Unpublished PhD thesis, University of Auckland.

Smith, J. and Elley, W. (1997) *How Children Learn to Write*. New Zealand: Longman.

Smith, L.T. (1999) *Decolonizing Methodologies: Research and Indigenous Peoples*. Dunedin: University of Otago Press.

Snowling, M.J. (2000) *Dyslexia*, 2nd edn. Oxford: Blackwell.

Stanovich, K. (1986) Matthew effects in reading: some consequences of individual differences in the acquisition of literacy, *Reading Research Quarterly*, 21(4): 360–406.

Stanovich, K. (1988) Explaining the difference between the dyslexic and the garden-variety poor readers: the phonological core model, *Journal of Learning Disabilities*, 21(10): 590–604.

Stevens, R.J. and Slavin, R.E. (1995a) Effects of a cooperative learning approach in reading and writing on academically handicapped and nonhandicapped students, *Elementary School Journal*, 95(3): 241–62.

Stevens, R.J. and Slavin, R.E. (1995b) The cooperative elementary school: effects on students' achievement, attitudes, and social relations, *American Educational Research Journal*, 32(2): 321–51.

Stokes, T.F. and Baer, D.M. (1977) An implicit technology of generalization, *Journal of Applied Behavior Analysis*, 10: 349–67.

Stone, C.A. (1989) Improving the effectiveness of strategy training for learning-disabled students: the role of communicational dynamics, *Remedial and Special Education* (10): 35–42.

Street, B. (ed.) (1993) *Cross-cultural Approaches to Literacy*. New York: Cambridge University Press.

Street, B. and Street, J. (1995) The schooling of literacy, in P. Murphy, M. Selinger, J. Bourne and M. Briggs (eds) *Subject Learning in the Primary Curriculum*. London: Routledge.

Strickland, D. and Cullinan, B. (1994) Afterword, in M.J. Adams (ed.) *Beginning to Read: Thinking and Learning about Print*. London: MIT Press.

Swanson, H.L., Hoskyn, M. and Lee, C. (1999) *Interventions for Students with Learning Disabilities: A Meta-Analysis of Treatment Outcomes*. New York: Guilford Press.

Taylor, A. (1992) Mana, in W. Ihimaera, H. Williams, I. Ramsden and D. Long (eds)

Te Ao Marama: Contemporary Maori Writing, Vol. 1: *Te Whakaahuatanga o te Ao* [Reflections on Reality]. Auckland: Reed Books.

Tharp, R.G. (1994a) Research knowledge and policy issues in cultural diversity in education, in B. McCloud (ed.) *Language and Learning: Educating Linguistically Diverse Students*, pp. 129–67. Albany, New York: State University of New York.

Tharp, R.G. (1994b) Instructional conversations in Native American classrooms. ERIC Clearinghouse on Languages and Linguistics, Washington, DC.

Tharp, R.G. (1994c) Intergroup differences among Native Americans in socialization and child cognition: an ethnogenetic analysis, in P. Greenfield and R. Cocking (eds) *Cross-Cultural Roots of Minority Child Development*, pp. 87–105. Hillsdale, NJ: Lawrence Erlbaum Associates.

Thomas, G. (1992) *Effective Classroom Teamwork – Support or Intrusion?*. London: Falmer.

Timperley, H. and Phillips, G. (2003) Changing and sustaining teachers' expectations through professional development in literacy, *Teacher and Teacher Education*, 19: 627–41.

Tizard, J., Schofield, W.N. and Hewison, J. (1982) Collaboration between teachers and parents in assisting children's reading, *British Journal of Educational Psychology*, 52: 30–7.

Tomlinson, S. (1988) Why Johnny can't read: critical theory and special education, *European Journal of Special Needs Education*, 3(1): 45–58.

Topping, K. (1996) Tutoring systems for family literacy, in S. Wolfendale and K. Topping (eds) *Family Involvement in Literacy*. London: Cassell.

Topping, K. (2000) Paired collaborative writing, *Research in Education*, 67 (Winter), University of Dundee: SCRE Centre.

Topping, K. (2001) *Thinking, Reading, Writing*. London: Continuum.

Vargas, J. (1978) A behavioural approach to the teaching of composition, *Behavior Analyst* (Spring): 16–24.

Visser, J. (1993) *Differentiation: Making it Work*. Tamworth: NASEN.

Volk, D. and de Costa, M. (2001) Many differing ladders, many ways to climb: literacy events in the bilingual classroom, homes, and community of three Puerto Rican kindergartners, *Journal of Early Childhood Literacy*, 1(2): 193–224.

Volk, D. and de Costa, M. (2004) Mediating networks for literacy learning, in E. Gregory, S. Long and D. Volk (eds) *Many Pathways to Literacy: Young Children Learning with Siblings, Grandparents, Peers and Communities*, pp. 25–39. London: Routledge Falmer.

Vygotsky, L.S. (1962) *Thought and Language*. Cambridge, MA: MIT Press.

Vygotsky, L.S. (1978) *Mind in Society: The Development of Higher Psychological Processes*. London: Harvard University Press.

Vygotsky, L. (1981a) The genesis of higher mental functions, in J.V. Wersch (ed.) *The Concept of Activity in Soviet Psychology*. New York: M.R. Sharpe.

Vygotsky, L. (1981b) The instrumental method in psychology, in J.V. Wersch (ed.) *The Concept of Activity in Soviet Psychology*. New York: MR Sharpe.

Wearmouth, J. (1997) Prisoners' perspectives on what constitutes a 'good' education. Paper presented to the British Psychological Society Annual Conference (Education Section), Warwick, England.

Wearmouth, J. (1999) Another one flew over: 'maladjusted' Jack's perception of his label, *British Journal of Special Education*, 26(1): 15–23.

Wearmouth, J. (2000) *Co-ordinating Special Educational Provision Meeting the Challenges in Schools*. London: Hodder.

Wearmouth, J. (2002) Interview transcript in E801 *Study Guide* (appendix), Milton Keynes: Open University.

Wearmouth, J. (2003) Unpublished PhD thesis, Open University.

Wearmouth, J. (2004) Learning from 'James': lessons about policy and practice for literacy difficulties in schools' special educational provision, *British Journal of Special Education*, 31(2): 60–7.

Weiner, B. (1979) A theory of motivation for some classroom experiences, *Journal of Educational Psychology*, 71: 3–25.

Wenger, E. (1998) *Communities of Practice: Learning, Meaning and Identity*. Cambridge: Cambridge University Press.

Westby, C.E. (1991) Learning to talk – talking to learn: oral – literate language differences, in C.S. Simon (ed.) Communication skills and classroom success: assessment and therapy methodologies for language and learning disabled students, pp. 334–57. EAU Claire, WI: Thinking Publications.

Westera, J. (2002) Reciprocal teaching as a school-wide inclusive strategy. Unpublished PhD thesis, University of Auckland, Auckland.

Westera, J. and Moore, D. (1995) Reciprocal teaching of reading comprehension in a New Zealand high school, *Psychology in the Schools*, 12: 225–32.

Westwood, P. (1997) *Commonsense Methods for Children with Special Needs*. London: Routledge.

Wheldall, K. and Glynn, T. (1989) *Effective Classroom Learning*. Oxford: Blackwell.

Wheldall, K. and Mettem, P. (1985) Behavioural peer tutoring: training 16 year old tutors to employ the Pause Prompt and Praise method with 12 year old remedial readers, *Educational Psychology*, 5(1): 27–44.

Whitehead, D. (1993) *Factual Writing Think Sheets*. Hamilton, New Zealand: Seaforth Education.

Wilkinson, I.A.G. (1998) Dealing with diversity: achievement gaps in reading literacy among New Zealand students, *Reading Research Quarterly*, 33(2): 144–67.

Williams, A. (2004) 'Right! Get your book bags!' Siblings playing school in multi-ethnic London, in E. Gregory, S. Long and D. Volk (eds) *Many Pathways to Literacy Early Learning with Siblings, Grandparents, Peers and Communities*. London: Routledge.

Wood, D. (1988) *How Children Think and Learn*. Oxford: Blackwell.

Wood, D. (1992) Teaching talk: how modes of teacher talk affect pupil participation, in K. Norman (ed.) *Thinking Voices: The Work of the National Oracy Project.* London: Hodder and Stoughton.

Wood, D., Bruner, J. and Ross, G. (1976) The role of tutoring in problem solving, *Journal of Child Psychology and Psychiatry*, 17: 89–100.

Wragg, E.C., Wragg, C.M., Haynes, G.S. and Chamberlain, R.P. (1998) *Improving Literacy in the Primary School.* London: Routledge.

Young, M. and McGeeney, P. (1968) *Learning Begins at Home.* London: RKP.

Ysseldyke, J. and Christenson, S. (1987) Evaluating students' instructional environments. Special issue: special education program evaluation, *Rase: Remedial and Special Education*, 8(8): 17–24.

Ysseldyke, J. and Christenson, S. (1993) *TIES II: The Instructional Environment System II*, 4th edn. Longmont, CO: Sopris West.

Ysseldyke, J. and Thurlow, M. (1994) What results should be measured to decide whether instruction is working for students with disabilities?, in J. Ysseldyke and M. Thurlow (eds) *Educational Outcomes for Students with Disabilities.* Minnesota: Haworth.

Web sites

www.tki.org.nz/r/assessment/exemplars/index_e.php

www.standards.dfes.gov.uk/primary/features/primary/1091819/1092063 (accessed 27 March 2005)

www.standards.dfes.gov.uk/personalisedlearning/five/afl/ (accessed 27 March 2005)

Glossary

Word	Meaning	Pronunciation
awhi	support	ɑfi
e kori	play, physical exercise	ɛ kɔri
hangarerenga o te reo	use of effective language structure	hʌŋʌrɛrɛŋʌ ɔ tɛ rɛɔ
hāngi	food cooked in an oven in the ground	hɑŋi
harakeke	flax	hɑrakɛkɛ
hapū	sub-tribe	hʌpu
he awa kōpikopiko	a river with many bends	hɛ ɑwa kɔpikɔpikɔ
he tuna kei roto i te awa	there are eels in the river	hɛ tunʌ kei rɔtɔ i tɛ ɑwa
hopungia	pick up the language	hɔpuŋiʌ
horahia	spread out	hɔrahiʌ
hū	shoe	hu
iti	small, tiny	ɪtɪ
iwi	tribe	iwi
ka waiata	(it) is singing	kɑ waɪʌtʌ
kaiarahi i te reo	language specialist	kaiɑrɑhi i tɛ rɛɔ
kai moana	seafood	kaɪ mɔɑnʌ
kapa haka	traditional Māori cultural performing group	kʌpʌ hʌkʌ
karakia	prayer	karakɪʌ
kaumātua	elders	kəʊmatuʌ
kei hea?	where?	keɪ hɛʌ ?
kei runga i te rākau	in the tree	keɪ rʌŋʌ i tɛ rakəʊ
kia tere tonu	be very quick	kiʌ tɛrɛ tɔnu
kīwaha	colloquialism	kiwahʌ
kohatu	stone	kɔhatu
kōrero	talk, story	kɔrɛrɔ
koro	grandfather	kɔrɔ

Word	Meaning	Pronunciation
kura kaupapa Māori	schools that operate within a Māori worldview and deliver the curriculum through the medium of Māori language	kurʌ kəʊpʌpʌ maɔri
kuia	grandmother	kuiʌ
maeneene	smooth	maɛnɛɛnɛ
mana	acknowledged authority and standing	mʌnʌ
manu	bird	manu
Māori	people of the land, indigenous people of New Zealand	maɔri
marae	meeting area, focal point of settlement, space in front of a meeting house	mʌraɪ
maramatanga	understanding of meaning or enlightenment	maramataŋʌ
maunga tino teitei	very tall mountain	məʊŋʌ tino teɪ teɪ
mau rakau	traditional form of Māori martial arts, employing weapons	məʊ rakəʊ
ngā	the, plural form	ŋa
ngā kete kōrero	the Language Baskets, name given for the framework for levelling Māori readers used in junior Māori immersion classrooms	ŋa kɛtɛ kɔrɛrɔ
ngā purapura	the seeds	ŋa purʌpurʌ
nunui	big, many	nunui
pakari	the level of students' overall language competency	pakarɪ
pākehā	New Zealander of European descent	pakɛha
pango	black	paŋɔ
paraoa rewena	Māori bread (unleavened)	paraʊʌ
patipati	encouragement	pʌtipʌti
pipi	cockles	pɪpi
pikopiko	type of asparagus	pikɔpikɔ

(*continued*)

Word	Meaning	Pronunciation
ponaho	useless	pɔnahɔ
pōwhiri	formal rituals of encounter	pɔfiri
putawhakaaro	brainstorm	pʊtəfʌkarɔ
reo whakaputa	productive language	rɛɔ fʌkʌputʌ
rikiriki	small	rikiriki
rorohiko	computer	rɔrɔhikɔ
taiaha	long weapon used in traditional Māori martial arts	taɪʌha
takapiringa	set them out	tʌkʌpiriŋʌ
tamariki	children	tamariki
tangihanga	gathering to say farewell to the dead, conducted according to appropriate Māori protocol	taŋihaŋʌ
taratara	coarse, jagged	tʌrʌtʌrʌ
te akau	shore, beach, riverside	tɛ akəʊ
teina	younger sibling or younger cousin	teinʌ
teīna	plural form of *teina*	teinʌ
te kōhanga reo	the Language Nest, Māori immersion early childhood centre	tɛ kɔhaŋʌ rɛɔ
te manu	the bird	tɛ mʌnu
te reo pākehā	the English language	tɛ rɛɔ pakɛha
te pakari o te reo	language competency	t ɛ pakarɪ ɔ tɛ rɛɔ
te tāhuhu o te matauranga	the Ministry of Education	tɛ tahuhu ɔ tɛ matəʊraŋa
te toi huarewa	name given to an evaluation of effective literacy teachers from Māori immersion junior classrooms	tɛ tɔɪ huərɛwa
titiko	shellfish, winkle	titɪkɔ
tuakana	older sister or brother or cousin	tuəkʌnʌ
tuākana	plural form of *tuakana*	tuɑkʌnʌ
tuhi atu tuhi mai	responsive writing	tuhi atu tuhi mai
tukuna kia rere	let the language flow	tukinʌ kiʌ rɛrɛ
wā	space, time, place, season, opportunity	wɑ
waka	canoe, vehicle	wakʌ
wakarererangi	aeroplane	wɔkʌrɛrɛraŋi
wakatopatopa	helicopter	wɔkʌtɔpʌtɔpʌ

Word	Meaning	Pronunciation
whaea	senior Māori women	faɪʌ
wharenui	meeting house	fɑrɛnui
whānau	family	fɑnəʊ
whanaunga	relationships through marriage rather than blood links	fɑnəʊŋʌ
whanaungatanga	the construct of relationships, and interconnectedness based on personal relationships	fɑnəʊŋʌtɑŋʌ
whakawhanaungatanga	the process of making, forging or maintaining relationships	fʌkʌfɑnəʊŋʌtɑŋʌ
whakaputa whakaaro	creating a brainstorm	fʌkʌpʊtəfʌkɑrɔ

Index

Page numbers in *italics* refer to tables

CLASSROOM INTERACTIONS IN LITERACY

Eve Bearne, Henrietta Dombey and Teresa Grainger

- How important is professional knowledge and an informed understanding of pedagogy?
- What are the key issues in the unfolding language and literacy agenda?
- How can the profession encompass a more interactive and informed view of pedagogy?

This book examines some of the complexities and debates about language, literacy and learning, challenging current assumptions about shared understanding of pedagogical principles. It foregrounds social and cultural issues and the nature of interaction between children and teachers; children and children; children and texts of all kinds; and the significance of wider interactions within the teaching profession.

The contributors revitalise debate about the nature of professional knowledge, provide insights into the detail of classroom discourse and teacher interventions, and examine the transformative possibilities of literacy. They argue for a more open and expansive agenda informed by an analytically constructive view of pedagogy and challenge the profession to move from restrictive certainties to the potent possibilities of development through uncertainty and risk.

Classroom Interactions in Literacy is key reading for primary teachers, students in initial teacher education, teacher educators, researchers in the field, literacy consultants in LEAs, inspectors and advisors.

Contents
Introduction – Part 1: Revisiting the Web of meaning – Keywords: a vocabulary of pedagogy and new media – Part 2: The Detail of Classroom Discourse – Oracy, literacy and pedagogy: international perspectives – Moving forward together – Part 3: Professional Knowledge and Understanding – The subject of literacy: what kind of knowledge is needed to teach literacy successfully? – Beyond the curriculum: learning to teach primary literacy – Part 4: Children's knowledge and teachers' interventions – Getting inside Anthony Browne's head: pupils and teachers asking questions and reading pictures – An interactive pedagogy for bilingual children – Part 5: The Play of Ideas – Exploring the unknown: ambiguity, interaction and meaning making in classroom drama – Six fingers with feeling: play, literacy and politics – Part 6: New texts and textual dimensions – Playing with possibilities: children's multidimensional texts – Back to the future: developing children as writers – Part 7: The social construction of literacy – Social and cultural influences on literacy – Action, talk and text: integrating literacy with other modes of making meaning – References – Author index – Subject index.

Contributors
Robin Alexander, Evelyn Arizpe, Eve Bearne, Kathy Coulthard, Henrietta Dombey, Peter Geekie, Teresa Grainger, Charmian Kenner, Trinka Messenheimer, Angela Packwood, Louise Poulson, Sandra Smidt, Ilana Snyder, Morag Styles, Sam Twiselton, Gordon Wells.

232pp   0 335 21385 5 (Paperback)   0 335 21386 3 (Hardback)

TEACHING MULTILITERACIES ACROSS THE CURRICULUM
CHANGING CONTEXTS OF TEXT AND IMAGE IN CLASSROOM PRACTICE

Len Unsworth

Teaching literacy in today's primary and junior secondary schools involves both teaching children what people understand as traditional literacy and also teaching children how to read and produce the kinds of texts typical of the current and emerging information age. This still means understanding grammar as a functional tool in reading and writing but it also now necessarily entails explicit knowledge about how images and layout can be structured in different ways to make different kinds of meanings and how both text and image are used in electronic formats. This major new textbook outlines the basic theoretical knowledge teachers need to have about visual and verbal grammar and the nature of computer-based texts in school learning. In doing so it:

- addresses both the present demands in literacy teaching and the emerging demands for teaching the multiliteracies of the information age;
- provides accessible, integrative, classroom oriented coverage of the complex range of current and emerging issues (like teaching grammar, visual literacy, the role of computer-based information and communication technology, critical literacy, literacies and learning in English and other curriculum areas);
- includes both theoretical frameworks and detailed practical guidelines with examples of classroom work;
- deals with the continuities and differences in the teaching of infants, children in the primary school and the transition to the first years of secondary education.

Contents
Introduction – Changing dimensions of school literacies – Learning about language as a resource for literacy development – Describing visual literacies – Distinguishing the literacies of school science and humanities – Exploring multimodal meaning-making in literature for children – Developing multiliteracies in the early school years – Developing multiliteracies in content area teaching – Teaching multiliteracies in the English classroom – References – Index.

320pp   0 335 20604 2 (Paperback)   0 335 20605 0 (Hardback)

NEW LITERACIES
CHANGING KNOWLEDGE AND CLASSROOM LEARNING
Colin Lankshear and Michele Knobel

An intriguing book which argues why the use of new media is transforming ways of knowing and making meaning in the digital age. Essential reading for anyone who cares about literacy education.

Associate Professor Ilana Snyder, Monash University

A good book opens a window onto new vistas; an excellent one, on the other hand, pulls readers through the opening and beyond, inviting critical dialogue at every turn. *New Literacies* belongs in the excellent catagory.

Donna Alvermann, University of Georgia

Literacy education continues to be dominated by a mindset that has passed its use-by date. Education has failed to take account of how much the world has changed during the information technology revolution. It proceeds as though the world is the same as before – just somewhat more technologised. This is the hallmark of an 'outsider' mindset. In fact, qualitatively new literacies and new kinds of knowledge associated with digitally saturated social practices abound. 'Insiders' understand this, 'outsiders' do not. Yet 'outsider' perspectives still dominate educational directions. Meanwhile, student 'insiders' endure learning experiences that mystify, bemuse, alienate and miseducate them.

This book describes new social practices and new literacies, along with kinds of knowledge associated with them. It shows what is at stake between 'outsider' and 'insider' mindsets, argues that education requires a shift in mindset, and suggests how and where pursuit of progressive change might begin.

Contents

240pp   0 335 21066 X (Paperback)   0 335 21067 8 (Hardback)